Trade Unions and Re

Trade Unions and Regions: Better Work, Experimentation, and Regional Governance is about the place of workers and their unions in the modern world. It addresses current challenges for unions working in regions and the experiments that may take place at this level of governance.

The book addresses pressing questions concerned with the conditions for better work and a humane society. The focus is on the capacities of unions to address questions relating to regional governance, in both supranational and sub-national regions. It examines workers and their unions in a variety of contexts: multinationals, industries, workplaces, and communities. The authors address the experiments that can be initiated by unions, governments, or employers and the ways in which collective organisations engage to address these matters in regional contexts. The analysis takes as a starting point the fracturing and divisions evident in various regions, in Australia, Canada, Mexico, Spain, the United Kingdom, and USA. The contributors propose novel analyses with lessons for unions. It should be of interest to union activists and leaders, political parties, governments, and those who make decisions in and about regions.

Researchers and students of labour markets, political mobilisation, and employment relations will take the analyses further.

Christian Lévesque is Professor of Employment Relations at HEC Montréal, Canada and the co-Director of the CRIMT (Interuniversity Research Centre on Globalization and Work).

Peter Fairbrother is Professor of Management and Labour, Tasmanian School of Business and Economics, University of Tasmania, Australia and Affiliated Professor, HEC Montréal, Montréal, Canada.

Blandine Emilien is Associate Professor in Human Resource Management (HRM) at the Université du Québec à Montréal (UQAM), Canada.

María C. González is tenured Associate Professor of Sociology at the University of Oviedo, Spain.

Lucie Morissette is Associate Professor of Employment Relations in the Department of Human Resource Management at HEC Montréal, Canada.

Routledge Studies in Employment and Work Relations in Context
Edited by Tony Elger and Peter Fairbrother

The aim of the *Employment and Work Relations in Context Series* is to address questions relating to the evolving patterns and politics of work, employment, management, and industrial relations. There is a concern to trace out the ways in which wider policy-making, especially by national governments and transnational corporations, impinges upon specific workplaces, occupations, labour markets, localities, and regions. This invites attention to developments at an international level, marking out patterns of globalisation, state policy, and practices in the context of globalisation and the impact of these processes on labour. A particular feature of the series is the consideration of forms of worker and citizen organisation and mobilisation. The studies address major analytical and policy issues through case study and comparative research.

Wildfire and Power
Policy and Practice
Edited by Peter Fairbrother and Meagan Tyler

Crossing Boundaries
Work and Industrial Relations in Perspective
Russell Lansbury

The Regulation and Management of Workplace Health and Safety
Historical and Emerging Trends
Edited by Peter Sheldon, Sarah Gregson, Russell Lansbury, and Karin Sanders

Contesting Inequality and Worker Mobilisation
Australia 1851–1880
Michael Quinlan

Trade Unions and Regions
Better Work, Experimentation, and Regional Governance
Edited by Christian Lévesque, Peter Fairbrother, Blandine Emilien, María C. González and Lucie Morissette

For more information about this series, please visit: https://www.routledge.com/Routledge-Studies-in-Employment-and-Work-Relations-in-Context/book-series/SE0840

Trade Unions and Regions

Better Work, Experimentation, and Regional Governance

Edited by Christian Lévesque, Peter Fairbrother, Blandine Emilien, María C. González, and Lucie Morissette

Routledge
Taylor & Francis Group
NEW YORK AND LONDON

First published 2023
by Routledge
605 Third Avenue, New York, NY 10158

and by Routledge
4 Park Square, Milton Park, Abingdon, Oxon, OX14 4RN

Routledge is an imprint of the Taylor & Francis Group, an informa business

Library of Congress Cataloguing-in-Publication Data
A catalog record for this title has been requested

ISBN: 978-0-367-37012-1 (hbk)
ISBN: 978-1-032-32009-0 (pbk)
ISBN: 978-1-003-00108-9 (ebk)

DOI: 10.4324/9781003001089

Typeset in Bembo
by MPS Limited, Dehradun

Contents

Figures

Tables

Contributors

Ruth Barton is a Senior Lecturer at the Tasmanian School of Business and Economics at the University of Tasmania. She is a co-researcher at the Interuniversity Research Centre on Globalization and Work (CRIMT). Her research interests lie in deindustrialisation, place, regeneration, and trade unions and their interaction, especially in Tasmania. As well, she is interested in ideas, narratives, and imagery and their role in mobilising trade union and community members.

Lucy Brill is the Director of the international labour rights charity, Homeworkers Worldwide (HWW). She joined HWW in 2017, initially researching precarious working conditions in UK garment manufacturing, and currently leading work in South Asia, with brands sourcing leather footwear and clothing from homeworker supply chains in South Asia. Lucy's doctoral thesis (Bradford 2004) explored gender and precarious work under globalisation, and civil society responses, based on fieldwork in the UK and Chile. Lucy also worked for Oxfam, managing their livelihoods programme in England (2007–2014), and as a researcher at universities in Bradford (2003–2007) and Manchester (2015–2017).

Cassandra Bowkett is a Lecturer in Human Resource Management and Employment Relations at the University of Manchester. She completed her post-doctorate at HEC Montréal, affiliated with the CRIMT research network and associated research centre, following her PhD research at Cardiff University. Her interests focus on the future of work and skills, particularly around the impacts of new technologies on HRM and employment relations in the manufacturing industries.

Jorge Carrillo has a PhD in Sociology from COLMEX and is a co-founder and has been a researcher at the El Colegio de la Frontera Norte (COLEF) since 1982. He is Emeritus Researcher of the National System of Researchers (SNI). In 2015, he received the State Prize of Science and Technology of Baja California. He has wide recognition in Mexico and abroad for his studies on the maquiladora industry, the automotive, electronics and aerospace sectors, multinationals and SMEs, the quality of employment and technology. His current research projects are about the impact on employment derived from digitalisation and robotisation, as well as labour outsourcing and social innovation.

Urwana Coiquaud is an Associate Professor of Labour Law at HEC Montréal and a co-researcher at the Interuniversity Research Centre on Globalization and Work (CRIMT). Her interests include the development of the notion of subordination and the regulation of precarious work. Her current research focuses on platform economies and their impact on public policies.

Blandine Emilien is an Associate Professor in Human Resource Management (HRM) at the Université du Québec à Montréal. Her research agenda bears comparative analyses across various industries and types of organisations, with the aim of identifying decent management practices in favour of Better Work. After a PhD exploration of the call centre industry in the Global South, a postdoctoral research fellowship enabled her to explore the realms of the aerospace industry in Canada and abroad. Her current projects focus on the staffing process involving migrant workers in the Quebec food-processing industry. She is also studying non-profit organisations, such as union confederations, which, as employers, face succession planning and talent management challenges in Quebec and Spain.

Peter Fairbrother is a Professor in the Tasmanian School of Business and Economics, University of Tasmania and Affiliated Professor, HEC Montréal, Montréal. He is a co-researcher at the Interuniversity Research Centre on Globalization and Work (CRIMT). His long-standing research interests involve theories of union renewal and revitalisation, the recomposition and restructuring of the modern liberal state and the political economy of work and employment. Currently, his research focuses on unions and their federations, regional governance and labour, with a second program addressing the ways farming households are addressing the climate crisis in sub-national regions.

Redi Gomis has a PhD in Social Science. He is a Research Professor of the Social Studies Department at *El Colegio de la Frontera Norte* in Tijuana, Mexico, since 1992. He is member of the Mexican National System of Researchers. He has published several scientific articles in journals and specialised books. Among the most recent are *The Four Stages of Lean in Mexico*; *Human Resource Management and Sector Analysis in Emerging Countries. A Comparative Study of Automotive Subsidiaries Operating in Latin America*; *The role of multinational enterprises in the aerospace industry clusters in Mexico: The case of Baja California*.

María C. González Menéndez is a tenured Associate Professor of Sociology at the University of Oviedo and a researcher on the CRIMT International Partnership Project. She has expertise in the cross-country and cross-regional comparative analysis of the governance of work and employment and has led international teams of researchers in projects funded by the Government of Spain and by the European Commission. She has published on workers' workplace participation; women on corporate boards; part-time employment; policy transfer and innovation in youth labour market policies; and human resource management and the sub-national governance of foreign direct investment.

Nikolaus Hammer is an Associate Professor in Work and Employment, co-director of the Centre for Sustainable Work and Employment Futures (CSWEF) at the University of Leicester, and co-researcher at the Interuniversity Research Centre on Globalization and Work (CRIMT). His core research interests focus on the restructuring of global value chains, particularly as regards to work and employment and the role of social standards. Recent work has focused on the reshoring of garment manufacturing in the rise of fast fashion in Europe.

Marc-Antonin Hennebert is a full Professor at the Department of Human Resource Management HEC Montréal and associate researcher at the Interuniversity Research Centre on Globalization and Work (CRIMT) and the International Observatory on the Societal Impacts of Artificial Intelligence and Digital Technologies (OBVIA). His research focuses on industrial relations, trade unionism, collective bargaining, and social dialogue, which he studies from both the national and international perspectives. At the international level, he is particularly interested in the social regulation of multinational enterprises and international framework agreements. His field studies carried out with international trade union representatives and the management of multinational enterprises have been the subject of several publications.

John Holmes is a Professor Emeritus of Geography at Queen's University in Kingston, Ontario, Canada and a former Faculty Associate in the Queen's School of Industrial Relations. He holds a BSc and MA (Social Science) from the University of Sheffield and PhD from The Ohio State University. His research and writing on the political economy of the North American automotive industry spans four decades. He sits on the Automotive Policy Research Centre's Board of Directors (https://automotivepolicy.ca/) and is an Honorary Life Member and Trustee of the Kingston and District Labour Council.

Christian Lévesque is a full Professor at HEC Montréal and the Co-Director of the Interuniversity Research Centre on Globalization and Work (CRIMT) and co-responsible for the research activities on Industry 4.0, Work, and Employment undertaken at the International Observatory on the Societal Impacts of AI and Digital Technology OBVIA. He has conducted several long-term research projects, including one recent international project on the aerospace industry. His current research interests focus on the impact of emerging technologies on future work.

Ian MacDonald is an Associate Professor at the École de relations industrielles, Université de Montréal. His research interests include labour geography, Marxist political economy, precarious work, and trade union strategy, particularly at the urban scale. *Unions and the City: Negotiating Urban Change* (Cornell ILR 2017), published under his direction, explores how unions shape urban everyday life in the course of pursuing collective bargaining and organising strategies. He holds a PhD in political science from York University.

Glenn Morgan is an Honorary Professor of Management at the University of Bristol. He has held chair appointments at Cardiff Business School and Warwick Business School and as a Velux Guest Professor at Copenhagen Business School. He was editor of the journal *Organization* from 2005 to 2009. In 2015, he was President of SASE (Society for the Advancement of Socio-Economics).

Lucie Morissette is an Associate Professor in Employment Relations at HEC Montréal, Quebec, Canada. Her recent studies and publications have addressed the issue of platform economies, and more specifically, their impact on public policies, actors, and political processes. Her previous publications focus on the role of institutions in industrial clusters and institutional entrepreneurs in bringing about innovations in labour unions.

Aroa Tejero, PhD in Sociology, is an Assistant Professor and a member of the Research Group 'Promoting Employment and Welfare in Europe' (PROMEBI) at the Department of Sociology, University of Oviedo (Spain). Her research focuses on socio-economic inequalities, mainly from a quantitative perspective. Her research interests include poverty, labour market, gender inequalities, and social policy analysis.

Malu Villela is a Senior Research Associate at the University of Bristol School of Management and a member of the Bristol Inclusive Economy Initiative. She currently holds an AXA fellowship and is leading the project Resilience through Inclusive and Sustainable Economies (RISE). For the past years, she has been researching and engaging with topics such as social economies and social enterprises, alternative types of organisation, networks, and cross-sector collaboration.

Thorben Wieditz is a campaigner and creative strategist with a record of successful worker, community, and municipal campaigns. He has worked for several labour unions and helped extract concessions from a variety of employers, real estate developers, and big tech platforms. Thorben trained as an urban geographer and planner at York University and TU University of Dortmund. He co-leads MetStrat, a public campaign firm based in Toronto, Canada. His academic work focuses on urban development processes and the role labour unions play in the re-structuring of urban regions.

Acknowledgements

This book is the product of a collaborative process. It benefits from the support of colleagues in the Inter-university Research Centre on Globalization and Work (CRIMT). The research activities of CRIMT focus on the theoretical and practical challenges of institutional and organisational renewal in the areas of work and employment in the global era. Its Institutional Experimentation for Better Work Partnership Project – funded by the Social Sciences and Humanities Research Council of Canada and the Canada Foundation for Innovation – brings together CRIMT (funded by the Fonds de recherche du Québec – Société et culture) and an international network of leading partner centres (20) and co-researchers (180). This multi-year project aims to build knowledge on and understanding of how to make work better.

This book seeks to contribute to this endeavour. It was crafted out of an international workshop that we organised at HEC Montréal in October 2018, entitled 'Unions at Work in Regions and Sectors: understanding institutional changes and stability for economic and social development'. We gratefully acknowledge the generous support for the seminar and publication received from Social Sciences and Humanities Council of Canada. Francine Jacques and Nicholas Roby of CRIMT provided superlative support to the workshop, and we acknowledge with thanks their ongoing guidance in the preparation of this publication. Staff at the HEC Montréal were wonderful hosts.

We wish to thank the many participants in the workshop for contributing their chapters for this book. This has been a long journey in the context of the Covid-19 pandemic, and we wish to thank them for their resilience and patience. We wish to thank the dedicated CRIMT students who provided research assistance and general support in preparing the workshop and this volume. Sincere thanks are extended to Annette Hayden who provided excellent editing services. Finally, we extend special thanks to the editorial staff at Routledge for their strong support throughout the publication process.

Co-editors of the book: Christian Lévesque, Peter Fairbrother, Blandine Emilien, María C. González Menéndez and Lucie Morissette

1 Understanding Union Power and Regional Governance

Peter Fairbrother and Christian Lévesque

Unions are or should be engaged with regional levels of governance to realise their purpose and exercise their capacities. Regions are increasingly considered as a relevant space to shape the future of work, to create good or bad jobs or to transform bad (good) jobs into good (bad) jobs. This book seeks to address these possibilities. In various ways, all contributors add to the development of a distinctive approach to understanding the role and place of trade unions in the processes and dynamics of regional institutional and organisational experimentation for better work. It may be that during such experimentation, unions can begin to address the challenges arising in the field of work and employment.

Over the last few decades, in the context of state restructuring and socio-economic development, regional forms of governance have acquired a saliency that has implications for workers and their unions. This focus draws attention to the spatial boundaries of regions, the patterns of relations within regions, the way regions cut across and are connected to local, national, and international spaces, and the place of various actors in regional governance. There is thus the prospect of opening up new avenues of understanding about the spatial extension of trade union action at the regional level. Such moves may result in the emergence of new forms of collective mobilisation and coalition-building, drawing on the diverse resources and capabilities of workers and their communities.

Under neo-liberalism, regions have been placed under increasing pressure to strengthen their economies by making their territories attractive to business investment. Such developments can threaten democratic institutions within governance and may make regional political authorities dependent upon corporate interests. There is evidence that regional economic development authorities claim to retain local democratic accountability, but that democracy becomes more indirect as these bodies are accountable to their councils and not directly to citizens (e.g. Pape et al. 2016). Indeed, attempts to produce more flexible local and regional authorities and governance can lead to the decline of political government and a diminishing policy influence by collective organisations such as trade unions.

DOI: 10.4324/9781003001089-1

To address these themes, we focus on regional governance and the ways in which workers and their unions address activities and policies. It may be that workers do not look to unions to address their concerns, either individually or collectively; alternatively, unions may be organised and operate in relation to regional-level matters or concerns that in turn can be leveraged in a variety of ways.

Unions

Unions are important forms of collective organisation for workers across the world. Faced with a changing political economy, labour unions can draw on ideas and understandings to articulate their concerns in conditions of uncertainty. In various ways, unions become the voice of their membership, as well as that of the broader population sympathetic and supportive of the aspirations embodied by unions. Utilising their capacities, they can seek to pursue their purposes to represent and express the interests of their members. These capacities can be exercised when labour unions have the capabilities to do so, knowledge, skills, and abilities that can be 'developed, transmitted and learned' (Lévesque and Murray 2010: 341). Nonetheless, capabilities without resources, particularly power resources, are not enough and vice versa. Even so, the ways that they organise and operate can vary from hierarchical and exclusive forms of representation to more inclusive and participative arrangements and modes of leadership. Hence, the conditions to realise these steps are complex and the settlements reached are often contested.

The foundation for trade unions as collective organisations is where people work. Much attention has been given to the ways that unions are shaped by and frame their activity at a workplace level (Hyman 1979; Cohen 2006; Fairbrother 2014; Haipeter 2020). In principal, all unions operate from this base, although the texture and profile of workspaces vary from single sites, where relatively large numbers of people are employed, such as a manufacturing establishment or an office complex, to household places where textile workers or displaced workers in a pandemic may be located, to the mobile workplace of an Uber food delivery worker and a long-distance vehicle driver. Moreover, the socio-demographic bases of workforces irrespective of workplace also shape union capacities and unions have belatedly begun to recognise gender, racialisation, age, and sexual orientation as primary organisational and representational concerns. Hence, the workspace base of trade unionism matters and is often contested by and within labour unions.

While much union activity is located in the workplace, it is also the case that the workspace is defined by a complex of relations that involve the union as well as the employer. Therefore, attention must be paid to the forms of organisation of individual unions and their confederations as well as to the ways in which workspaces may stand alone or be part of larger entities such as corporations, state administrations, and other arrangements. The workspace is often part of a set of institutionalised relations that involve various forms of ownership, sourcing, production and servicing activity, and provision. For both unions and employers, these relationships can be local, regional, national, and global. Moreover, the boundaries of the workspace frequently are blurred by the unbundling of the firm and the recomposition and decentring of the public and private services. There is thus a fissuring of the workplace (Weil 2014) recently enhanced by the diffusion of technological intermediation and the possibility of working remotely, accelerated by the COVID-19 pandemic (Pawel 2020). Such features of work and employment raise important questions about representational issues for trade unions.

Unions realise their ambitions in relation to specific socio-economic contexts. These contexts are the base from which unions organise, act, and shape their purposes. In situations where these organisations face multinational capital, for example, they face circumstances where they must deal with distanced and often disconnected management or suffer parochial irrelevance (Fairbrother 2015). Employers often seek to undermine the bases of solidarity within unions, via differentiated terms and conditions of employment as well as spatial fragmentation of work tasks. Increasingly, it is likely that unions will construct their approaches and foci, at the local, regional, national, and international levels, frequently involving 'complicated scalar practices' (Mansfield 2005: 459). In this circumstance, unions draw on internal and, increasingly, external resources when dealing with the impact and outcomes of these relations. These institutional and relational dimensions of trade unionism play out in complex and contingent ways. In such circumstances, the responsibilities facing union leaders and activists are to frame their interests in collective terms. To explore these dimensions, we begin with a consideration of the idea of region and the evident forms of regional governance.

Regions and Regional Governance

There is an ongoing debate in the regional studies literature about the concept of region (Massey 2004; Morgan 2007: 2014; Goodwin 2012). In these debates, the role of unions in economic and social development with reference to skills and employment tends to be overlooked. However, of note, regions have become the focus of economic development and transition. This spatial aspect is captured by the notion of territory, although this can cross national borders, as is the case of the Great Lakes region, a binational Canadian-US region, or it may be sub-national such as the Ruhr industrial region, the urban area of North Rhine Westphalia, Germany. The point is that there is no clear-cut definition of a region in terms of territory. Additionally, regions comprise a relational dimension defined by the connectivity of regions (Goodwin 2012). These two dimensions produce regions whose spatial boundaries are blurred by their interaction via social networks and connections (see Massey 2004).

These forms of governance comprise a range of actors, from governments to sectional interest groups. Often it is unclear how these actors and the diverse interests that they represent are interacting within processes of regional decision making and policy formation (e.g. Pape et al. 2016). Research has often highlighted the role of the state in combination with politically and economically dominant interest groups, generating an account of regional development that emphasises the interaction between state and market forces (e.g. Larner 2005). There has been far less consideration of the ways in which local interest groups, particularly those that are considered less economically or politically central, can contest and shape processes of regional development.

The relational characteristics of regional governance explain how, in the process of exercising state power, governments 'are able to "reach" into the politics of regions' (Goodwin 2012: 1183). Regional governance thus takes the form of fluid and at times ambiguous institutional arrangements that fall both within and outside formal government structures. While regional governance often appears institutionally bounded in some respects, it is porous and impermanent in others (Morgan 2007: 2014). Such arrangements are sufficient to allow diverse actors to focus their activities in relation to regional economic and social matters (Amin 2004).

Increasingly, research on regions focuses on different scalar relations such as city, sub-region, province or State, cross-national regions (e.g. Clarkson 2001). Attention has been given also to the complex relationships between the rural and the urban, with a focus on city-regions (Parr 2005). Indeed, this research opens up questions about city-regions as sites of political struggle, with implications for trade unions (Jonas 2012). These features of regions play out in relation to the varied dimensions of regional governance.

Workers, Unions, and Regional Governance

Regions are thus sites of contestation. However, it is not clear where workers are in these processes or the place of unions in them. The focus in many studies is on the institutional conditions for socio-economic regional development and change, drawing on the foundational work of Amin and Thrift (1996). In a variety of ways, research has sought to characterise and locate the place of collective actors in regional governance (Cooke 2004; Clark 2013; González Menéndez et al. 2018). Cooke (2004) proposes a typology of more or less centralised governance forms ranging from grassroots systems to network systems (where business and labour associations play a vital role) to dirigiste systems (where central government policies play a crucial role). In the same vein, González Menéndez et al. (2018) distinguish between market, state-led, and associational governance where trade unions have greater voice. Such studies tend to address a range of factors which enable or inhibit the possibilities of developing common agenda, across and by a range of actors.

More recently, these analyses have been extended with a systematic study of types of regional institutions (e.g. Zukauskaite et al. 2017: 337–338). This involves distinguishing regional governance according to their institutional thickness: the variety of organisations and actors (e.g. firms, unions, trade associations, training bodies), patterns of interaction between actors and organisations, the distribution and structure of power and the presence of common agenda. Given the economic and technological uncertainties occurring with increasingly globalised competition, these regional institutions are often unsettled, and actors reassess and revise their objectives through a process of mutual adjustment and collective learning (Heidenreich 2005). Hence, as actors face new challenges, it may be that a region must be reinvented, involving governance, structure, and organisation, as well as patterns of interaction across a region.

Of note here, collective actors such as trade unions may seek to deploy their resources anew in regional settings. Via narratives or visions of development, actors frame opportunities and challenges in specific and often targeted ways (see Lévesque and Murray 2013). This draws attention to the ways that the relationships and processes that comprise regional policy development are managed and navigated (see Garud et al. 2007; Klijn and Koppenjan 2012). It also raises the question of democratic legitimacy, about who is involved in decision-making processes and when. Such processes can claim to be participatory in nature, but in practice often fall short of being genuinely so, particularly in the absence of actual debate, reflection, and binding decision-making power (Morgan 2014). Some actors may be able to promote and extend their existing relations with state institutional and economic structures, while others experience limitations and inhibitions in relation to nodes of political or economic power.

Over the last four decades, many governments took on the question of union power. Notably, the Thatcher government (UK) and the Reagan administration (USA) in the 1980s laid the foundation for governments to use state power to reconfigure contemporary capitalism. Increasingly, the state re-regulated class relations in ways that undermined and inhibited collective power (Howell 2021). Irrespective of the state form (liberal market or coordinated market or combinations thereof), there has been a state-driven re-regulation (liberalisation) of employment relations, with implications for collective worker capacities. Nonetheless, the tasks facing workers are to realise their capacities via their collective forms of organisation and operation. Among other things, this requires developing and producing the narratives, the ideas, that challenge the exploitative conditions of their circumstances. This step involves a consideration of the social construction and organisation of these ideas (Morgan and Hauptmeier 2021).

At a regional level, the question for workers and their unions is how to articulate and pursue their purpose in relation to regional governance (Fairbrother 2015). Possibilities range from situations where workers lack capacity and resource to act collectively to situations where union forms of organisation are long established and often routinised. As we argue, the collective forms of worker organisation are a precursor to experimentation that may question or affirm established governance relations and practices. The outcomes are often contested.

The Making of Experimentation

Much has been written about institutional change over the last decade with the intent of injecting more agency into institutional analysis (Campbell 2004; Crouch 2005; Kristensen and Morgan 2012). Institutions can limit prospects for change by engaging actors in path-dependent ways and lock them into particular repertoires of action and constrain future options. However, institutions are also created and developed through actor contention and negotiation. They may offer resources that facilitate agency and can be mobilised to reshape patterns of relationship and behaviour. Further, Kristensen and Morgan (2012) argue that the distinction between actors and institutions is fading away since actors are continuously developing, adapting, and forming new institutions to cope with globalisation. More specifically, they develop the notion of experimental institutions to depict these change processes. Hence, in each territory, a variety of heterogeneous and complementary institutions coexist, gradually changing over time. In this process of experimentation, various actors incrementally co-construct new regulations, norms, and cognitive frames.

It is helpful to distinguish two forms of experimentation: organisational and institutional (Murray et al. 2020). Organisational experimentation is generally localised within a single or a few organisations within a region. To cope with uncertainties, actors use existing institutions to develop new resources, organisations, or networks although they do not seek to create new institutions. This form of experiment can modify the distribution of power resources and actor's agency but it does not change the rules of the game. Examples of such an experimentation range from trade union management representatives in a workplace introducing new forms of bargaining (Rutherford and Frangi 2020) to unions integrating new technologies to enhance their repertoire of action and develop new networks (Pasquier et al. 2020).

Institutional experimentation involves changing or creating new institutions. This takes the form of forging common understanding, norms and rules, scaling up and institutionalising such arrangements. It can involve non-state and state actors and can be triggered through bottom-up or top-down processes, often involving collective action and joint deliberative processes. This form of experimentation can draw on existing institutions, although actors try to modify them by recombining elements from various fields or even create new institutions. In the latter case, this may involve new understandings (cognitive), new beliefs about what is appropriate (normative), or new formal rules (regulative). It generally leads to new habits or ways of thinking and acting (Garneau 2021) and can have a transformative effect on power dynamics. Examples of such experimentation include the introduction of coordinated bargaining by business associations and trade unions illustrated in Ireland and Italy by Culpepper (2008). More extensively, it is demonstrated by the transformation of trade union purpose towards community unionism in the mining industry in Australia (Barton 2018). In both cases, the experimentation involves the social organisation of ideas (Morgan and Hauptmeier 2021) to create a new common knowledge as a response to the challenges faced by these collective actors.

These forms of experimentation are depicted in Table 1.1.

Table 1.1 Experimentation in the making

Experimentations	*Organisational*	*Institutional*
Scope	Localised within one or a few organisations	Spread within the region or across organisations
Nature	Bottom-up	Bottom-up or/and top-down
Actors involved	Limited coalition of non-state actors	Extended coalitions of non-state and state actors
Types of change	New resources, practices, and networks	New cognitive, normative, and/or regulative frame
Impact on patterns of behaviour and relationship	Shaping actor's agency and the distribution of power resources	Transforming power dynamics through new habits of thinking and acting

The idealised forms of experimentation described in Table 1.1 are in reality often unsettled and contested. Both forms of experimentation intersect in rather complex and often overlapping ways between the two forms of experimentation. Organisational experiments can be contained at a localised level, or they can be scaled up. Institutional experimentation can foster organisational experimentation, but it can also trap actors in a form of path dependency which reduces experimentation. One of the theoretical challenges that we seek to unpack in this book is the temporal dimensions and mechanisms that underline the movement and interaction between forms of experimentation.

A further key theoretical issue is related to the conditions enabling and constraining the development of these forms of experimentation. Existing regional institutional configurations can exert tight or loose constraints on experimentation. It may be the case that thin institutional configurations can foster organisational experimentation, while thick institutional configurations are more conducive to institutional experimentation. But there is more to these relationships. As highlighted by Morgan and Hauptmeier (2021) in their analysis of their German case, which is characterised by thick institutional arrangements, the consensual and incremental approach to decision making can narrow ideational options and result in path dependency, thereby limiting experimentation. The articulation between existing regional institutional configurations and forms of experimentation thus remains an open question.

The hidden aspect in this analysis is related to the autonomy of actors and their experimentational capacities. This draws attention to the ways in which actors may utilise the power dynamics available, in this case, as regionally focused actors.

Using Power Resources

The question of power is indeed central to our understanding of collective action and trade unionism and to their role in the on-going processes of experimentation. The very existence of trade unions indicates the presence of asymmetrical power relations between labour and capital. Power and its twin, domination, are embedded in employment relations and trade unions exercise power over other actors to realise their purpose (Edwards 1986). While there is much debate about the concept of power (Bourdieu 1980; Friedberg 1993; Lukes 2005), there is strong agreement over the fact that power encompasses a variety of logics and arrangements. Many scholars draw on the work of Wright (2000) and Silver (2003) and focus on the position of actors within the economic field. Others emphasise the position of an actor within the political field and, more broadly, within the capitalist system, allowing access and benefit from strategic resources (Culpepper 2015; Carstensen and Schmidt 2016). Recently, Schmalz et al. (2018) have tried to resolve this controversy by proposing a framework that distinguishes societal power (political field) from structural power (economic field). It is important and necessary to take account of these aspects of power resources, and build on previous understandings (Fairbrother et al. 2013).

Unions deploy power resources in various ways and combinations. We distinguish two broad dimensions of power resources. First, structural power is a resource associated with an actor's position in the economic and political fields and, second, dispositional power refers to forms of collectivity which, in turn, lead to a consideration of the various configurations of institutional and organisational power (see Gumbrell-McCormick and Hyman 2018). It may be that the utilisation of such resources is for defensive reasons where the fragmented circumstances of work and employment inhibit more traditional forms of collective organisation, such as is often the case with much homework, and sections of the gig economy. In contrast, overtime workers can build and develop their collective capacities to confront the harsher edges of employment, as experienced by many when founding union forms of organisation in previously unorganised sectors of the economy. In short, while power resources may be available, in different combinations and arrangements, the steps towards collective organisation and experimentation are not straightforward.

Nonetheless, these resources may be available to workers and their unions in uneven and, at times, contradictory ways. It is not given that accessibility provides the capacities to organise in collective ways or take steps to realise the aspirations of better work. Of note, trade unions operate at different spatial levels experimenting at times with new mechanisms, new rules, and, in the process, developing capacities to address the challenges they face. Such experiments are played out locally, nationally, and globally, depending on the circumstances faced by these unions and their members, as workers.

The Processes and Consequences of Experimentation

Thus far we have argued that regions are an important space for collective organisation, such as labour or unions, dealing with the uncertainties associated with the disruptive changes associated with globalisation. In such conditions of work and employment uncertainty, unions are a form of collective organisation that can draw on power resources to pursue their purposes. The actions with such resource use may begin to dislocate the valorisation of capital, in different ways, via industrial action, by petitioning and lobbying for change, by negotiating and seeking improvement to work and life conditions.

Currently, regions have become the focus of economic development and transition and are crucial spaces for unions to represent and express the interest of their members. They are sites of contention where actors seek to advance their interests and their visions of regional economic and social development. One analysis presents this circumstance and possibility as the ongoing interplay between 'institutional forms and political forces' (Macleod and Goodwin 1999: 523; see also Macleod and Jones 2007). Regions are also sites of experimentation where various actors mobilise existing regional institutions and utilise their capabilities and power resources to modify their organisation, their networks and to maintain, disrupt, or change existing arrangements.

Experimentation in and of regions is an unsettled and contested process that can take various shapes and forms. It can be localised within one or few organisations, which can be defined as an organisational experiment. Experimentation also can be distributed within a region or across organisations, defined as institutional experimentation. Both forms intersect in rather complex ways and one can lead into the other. These experiments can yield positive and negative consequences on both the power dynamic within the region and the quality of work. They can enhance or reduce inequalities, increase or reduce the asymmetries of power, and be more or less inclusive, democratic, and participatory. They can also shape the future of work by worsening or improving working conditions, creating good or bad jobs and transforming bad jobs (good) into good jobs (bad).

Figure 1.1 schematically presents the link between the conditions of experimentation, the forms of experimentation, and their consequences in terms of both power dynamics and the quality of work.

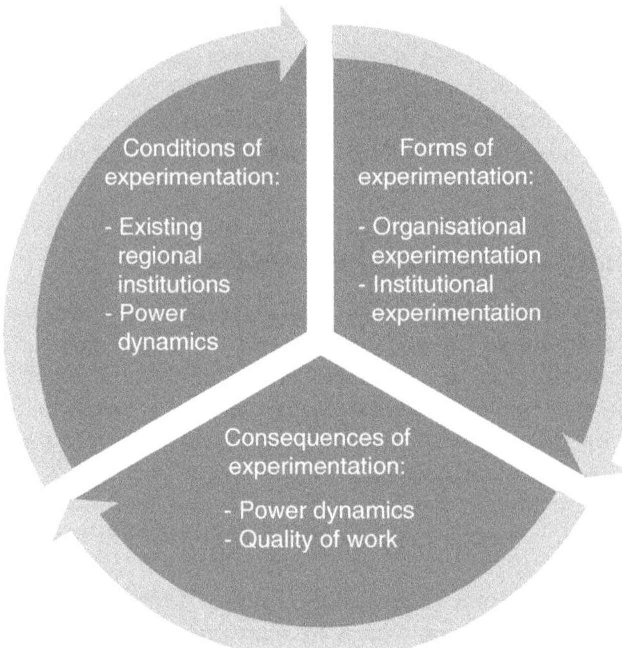

Figure 1.1 Conditions, forms, and consequences of experimentation.

Our main theoretical point is that the deployment and mobilisation of workers' capabilities and power resources is a critical condition to mitigate the negative consequences of experimentation. The conditions for regional experimentation by unions involve a drawing down of power resources, addressing regional institutions. Experimentation in relation to regional governance allows a focus on collective actors, such as labour unions, often expressing different socio-spatial interests and resulting in forms of regulation in relation to these dimensions. There are two dimensions to these logics. First, unions as collective organisations may be historically and institutionally circumscribed, leading to restricted foci associated with past practice. There may be a narrowing of union purpose, which raises questions about what constitutes legitimate and acceptable objectives in relation to regional change. Second, unions organise in multiple contexts, in the workplace, industry, with reference to the state and across global production networks. Their success depends in part on their capacities as collective organisations. As we argue, the collective forms of worker organisation may question or affirm established governance relations and practices.

The Book and Its Focus

The book provides positive examples of experimentation, including experiments where there are limited outcomes or where an experiment has been compromised. In some situations, unions have played a key role in initiating and promoting the experiment while other unions in effect were excluded both from the process of experimentation and from regional governance. Some contributions focus on either organisational experimentation or institutional experimentation, while others focus on the movement from one form of experimentation to the other.

We have focused and organised the contributions in thematic ways to demonstrate the circumstances in which our understandings of unions in and of regions can be further developed. Each set of contributors focused on workers, unions, and regions. They presented and crafted their chapters in terms of their specialist focus. The result is an engagement with the themes outlined, from different perspectives and focusing on illustrative exemplars. The chapters are presented in four parts focusing on the forms of experimentation addressed.

Organisational Experimentations

Part 1 includes two chapters that explore the consequences of organisational experimentation. The first (Morgan and Villella) locates the experiment in relation to urban-based form of governance where unions found themselves in a reactive rather than proactive stance. The second (Holmes), in contrast, examines an inter-state form of industry governance, where unions sought to establish a solidaristic response to corporate supra-regional initiatives; the unions struggled in these circumstances.

The chapter by Glenn Morgan and Manu Villela employs a historical approach to analysing the city's urban regime from its medieval trade origins to its current partnership and networked governance configuration and explores the different experimentations in these different phases. It examines how the shift from manufacturing to services, followed by the emergence of high technology industries, ultimately undermined the role of trade unions, which, in turn, failed to engage with the new organisational experimentations born out of the blurring of boundaries between sectors. It also explores how the different groups leading each of these phases exerted power and influence over the urban political context and how trade unions reacted to these changes in leadership. It concludes by proposing four steps to analyse how urban regimes evolve, experiment, and innovate at the local and regional levels.

This is followed by the chapter by John Holmes that focuses on the automotive industry in the Great Lakes region of North America; an integrated cross-border region that encompasses several US states and southern Ontario in Canada. It argues that when the longer-term viability of vehicle manufacturing in the region was challenged by the emergence of lower-cost automotive regions elsewhere in North America, collective bargaining played a pivotal role in ensuring the resilience of Great Lakes automotive manufacturing. Nonetheless, this was achieved only at a very real cost to autoworkers. The chapter emphasises the dynamic interplay of collective bargaining outcomes between the American and Canadian unions representing autoworkers in the region and how union bargaining priorities underwent a fundamental shift. Over the course of several rounds of bargaining between 2003 and 2016, auto unions on both sides of the border reluctantly accepted wage and benefit concessions, including tiered wage systems for newly hired workers. In a significant departure from past bargaining practice, the unions shifted their primary bargaining demands from economic gains to securing new investment commitments for specific manufacturing plants. Some commitments that were won proved transitory as rapidly shifting market conditions led to further restructuring and plant closures. This caused some to question the efficacy of the switch in bargaining strategy. As more and more new workers were hired, the union's failure during bargaining to eliminate the tiered wage structure coupled with the focus on securing investment commitments for specific workplaces, severely tested traditional rank-and-file solidarity within and across plants and the ability of the union leadership to secure ratification of new agreements. Hence, support for the switch in bargaining strategy proved tenuous and points to the continued challenges facing the union leaderships and their members.

Institutional Experimentations

Part 2 provides cutting-edge, theoretically informed empirical studies on the process of institutional experimentation. The first (MacDonald and Wieditz) focuses on the ways unions may be able to engage in cross-class alliances to promote the possibility of decent jobs and supportive arrangements for the social reproduction of labour. In the second chapter, the authors (Coiquaud and Morissette) focus on regulatory experimentation in relation to the Montreal taxi industry.

The chapter by Ian MacDonald and Thorben Wieditz examines how unions have joined in cross-class territorial alliances to shape labour markets, employment relations, public services, and housing markets across a variety of sectors. It analyses various campaigns as attempts to make labour markets and employment practices conform to a model that is more conducive to union organisation and bargaining in a challenging environment, characterised by the loss of 'good jobs' with deindustrialisation and the rise of new business models in the service economy. The intention of the authors is to produce a map of the terrain which would permit decision-making in full view of the variety of strategies available to unions. They identify the common ground between unions and other class actors, class fractions and the local state, to understand how it is possible for trade unions to advance their priorities in urban and regional governance. The chapter concludes with a reflection on the limits of cross-class alliances and the potential for union strategies beyond the reproduction of capitalist social relations.

The chapter by Urwana Coiquaud and Lucie Morissette seeks to understand how, through experimentation, the state and collective actors endeavoured to structure the taxi industry in Montreal, and why this institutional architecture was weakened with Uber's arrival. The conceptual framework developed in this chapter allows the authors to qualify the institutional transformations through time and to understand how the actors organised themselves around these change processes. To this end, regulatory experimentation was used as a strategic tool in the hands of the actors, with the state and Uber at the forefront. Institutional transition was then forced and processes of mitigating radical change were expressed.

Comparative Studies of Experimentation

Part 3 presents two comparative studies addressing experimentation in a variety of ways involving a range of regions. The first (Hammer and Brill) shows how lead firms in the UK apparel manufacturing play a crucial role in the processes of experimentation but that initiatives undertaken by trade unions and NGOs gradually increase union access and community engagement. In the following chapter, the authors (Lévesque, Gomis, Emilien, and Carrillo) investigate the possibilities and limits of trade union engagement in the processes of organisational experimentation and how these are shaped by the dynamic interplay between structural and dispositional power.

The chapter by Nikolaus Hammer and Lucy Brill argues that economic restructuring concomitantly reshapes the regional and functional division of labour as economic activities are necessarily embedded in specific localities as well as value chain strands. Restructuring, therefore, not only puts regions in competition with other regions, but it also puts them in competition over specific roles in the production of goods and services. Processes of competition and contestation are intertwined in complex ways at different levels. Research at the intersection of institutional and value chain analysis has begun to differentiate between societal dynamics and those at the level of specific value chains. These themes are addressed in this chapter in relation to the growth of UK apparel manufacturing over the last ten years, specifically driven by fast fashion. It has profoundly reshaped the regional and functional division of labour. This renewed growth of apparel manufacturing provides the context for three steps in the analysis. First, the authors argue that in order to understand how local and global dynamics of restructuring interact, it is crucial to differentiate regions and industrial subsectors (Froud et al. 2017). Second, they then investigate to what extent the fruits of this growth in apparel manufacturing have been shared. Third, these developments reveal the underlying politics of these processes. The specific focus is an analysis of two political 'projects' in Leicester and Manchester, two key sourcing hubs for fast fashion.

The next chapter by Christian Lévesque, Redi Gomis, Blandine Emilien, and Jorge Carrillo examines how various actors, in the aeronautic industry in two regions of Mexico, Baja California and Queretaro, engage in organisational experimentation to attract new investment and create high-skill jobs. A striking difference between the two regions lies in the role of trade unions in the process of experimentation. In Baja California, trade unions are not involved in the process of organisational experimentation. Often labelled as 'ghosts unions', these unions are virtually absent from the workplace as well as at the regional level. The coordinated approach developed in Queretaro seems to open up more space for workers and trade unions to participate in the processes of organisational experimentation. Despite the absence of union representation within the cluster association, trade unions can voice workers' concerns and interests through workplace bargaining and regular interactions with both firms and regional organisations (e.g. vocational training institute). The mobilisation of both associational and organisational power provides trade unions with more opportunities to voice their concerns. However, these power resources are not sufficient to overcome the pressures to conform to the export-oriented imperative of the national State and foreign capital (structural power).

The Interconnections between Organisational and Institutional Experimentation

In Part 4, we present three studies that capture the complexity and tenuousness of the movements and shifts between organisational and institutional forms of experimentation. These three chapters focus on how trade union strategic capabilities and power dynamics shape their engagement in the process of experimentation with regional governance. They address different faces of regional governance. The first (González Menéndez and Tejero) focuses on the development of institutions supporting worker skills. The second (Lévesque, Bowkett, Hennebert, and Morissette) examines the promotion and elaboration of industrial experimentation to co-construct the regional governance institutions to address key features of the industry as a global industry. To extend the debate, the last chapter (Barton and Fairbrother) focuses on different forms of union engagement in and of regions to extend the union remit beyond an industrial focus; they note the fragility and challenge of such endeavours.

The chapter by Maria González Menéndez and Aroa Tejero focuses on an innovative Dual Vocational Education and Training (VET) scheme, developed in Asturias, Spain, as an instance of collaborative institutional work of regional unions, employers, and government creating a new institution to address a labour market mismatch. A key sector in the regional development strategy in which employers had often voiced concerns about future skill shortages, the metal sector, was chosen to carry out a Dual VET experiment. The innovative design of the scheme – targeting low-skilled youth, promoting their being at the workplace from day one, and being paid workers – was clearly union-led. Government, trade unions, and employers combined efforts in attracting prospective student-workers and trainers-employers and in supervising the scheme. Tracing the negotiation (2005–2014), implementation (2014–2017), and appraisal (2019) processes, the chapter reveals the key role of trade unions in shaping the scheme. These trade unions used all four strategic capabilities identified by Lévesque and Murray (2010): intermediating between contending interests to foster collaborative action and to activate networks; framing; articulating actions over time and space; and learning. Trade unions' capacity to dominantly frame issues in an unfavourable political and economic national context is explained by the trade unions' power, both structural and associational. Structural, because of the high membership in the sector and more generally in the region, and associational, due to the unions' presentation of a common front of demands and the use of ties to the party in government. The chapter reflects also on the mix of experimentation and of institutional inertia involved in the creation of the new institution, and on the political climate impact on the assessment of the role of social actors as regional regulators of the labour market and its institutional outcomes (labour market inclusion vs employment).

This is followed by the chapter of Christian Lévesque, Cassandra Bowkett, Marc-Antonin Hennebert, and Lucie Morissette who analyse the roles of trade unions in the co-construction of regional governance institutions in the Montreal aerospace industry. These arrangements focus on the challenges facing the industry as a regional employer. The industry operates globally and thus the capabilities and resources for the industry in Montreal are a focus of marked union concern and interest. The chapter analyses the dynamic interplay between organisational and institutional experimentation and how they can transform the rules of the game and lead to new understanding, norms, and rules. It also highlights the necessity for trade unionists to build new resources and capabilities to cope with the challenges of this global industry and, furthermore, to play a leading role in the processes of experimentation. The authors show that the gradual involvement of the union in the processes of experimentation required the development of new strategic capabilities (framing, mediating, learning, articulating). This transformative process was a prerequisite for experimentation, and it compelled the trade union to pursue the experimentation within their own organisation. The development of new ways of thinking and acting put into question the traditional logics on which trade unions have had to rely to build their power at the local, regional, and global levels.

The last chapter by Ruth Barton and Peter Fairbrother explores how unions can engage in experiments in relation to regional transition and change. Of note, unions tend to organise in relation to sectors and occupations and not regions *per se*. Hence, the unions representing these place-based members often appear to connect with questions about the specificities of regional economic and social development in uneven ways. These conundrums are addressed via a study of union representation and engagement in two sub-national regions in Australia, Gippsland in the State of Victoria, and North West Tasmania in the State of Tasmania. Both regions have undergone major restructuring in recent decades, which has created challenges for unions. These engagements range from activity around a specific crisis, such as a closure, and more diffuse concerns to do with climate change in energy processing areas or industrial restructuring and transition. The challenge for unions is that where institutional experimentation remains informal and disconnected from the furtherance of organisational capacities and resources, the experiments are likely to be unstable in the long run. Even where unions have formalised these arrangements organisationally, for example, via a hierarchical confederation structure, inclusive engagements in regional governance can be negated with changes in union leadership and composition. The conclusion is that without a strong and inclusive narrative of engagement in relation to regional governance, based on an inclusive organisational base, the outcome is likely to be *ad hoc*, often responsive, and not purposeful and a changeable position.

References

Almond, P., Gonzalez, M., Gunnigle, P., Lavelle, J., Luque, D., Monaghan, S. & Murray, G. (2014) Multinationals and regional economies: embedding the regime shoppers? *Transfer*, 20(2), 237–253.

Amin, A. (2004) Regions unbound: towards a new politics of place. *Human Geography*, 86(1), 33–44.

Amin, A. & Thrift, N. (1996) Living in the global. In Amin, A. and Thrift, N. (eds.) *Globalization, Institutions and Regional Development in Europe*. Oxford: Oxford University Press, pp. 1–22.

Barton, R. (2018) 'Our tarkine, Our future': the Australian Workers Union use of narratives around place and community in West and North-West Tasmania, Australia. *Antipode*, 50(1), 41–60.

Boeger, N. & Villiers, C. (eds.) (2018) *Shaping the Corporate Landscape: Towards Corporate Reform and Enterprise Diversity*. Oxford: Hart Publishing.

Bourdieu, P. (1980) *Le sens pratique*. Paris: Les Éditions de Minuit.

Campbell, J. (2004) *Institutional Change and Globalization*. Princeton: Princeton University Press.
Carstensen, M. B. & Schmidt, V. (2016) Power through, over and in ideas: conceptualizing ideational power in discursive institutionalism. *Journal of European Public Policy*, 23(3), 318–337.
Clark, J. (2013) *Working Regions: Reconnecting Innovation and Production in the Knowledge Economy*. New York: Routledge.
Clarkson, S. (2001) The multi-level state: Canada in the semi-periphery of both continentalism and globalization. *Review of International Political Economy*, 8(3), 501–527.
Cohen, S. (2006) *Ramparts of Resistance: Why Workers Lost Their Power and How to Get It Back*. London: Pluto Press.
Cooke, P. (2004) Introduction: regional innovation system. An evolutionary approach. In Cooke, P., Heidenreich, M. & Bracyk, H.-J. (eds.) *Regional Innovation Systems*, 2nd ed, London: Routhledge, 1–18.
Crouch, C. (2005) *Capitalist Diversity and Change: Recombinant Governance and Institutional Entrepreneurs*. Oxford: Oxford University Press.
Culpepper, P. (2008) The politics of common knowledge: ideas and institutional change in wage bargaining. *International Organization*, 62(Winter), 1–33.
Culpepper, P. D. (2015) Structural power and political science in the post-crisis era. *Business and Politics*, 17(3), 391–409.
Driver, C. & Thompson, G. (eds.) (2018) *Corporate Governance in Contention*. Oxford: Oxford University Press.
Edwards, P. K. (1986) *Conflict at Work: A Materialist Analysis of Workplace Relations*. London: Blackwell.
Fairbrother P. (2008) Social movement unionism or trade unions as social movements. *Employee Responsibilities and Rights Journal* 20(2), 213–220.
Fairbrother, P. (2014) Unions: Practices and Prospects. In Wilkinson, A., Wood, G. & Deeg, R. (eds.) *The Oxford Handbook of Employment Relations: Comparative Employment Systems*. Oxford: Oxford University Press, 637–654.
Fairbrother, P. (2015) Rethinking trade unionism: union renewal as transition. *The Economic and Labour Relations Review*, 26(4), 561–576.
Fairbrother, P., Hennebert, M.-A. & Lévesque, C. (eds.) (2013) *Transnational Trade Unionism: Building Union Power*. New York and London: Routledge.
Fairbrother, P., Walker, M. & Phillips, R. (2018) Unions and regional governance: the case of North West Tasmania, Australia. *Regional Studies*, 52(11), 1502–1511.
Fairbrother, P. & Webster, E. (2008) Social movement unionism: questions and possibilities. *Employee Responsibilities and Rights Journal*, 20(3), 309–313.
Friedberg, E. (1993) *Le pouvoir et la règle*. Paris: Seuil.
Froud, J., Hayes, S., Wei, H. & Williams, K. (2017) *Coming Back? Capability and Precarity in UK Textiles and Apparel*. Manchester: CRESC, University of Manchester.
Garneau, J. (2021) *Relations d'emploi à l'ère de l'industrie 4.0: Un cas d'expérimentation institutionnelle dans le secteur manufacturier de l'aérospatiale au Danemark, Thèse de doctorat*. Québec: Université Laval.
Garud, R., Hardy, C. & Maguire, S. (2007) Institutional entrepreneurship as embedded agency: an introduction to the special issue. *Organization Studies*, 28, 957–969.
González Menéndez, M., Almond, P. & Murray, G. (2018) Regional Business Systems and the Governance of Foreign Direct Investment in Canada, Spain and the UK. *Revista Española de Investigaciones Sociológicas (REIS)*, 3(163), 3–20.

Goodwin, M. (2012) Regions, territories and relationality: exploring the regional dimensions of political practice. *Regional Studies* 47, 1181–1190.

Gumbrell-McCormick, R. & Hyman, R. (2018) *Trade Unions in Western Europe: Hard Times, Hard Choices*. Oxford: Oxford University Press.

Haipeter, T. (2020) Digitalisation, unions and participation: the German case of 'industry 4.0'. *Industrial Relations Journal*, 51, 242–260, 10.1111/irj.12291.

Heidenreich, M. (2005) The renewal of regional capabilities: experimental regionalism in Germany. *Research Policy*, 34(5), 739–757.

Howell, C. (2021) Rethinking the role of the state in employment relations for a neoliberal era. *IILR Review*, 76(3), 739–772.

Hyman R. (1979) The politics of workplace trade unionism: recent tendencies and some problems for theory. *Capital & Class*, 8, 54–67.

Jonas, A. (2012) City-regionalism: questions of distribution and politics. *Progress in Human* Geography, 36(6), 822–829.

Klijn, E. & Koppenjan, J. (2012) Governance network theory: past, present and future. *Policy and Politics*, 40, 587–606. 10.1332/030557312X655431

Kristensen, P. & Morgan, G. (2012) From institutional change to experimentalist institutions. *Industrial Relations*, 51(1), 413–437.

Larner, W. (2005) Neoliberalism in (regional) theory and practice: the stronger communities action fund in New Zealand. *Geographical Research*, 43, 9–18.

Lévesque, C. & Murray, G. (2010) Understanding union power: resources and capabilities for renewing union capacity. *Transfer*, 16(3), 333–350.

Lévesque, C. & Murray, G. (2013) Renewing union narrative resources: how union capabilities make a difference. *British Journal of Industrial Relations*, 51, 777–796.

Lukes, S. (2005) *Power: A Radical View*. 2nd ed. Basingstoke: Palgrave Macmillan.

Macleod, G. & Goodwin, M. (1999). Space, scale and state strategy: rethinking urban and regional governance. *Progress in Human Geography*, 23(4), 503–527.

Macleod, G. & Jones, M. (2007) Territorial, scalar, networked, connected: in what sense a 'regional world'? *Regional Studies*, 41(9), 1177–1191. 10.1080/00343400701646182

Mansfield, B. (2005) Beyond scaling: reintegrating the 'national' as a dimension of scalar relations. *Progress in Human Geography*, 29(4), 458–473.

Massey, D. (2004) Geographies of responsibility. *Geografiska Annaler Series B*, 84(1), 5–18.

Morgan, G. & Hauptmeier, M. (2014) Varieties of institutional theory in comparative Employment Relations. In Wilkinson, A., Wood, G. & Deeg, R. (eds.) *The Oxford Handbook of Employment Relations: Comparative Employment Systems*. Oxford: Oxford University Press, 190–221.

Morgan, G. & Hauptmeier, M. (2021) The social organisation of ideas in employment relations. *ILR Review*, 74(3), 773–797.

Morgan, K. (2007) The polycentric state: new spaces of empowerment and engagement? *Regional Studies*, 41, 1237–1251.

Morgan, K. (2014) The rise of metropolitics: urban governance in the age of the city-region. In Bradford, N. & Bramwell, A. (eds.) *Governing Urban Economies: Innovation and Inclusion in Canadian City-Regions*. Toronto: University of Toronto Press, 297–318.

Murray, G., Lévesque, C., Morgan, G. & Roby, N. (2020) Disruption and re-regulation in work and employment: from organisational to institutional experimentation. *Transfer: European Review of Labour and Research*, 26(2), 135–156.

Parr, J. (2005) Perspectives on the city-region. *Journal of Regional Studies*, 39(5), 555–566.

Pape, M., Fairbrother, P. & Snell, D. (2016) Beyond the state: shaping governance and development policy in an Australian region. *Regional Studies Journal*, 50(5), 909–921.

Pasquier, V., Daudigeos, T. & Pereira Fernandes De Barros, M. (2020) Towards a new flashmob unionism: the case of the fight for 15 movement. *British Journal of Industrial Relations*, 58(2), 336–363.

Pawel M. (2020) Is the Coronavirus Shaping the Future of How We Work? *The New York Times*, 20 March. Available at: https://www.nytimes.com/2020/03/20/opinion/coronavirus-california.html (accessed 21 March 2020).

Rutherford, T. & Frangi, L. (2020) Is Industry 4.0 a good fit for high performance work systems? Trade unions and workplace change in the Southern Ontario Automotive Assembly Sector. *Relations industrielles/Industrial Relations*, 75(4), 751–773.

Schmalz, S., Ludwig, C. & Webster, E. (2018) The power resources approach: developments and challenges. *Global Labour Journal*, 9(20), 113–134.

Silver, B. J. (2003) *Forces of Labor: Workers' Movement and Globalization since 1870.* Cambridge: Cambridge University Press.

Snell, D. & Fairbrother, P. (2011) Toward a theory of union environmental politics: unions and climate action in Australia. *Labor Studies Journal*, 36(1), 83–103.

Streeck, W. (1991) More uncertainties: German unions facing 1992. *Industrial Relations: A Journal of Economy and Society*, 30(3), 317–349.

Thelen, K. (2009) Institutional change in advanced political economies. *British Journal of Industrial Relations*, 47(3), 471–498.

Weil D. (2014) *The Fissured Workplace: Why Work Became So Bad for So Many and What Can Be Done to Improve It.* Cambridge: Harvard University Press.

Wright, E. O. (2000) Working – Class power, capitalist-class interests, and class compromise. *The American Journal of Sociology*, 105(4), 957–1002.

Zukauskaite, E., Trippl, M. & Plechero, M. (2017) Institutional thickness revisited. *Economic Geography*, 93(6), 325–345.

Part I

Organisational Experimentations

2 Urban Regimes: Experiments and Institutional Innovation

Glenn Morgan and Malu Villela

Introduction

How do urban regimes evolve and what role do trade unions play in these processes? Space for this sort of analysis has begun to open up in the field of industrial relations and employment systems as greater recognition has emerged of the internal differentiation within various forms of capitalism (Almond 2011). Whilst core national institutional features may place constraints on institutional experimentation at the local level, the way in which local patterns of employment interact with and shape the geographical distribution of job opportunities leads to regions and cities with very distinctive social and economic histories and paths of development. As recent research is uncovering, the result is that the ability of actors to engage locally with institutional experimentation and shape policy outcomes at the local and regional level is likely to vary both within and across capitalisms.

In this chapter, we take the particular location of Bristol in the United Kingdom as our example. We build a generalisable analytical framework to understand the role of what we describe as 'urban regimes'. Based on this, we show how over a 50-year period from the 1970s to the late 2010s, the nature of the actors in the local area, and their scale and influence on the politics of the city has changed. We identify three main phases in the development of Bristol in which the role of trade unions gradually changes – the Fordist/Labourist urban regime up to the 1970s; from the late 1970s through to the New Labour victory in 1997, an emergent neo-liberal urban regime characterised by a changing industrial and employment structure and a struggle between the local council and the Tory central government over implementing neo-liberal policies; and finally, as the negative consequences of this became clearer to local actors, the emergence locally within a national framework of neo-liberalism and austerity of a networked governance structure where collaboration between public and private organisations gradually developed.

The chapter is constructed in the following way. Firstly, we develop our analysis of urban regimes and the dimensions across which such regimes can vary. Theoretically, we take a broad pragmatist approach in which urban

DOI: 10.4324/9781003001089-3

regimes evolve, as actors face new contexts and new problems, leading to efforts at creative institutional experimentation that never fully close the circle in the sense of producing institutional stability. Rather, tensions and conflicts are built into the development of urban regimes as actors seek to negotiate their different interests within the urban space through formal and informal systems of representation and organisation whilst all the time being under the pressure of external forces such as outside investors and central government. Secondly, we provide our analysis of how the urban regime evolved in the Bristol context over the period under study. We pay particular attention to the emergence of new forms of governance reflected in forms of institutional experimentation in terms of new partnerships, new organisational structures, and new discursive identities. In the final section of the chapter, we consider the implications of our example for the wider analysis of the role of trade unions in regional and local forms of experimentation.

Urban Regimes and Forms of Governance

Drawing on Stone's classic study, we begin with the idea that an urban regime consists of 'the informal arrangements by which public bodies and private interests function together in order to be able to make and carry out governing decisions' (Stone 1989: 6, 1993). However, unlike Stone, we seek to distinguish between different levels of analysis. Firstly, the concept of 'private interests' needs to be more explicitly embedded in an analysis of the range and form of capitalist enterprises in a particular local area. By private interests in this context, therefore, we are concerned with the nature of private sector employment in a particular location and whether it is primarily owned and governed by those in the locality or is it part of a national or international concern headquartered elsewhere. Part of the issue here also relates to the degree to which local ownership leads to the formation of local status orders reflected in shared social relationships amongst the high-status group, embedded in particular organisations such as Chambers of Commerce and a particular political party (in the United Kingdom, the Conservative party), etc., which articulate a 'business interest' either formally or informally. As authors developing structural power theory have suggested with regard to national governments (Przeworski and Wallerstein 1988; Lukes 2005; Culpepper 2011, 2015), we assume that local governments will also broadly recognise that their fate is intertwined with keeping private sector interests committed to their 'place' in the local community. Therefore, their policies will be concerned to maintain an environment that is favourable to existing and potentially incoming business interests. Challenge to the priorities of the private sector will be limited but in so far as local democratic governance exists (and the terms under which it exists, i.e. how much power does the local have relative to the national government) and becomes salient and relevant for the population, conflicts may arise.

Ownership issues are crucially embedded at the local level with structures of employment. Urban areas are characterised by a mix of employment sites. Certain industry sectors, particularly in assembly manufacturing, have been characterised by large factory workplaces which, in turn, offer opportunities for collective trade union organisation. Smaller workplaces, retail locations, and many professional and technical businesses are less likely to be unionised. Gender and ethnic differences in the workforce can also weaken collective solidarities. Any analysis of an urban regime and the role of trade unions, therefore, needs to investigate how this sectoral division of labour in the local area evolves and influences the degree of collective organisation that is emergent and the degree to which this organisation acts as a counterweight to the structural power of capital.

Alongside the private sector, major public organisations exist representing local government activity (e.g. social care, waste, schools, etc.) and other areas such as local health services, transport, universities, and local branches of central government departments. The boundaries of the public sector vary over time and are in constant play with actors from the private sector. In the UK case, the shift of many of these activities over to the private sector during the neo-liberal era has been a major change in local areas. Conditions of work in terms of wages, hours of work, and other employment conditions, including trade union representation, have been fundamentally altered by these processes, particularly through splitting what were once relationships between a single employer and a wider range of different occupations often represented by a single trade union into a series of separate bargaining units where trade unions are weaker, if not entirely excluded. One area of conflict which is seen therefore in the Bristol context is the struggle by trade unions based in the public sector to resist privatisation and contracting out of services. The size of workplaces and the collective nature of work in many of these organisations led to relatively high levels of unionisation, supporting collective bargaining. Efforts to privatise or contract out many of these activities have been accompanied by declining trade union membership and an overall weakening of bargaining rights and lowering of wages.

An urban regime is also constituted through collective decision making, which shapes the context in which local economic development occurs. In the UK context, locally elected councils with distinctive powers delegated by national governments (but subject to continued monitoring, control, and change) potentially act as an arena in which on the one hand constraints can be placed on market processes and capitalist development, e.g. through planning law, through control of key infrastructure projects and, on the other hand, public goods can be created which have positive effects for business, e.g. education and skill provision, the creation of safe, secure, hygienic and healthy urban environments, the provision of adequate housing, support for new business development, etc. How far local governments go in being active in these areas relates to the nature of the underlying forces within the urban area, the powers which they have in general and, in particular, their ability to raise revenue and articulate a discourse that sustains an electoral coalition giving stability to a particular direction of travel. Beyond the political dynamics of party formation in the local council, important actors in shaping the urban regime are employers and their collective organisations and trade unions working separately or together through institutions such as local Trade Councils. These groups are also key in providing personnel and support for the elected councillors. This terrain is subject to change and, in the United Kingdom, there have been a number of systems of local government with a division of power between them. Post-2010, larger council electorates have been able to choose executive mayors who have formed cabinets rather than rely on older style committee systems.

The 'urban regime' concept suggests that the representatives and leaders of these various groups evolve patterns of working together over time that entrench certain powers and certain ways of doing things. This pattern is not necessarily visible in the formal institutions of local power such as the council, but lies behind the sorts of decisions which emerge into the public arena. Drawing on Lukes' theory of power (2004), one might argue that power in an urban regime is partly visible when decisions advantage one group at the expense of another, but power may also be invisible in the sense that keeping specific issues off the agenda is an important way to exercise power. Finally, power is exercised in an urban regime by the creation of a hegemonic and unquestioned view of what any particular city or region is about; what are the unquestioned assumptions about how it should develop? The focus on power alerts us also to the idea that urban regimes are not static; they evolve and change as power asymmetries are challenged or reconfigured in order to enable old actors to reassert themselves or new actors to find a place for themselves in the urban regime. As new industries rise and old industries fall, institutions and the actors which control them are subject to change as well as being subjects who initiate change.

The key concepts in our extended version of 'urban regimes' and the structures and actors which lie at its core are presented in Figure 2.1.

Outside this core, but continually interacting with it in various ways, disturbing and disrupting emergent institutional equilibrium, lie two main factors – firstly national government and its view of the role of local autonomy/dependence in its wider strategic vision of economic policy and secondly, developments in business and markets which impact on the viability of local economic orders. The result is a continuing challenge to actors in the urban regime to respond to these disruptions by experimenting with and building new institutions. As we shall describe, this is not an easy task and urban regimes can undergo long periods of stagnation and decline from the point of view of employment conditions; whether they are ever able to rebuild and in what ways and with what costs is a key question.

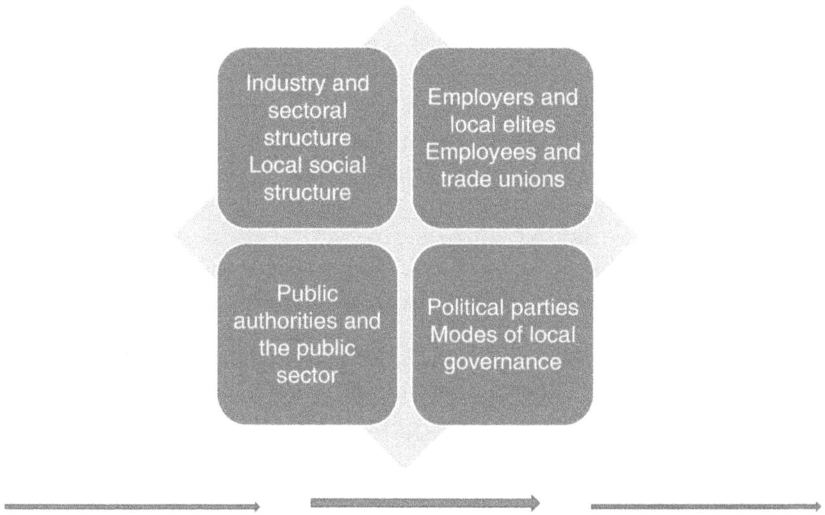

Figure 2.1 Elements of the urban regime: changing over time.

Bristol: Understanding Urban Regimes

Bristol's origins lie in the fact that, from the medieval period, it was an important port through which various agricultural, textile, and raw material products were exported and imported to the wealthy towns and villages of the Cotswolds and Wiltshire. By the 18th century, it was England's second city and port. Because of its easy access to the Atlantic, its importance grew with the discovery of the Americas. It was a central node in the Triangular slave trade, exporting goods and textiles to be traded for slaves in Africa which were, in turn, traded for sugar and tobacco in the Americas. Bristol's Society of Merchant Venturers formed in the early 18th century was made up of local and London-based merchants that funded these trades. They founded various charitable foundations in the City, built a mansion to house their activities in the fashionable neighbourhood of Clifton, and donated part of the open area known as the Downs to the City. Membership of the Merchants is by invitation only – and until very recently only men were allowed – and the organisation remains a self-perpetuating oligarchy of the wealthy in Bristol and the surrounding area, still engaging in educational and philanthropic activities.

From early on, Bristol was a divided city, not just in terms of the contrast between rich and poor, but also in terms of the physical structure of the place. The Harbourside area of the city first developed large warehouses for storage and then began to be the site of processing as tobacco factories, sugar refining, and chocolate production were established as well as a range of shipbuilding, dry dock ship repair, and ships stores. Working-class housing in crowded and insanitary conditions down by the docks contrasted with the mansions of the Merchants and others up on the hill where the graceful village of Clifton characterised by Georgian mansions and squares developed. The dock area and the processing factories were, however, constrained by the tidal nature of the access to the harbour and, as larger ships developed, a new dock was established directly on the Severn at Avonmouth with easy access to the Atlantic from where materials could be taken into the city in smaller vessels for processing. By the late 19th century, a series of 'spin-off' industries had developed in light engineering production sites, e.g. to provide machinery paper and packaging to the tobacco and chocolate factories. Related to this, Bristol was also an early innovator in producing cars and buses and most importantly aircraft. By the inter-war years, Bristol's industrial structure was based on the docks, on tobacco, sugar, and chocolate manufacture and on mechanical engineering with particular expertise in aircraft and buses. This was the legacy Bristol carried into the second half of the 20th century.

The Fordist/Labourist Urban Regime 1950s–1970s

In the post-war period, Bristol experienced a period of growth driven mainly by its manufacturing sector. Boddy et al. (1986) report that 'in 1961 the manufacturing sector in Bristol accounted for 44% of total employment, with 64% of this employment concentrated in three major sectors' (10) – Vehicles (mainly aircraft), Food, Drink and Tobacco, and Paper, Printing and Publishing, often concentrated in relatively large Fordist workplaces with strong trade union presence (especially in aircraft manufacture: Danford et al. 2005). During much of this period, economic conditions were relatively positive for many of these groups of workers. Boddy et al. (1986) argue that 'the long history of relative prosperity in Bristol, together with the welfare paternalism of some of the traditional employers, helped to sustain a tradition of "cordial" labour relations' (11). Trade unions in the area were well organised but, in general, were not seen as particularly militant. Employers responded to tight labour market conditions during these prosperous years by agreeing the moderate wage demands made by the trade unions and although tensions existed within the aircraft sector, in particular, regarding piecework rates, industrial disruption was relatively rare.

The largest companies in the area were British-owned and there were few foreign multinationals in the locality. In his study of 'local notables' in the Bristol area conducted in the mid-1960s and published in 1969, Clements (1969) pointed to the 'often close personal and social relationships between members of sample [of local notables]; according to one informant all the prominent businessmen live outside Bristol and know each other – they can't disentangle their business and private lives' (115). Clements also identified a sense amongst this group that they were highly influential in the city even if they were not councillors. 'The sources of this influence and superiority in the social hierarchy are manifold and complex. Amongst them is the fact that they possess social prestige and important friendships and many are endowed with a kind of traditional legitimacy based on family descent … They also often feel themselves and are acknowledged to fill representative roles as spokesmen of important associations, firms, societies, industries, interest groups or trades which gives them weight, authority and receptive audiences … Many are closely associated with the leadership of institutions of real economic power' (Clements 1969: 120).

At the level of the local Bristol City Council itself, the Labour Party was mainly in control throughout this period. It had strong links to the local trade unions and to the Trades Council. The agenda of the council through much of this time was with rebuilding Bristol from the severe impact of bombing in World War Two when its manufacture of aircraft had made it a major target for the German air force. The old centre of the city had been severely damaged, reducing retail space but also impacting on housing. The Labour Council and the trade unions were united in supporting a rapid modernisation of the city and, from much of the 1950s and 1960s, this involved bulldozing many areas of old Bristol and replacing them with new concrete buildings and road systems in the centre and creating large public housing estates on the edge of the city or in tower blocks nearer to the centre. The lead taken by the council and the fact that being in Labour hands was supportive of collective bargaining enabled trade unions to spread their membership further into the local government sector. The private sector, the 'local notables', and the Conservatives on the council were broadly part of this consensus supporting the redevelopment programme, both for its social effects and for some of the business opportunities it opened up for building contractors and later property developers. Clements (1969) argues that, in this phase, 'the typical relationship between notables and the local political system … was commonly one of business-like cooperation, "give and take", in enterprises in which both or all sides are recognized to have legitimate, if somewhat differing, interests' (137). Finally, it is noticeable that this Fordist reconstruction of Bristol in both production and consumption terms was accomplished with little direct input from central government and/or multinational capital. It reflected the long-term development of a particular combination of capitalist development and local political and social hierarchies that gave Bristol distinctive advantages and strengths stretching back to its early insertion in global value chains and mercantile capitalism in the 17th and 18th centuries.

Bristol and the Neo-liberal Revolution 1970s–2000s

From the 1970s, this model of Bristol's urban regime was put under pressure from both outside and inside. Outside pressures were of two main sorts. Firstly, the manufacturing industries which had employed so many people in Bristol were becoming increasingly uncompetitive as old markets declined (such as tobacco) and new competitors entered traditional markets. In the period 1971–1978, manufacturing employment in Bristol fell by 14.3% with more than 78% of the losses being in the three main sectors of Food, Drink and Tobacco; Vehicles; and Paper and Print. Reflecting the gendered division of labour that existed in Bristol where men were over-represented in manufacturing, the result was the loss of significantly more male jobs than female jobs. Secondly, as the UK's competitive position deteriorated more generally against other countries, government finances became increasingly constricted. By the late 1970s, and in particular during the Thatcher years of the 1980s, central government began firstly to impose a series of restrictions on the revenue-raising powers of councils, then on what they could spend on and, finally, on what services they could provide in-house as opposed to privatizing. For councils traditionally run by Labour, the Thatcher years posed particularly hard choices about spending and services and whilst Bristol's conflicts with Whitehall were not as well known as those which gripped cities such as Liverpool and London, they were nevertheless highly consequential for the city, for Labour politics, and for the influence of trade unions. The latter was particularly undermined by the liberalisation and reregulation of employment relations.

On the other hand, Bristol did not turn into the wasteland that many British cities did during the 1980s. Instead it became hailed as a 'boom city'. In the first instance this reflected the growing importance of services in the city's economy. Its mercantile past had meant that it was always well served by professional groups such as lawyers, accountants, and bankers and a thriving retail sector serving a wealthy clientele as well as a more mass-market set of consumers. In turn, these groups had encouraged the development of a range of high-quality private schools in the area and, eventually, a civic university and, later, a large polytechnic which turned into a university. By the 1960s, these institutions were involved in a range of large science projects together with local businesses, e.g. on the supersonic Concorde project. This provided both a business and a social attraction for services companies wishing to move out of high rent London and for new start-ups. Even by 1971, Bristol had a higher proportion of service sector jobs than the country as a whole (57.3% compared to 54.2%: Boddy et al. 1986: 14) and this area of employment continued to grow particularly in Insurance, Banking, and Finance where the sector's employment grew by 73% between 1971 and 1981. Four UK insurance companies and the insurance subsidiary of one of the major clearing banks relocated to Bristol between 1972 and 1983, according to Boddy and Lovering (1986: 229).

Another area which became increasingly identified with employment growth in Bristol from the early 1980s was high technology electronics. Boddy and Lovering (1986) describe early predictions made in the *Sunday*

Times in 1981 that 'Bristol is on the way to becoming the high technology centre of Britain ... set to become Britain's Silicon Valley of the 1980s' (218). In their evaluation of these claims, Boddy and Lovering note that by far the most important sector has been aircraft manufacture and although this had stimulated a number of small sub-contracting companies, many of these were involved in low-level processes, not high technology. They found some evidence of advanced electronics companies often working in growing defence industries cluster in the Bristol area including participating in developing new weapons systems for the British military. In terms of employment and labour market impact, these sectors provided a range of opportunities at semi-skilled, technical, and managerial levels.

These changes in the industrial structure impacted differently on employers and employees. The era of 'local notables' declined as larger companies from London moved in bringing managers without long-term connections to the Bristol area or the networks embedded in family, school, and social ties that had linked together and solidified the status and position of the earlier groupings. Although old organisations such as the Merchant Venturers, the Chamber of Commerce, the Rotary Club, etc. continued to exist, they no longer carried the same long-term sense of entitlement to influence that had characterised the earlier era. Bristol's business community was becoming more diverse; there remained some substantial and important local companies but many of them were starting to headquarter themselves in the City of London and orient themselves to the London Stock Exchange and international shareholders, whilst London-based firms were moving some of their activities to Bristol and gradually a small number of foreign multinationals were beginning to enter.

These changes were having consequences for the trade unions. Expansion of service sector employment in private companies was often less helpful to trade union membership whilst some traditional manufacturing areas of strength were rapidly declining. Legislation in the Thatcher years made it more difficult to organise, as did the impact of major trade union defeats such as the Miners Strike. Government pressures on local government also had an impact. Council house sales and restrictions on public sector house building were soon followed by regulations forcing councils to privatise and contract out many services such as waste collection, direct labour organisations, highway maintenance services, managing leisure centres, etc. Although EU-backed TUPE (Transfer of Undertakings Protection of Employment) regulations reduced some of the changes to employment conditions which private-sector employers might have wanted to impose, over time, the worsening of wages, work conditions, and employee benefits was occurring.

In Bristol, trade unions supporting the Labour group on the council found themselves fighting a number of battles over specific privatisations in part because the council, during the previous era, had invested in infrastructure projects to help build the city's economy. Two of these were the

Royal Portbury Dock and Bristol Airport. The Docks project had begun in the 1950s when Avonmouth, built in the 19th century itself (and owned and controlled by the council), had seemed to be becoming obsolete for the size of ships that were emerging as the container revolution began to take hold. In 1971, the city managed to get the relevant legislation through Parliament to allow it to build new docks. There was to be no government subsidy and the council would have to finance the development itself. Work was completed by 1977 and, as Bassett states, 'to the Labour majority on the council the new dock was a triumph of municipal socialism; to the Conservatives on the council who were equally enthusiastic, it was a triumph of municipal entrepreneurialism' (Bassett 1993: 259). Unfortunately, however, it soon became obvious that with the United Kingdom becoming more integrated into the EU, ports on the West Coast such as Bristol were less in demand (Bassett and Hoare 1984). When the world economy stalled in the early 1980s, demand and revenues at the port fell further. To the dismay of the unions, the number of port employees was cut from around 2000 to 704. The annual financial deficit grew, and the gap had to be met by the City Council placing a burden on ratepayers at a time when the Thatcher government was already constraining spending and council revenue raising. By the late 1980s, the Conservatives on the council who briefly held power had decided to restructure the Port in order to make it ready for privatisation – effectively by taking its debt off the books and placing it in the council's accounts directly. A private company named First Corporate made an approach to the council in 1990 to buy the port. At first there was little opposition from the workforce, which had had to endure a long period of uncertainty. However, after the deal was done, Bassett reports that there was a political backlash when First Corporate announced that it had made a deal with National Power to build a facility at the port which would enable it to import millions of tons of coal. 'This provoked strong opposition by the small group of left-wing councillors who had opposed the sale and also alerted the National Union of Mineworkers (NUM) to a major threat to its members' (Bassett 1993: 263). The controversy that followed did nothing to change the outcome and subsequent to this, First Corporate made further deals including becoming the main site for the import of Japanese Honda cars into the United Kingdom and later importing liquid natural gas.

A second privatisation struggle took place over Bristol airport which had been owned by Bristol City Council since 1929 even though it has been located at Lulsgate in North Somerset since 1957. In 1986, the Thatcher government passed a law empowering the Secretary of State for Transport to 'order airports under complete or partial municipal ownership and with annual turnovers exceeding £1 million to be reconstituted as limited liability companies' (Hoare 1997). The Council was forced to reconstitute the governance structure, though in the early stages it retained full control. In 1997, a majority shareholding in the airport was sold to FirstGroup and then in 2001, the airport was sold to a joint venture of Macquarie Group and Cintra (a subsidiary of Ferrovial) which in turn sold it in 2014 to the Ontario Teachers Pension Plan (which had been building up its holdings since 2002). In 2018, Bristol airport reported that 3,978 employees were working at the airport for a range of companies including airlines, concessions, support, and operations. The council was unable to hold on to its control of the airport under pressure from central government to privatise. Instead, the ultimate ownership of the airport is currently vested in a Canadian public organisation, again undermining any sense of a set of 'local notables' coordinating the urban regime. The diversity of employers also militated against unified employee action even if some groups did pursue their own interests through various forms of collective activity.

Finally, a crucial area of conflict which occurred in the 1980s and 1990s was over the Council's role in city planning (Punter 1992; 1993). As the industrial structure of the city changed, demand grew for more office space. Under long-standing legislation, the City Council had the right to zone various areas in particular ways – residential, retail, office, manufacturing, etc. Any planning applications for new buildings had to be considered in the light of these zoning decisions and further criteria established regarding the nature and quality of buildings. During the period of the Fordist urban regime as described earlier, all groups were committed to speedy reconstruction and construction of housing and retail space with relatively little concern for aesthetic or other considerations. However, Bristol was a city with a long tradition and a number of areas in which architecturally distinguished residential, factory, port, and administrative buildings from the 18th and 19th centuries had retained a place, even if they had fallen into disuse. By the 1970s, therefore, there was an emerging conservation movement in the city that was beginning to challenge what they saw as the unnecessary destruction of the City's building heritage. By the 1980s, this was building into an area of conflict in part because property developers were starting to buy up old parts of the city, particularly in the docks area (an emerging trend globally), in order to provide office space for the new entrants and to develop new leisure and residential facilities. The old docks in the centre, in particular, were a major area of contention. A combination of war damage and then decline in their use had led to them being derelict, but given their location in the heart of the city and the growing example of other dockland-led city revivals in the United States and the United Kingdom, this area became the heart of the conflict (Punter 1992, 1993). The Labour Group, supported by trade unions, were against the emerging property speculation and property boom and sought to operate a more balanced planning agenda in which there was mixed usage of the inner city space with issues of conservationism and access to low-cost social housing as criteria to be taken into account in the planning process. However, the city was refused any central government assistance for this sort of inner-city regeneration on three separate occasions – 1978, 1980, and 1983, reflecting, firstly, a widely held view that Bristol was a wealthy city and did not need government money and, secondly, during the years of the Thatcher government, an unwillingness to support a Labour council which was hostile to the Tory project. Instead the government supported property developers as drivers of the regeneration process. This group, which had bought up many of the derelict sites in the docks area, became increasingly frustrated by the council's efforts to stymie their projects, claiming incompetence inside the council's planning department for long delays in reaching decisions. As such decisions could be overturned by inspectors sent from Whitehall who supported the government line that property development was generally positive, the Labour council were losing the battle. However, it was a long and arduous process in which the gap between Bristol's Labour council and its trade union supporters on one side and the Thatcher government on the other side was all the time growing. All around the docks area, struggles took place between the city planners and property developers about new buildings. As these heightened in intensity, the national government decided to try to wrest control of property permissions from the council by setting up Urban Development Corporations (UDC), the borders of which were to be carefully demarcated to take the most important areas of land in the city under the planning control of the UDC rather than the council. Within the UDC, property developers could expect to more quickly win permissions to build offices and to build in ways which might have contravened the city's zoning and quality specifications.

The most emblematic of the struggles was the conflict over a new office development right next to the water on a piece of land named Canon's Marsh. A group of property developers had purchased the land and buildings in the area and had entered into negotiations with Lloyds Bank to design a major new building to allow a large relocation of staff from London to Bristol. The council was concerned that the original design would block access to the waterfront as well as turn what was meant to be a large public open space combining different retail, entertainment, and housing uses with a restrictive private office building acting as a barrier along the harbourside. Concerned that if the decision was left to the UDC, the property developers might win everything they wanted, the city entered into a speedy set of negotiations which, in their view reduced the worst of the consequences of the plan whilst allowing the basic office building to be built. However, the UDCs went ahead and further exacerbated conflict between local government on the one side and property developers supported by the UDC and central government on the other.

The period under discussion saw a fundamental change in the nature of the industries and sectors which dominated Bristol. The shift from manufacturing to services and the emergence of some high technology industries were crucial to weakening trade unions on top of the active efforts of the government to reduce their power and influence. These same shifts also saw a decline of the system of 'local notables'. Firms from outside Bristol came with executives and leaders that had little knowledge of the city, few networks and even fewer social connections to each other and the city. New actors arose seeking to develop new businesses, particularly in finance and in property. On the council itself, conflicts between Labour and Conservatives deepened as ideological struggles at the national level translated into specific conflicts locally over privatisations, over cuts, and over property and planning. The urban regime was pushed by the power of central government down a neo-liberal policy route but actors in the council sought to resist this. However, their traditional allies in trade unions were weakening and new forces, particularly in finance and property development, were growing that were using the Thatcherite changes to their own advantage in terms of restructuring the landscape of Bristol as a city. Nevertheless, there was a sense in the mid-1990s that these conflicts were actually holding the city back as a whole. In the early 1990s, the city again failed to receive funding for regeneration under the City Challenges initiative. Partly, that was down to the council. As Malpass (1994), for example, argues, the message given to officers in Bristol council was that 'nothing should be done to compromise certain basic principles' (306), even if this meant that the bid failed. In particular, bids were more likely to succeed where they could show sustained partnership between different groups and particularly between the private sector and the council, but over the 1980s this had dwindled in Bristol. By the early 1990s, therefore, there was a growing recognition that these gaps needed to be bridged if the city was to move forward.

From Neo-liberalism to Partnership and Networked Governance?

In the 1990s and 2000s, the city's economic structure began to change again in ways which enabled various actors to develop new bridge building and partnership initiatives and experimentally and pragmatically create a new urban regime. At the level of employment and industrial structure, manufacturing employment continued to decline. The main exception to this was the continued importance of the aerospace and defence industries. At the ownership level, the internationalisation of the sector as a whole and its development towards global supply chains within integrated multinationals led to a series of changes in the local aerospace and defence industries. British Aerospace became BAE Systems in 1999 and, in 2001, spun off its business building aircraft wings based at Filton in Bristol to a new company, Airbus UK, which in turn became part of what was initially EADS and is now Airbus SE, a company registered in the Netherlands owned in part by the German, French, and Spanish states and in part by private funds. Being part of Airbus and its efforts at competing globally with Boeing and other suppliers of passenger jets has provided trade unions in Filton with a continuing source of membership and power. Upskilling and implementing high-performance work systems has been accompanied by efforts at developing a more partnership-oriented employment policy with trade unions (Danford et al. 2005), whilst at the same time leaving the workforce potentially vulnerable to relocation decisions made by a management based outside the United Kingdom, a vulnerability increased recently by Brexit pressures. At present, the Filton site remains the key producer of wings for Airbus and the main site for manufacturing-type employment in the Bristol area. The Airbus model also comprises a complex network of contracted out suppliers and service providers though detailed data on employment impact is not available. Overall, the 2011 census identified 6.5% of the employed population of Bristol in manufacturing. Financial and professional services have continued to be of importance in the area, constituting over 15% of people in employment in the 2011 census.

However, three trends have emerged that were not so obvious in the earlier period. Firstly, there has been a significant growth in the creative industries in the Bristol area. Historically, the BBC has had a significant programme making presence in Bristol which, post the Birt reforms, led to a spinning out of many creatives into setting up their own companies locally and a vibrant scene of independent film companies and film studios. In 2020, it was announced that the TV channel, Channel 4, would open a hub in Bristol, further consolidating the creative media cluster, including Oscar-winning Aardman Animations famous for 'Wallace and Gromit' animated films. Linked to the extension of the creative economy has been the powerful example of Banksy, a local graffiti artist whose works appear across the city at irregular intervals and who now has a global reputation. Musical innovation has contributed to the dynamic nature of the 'Bristol sound' in terms of both recording artists such as Massive Attack, Roni Size, Tricky and live performance venues in the area. All of these have come together more as digital technology has opened up the space for developing new artistic ventures, a process in which the Watershed Media Centre has played a major role, not just locally and nationally but also internationally, in leading the way to facilitating open access creative experiments through a mixture of public and private funding (Griffiths et al. 1999).

Secondly, and related to this, has been the development of many new business ventures. In 2016, Bristol had more than 2.5 times more jobs in visual arts, such as programming and broadcasting, than the English average (ONS 2017), and it was also the third city in the United Kingdom with the largest growth in the number of SMEs, just behind London and Birmingham (Centre for Economics and Business Research 2017). In the first half of 2017, there were around 3,500 new business start-ups in the region, mostly located in the professional, scientific, and technical activities sectors (Bristol City Council 2017a). By 2025, SMEs in Bristol are expected to contribute around £5 billion to the UK economy (Centre for Economics and Business Research 2017). Bristol has been listed as both a creative and a high-tech economy hotspot by

NESTA (Bakhshi et al. 2015), the UK global innovation foundation. It was also awarded a leading UK SMART City in May 2016 and in 2017, overtook London as the UK's leading SMART City (Woods et al. 2016). The 2016 report considered Bristol 'a leader in open data access, energy innovation, and imaginative forms of community engagement' and highlighted the role of Bristol is Open as 'a unique project that can put the city among the global leaders in urban innovation projects' (Woods et al. 2016: 7). Bristol is Open is a joint venture between the Bristol City Council and the University of Bristol focused on developing an open programmable city.

Thirdly, it is worth noting also that many of these new businesses have been developing with a strong social mission often around ethical and sustainability objectives. The Local Enterprise Partnership's last survey was undertaken in 2012 and identified around 600 social enterprises in the region, employing 10,000 people and with a turnover of 378 million pounds (Social Enterprise Works 2013). Research by Roger Tym & Partners in 2006 assessed the demand and supply of social enterprise business support in South West England and identified 5,500 organisations with potentially 2,200 of them generating at least 25% of their income from trading (Social Enterprise Works 2013). As for Bristol's region, the most recent report is from 2004/5 and covered the broader social economy, including trading social enterprises, as well as voluntary and community groups. According to the report, the social economy in Bristol was worth 240 million pounds, with 70% of the income coming from trading. It employed 15,000 staff and 20,000 volunteers. Around 35% of these organisations identified themselves as social enterprises and 10% as co-operatives. The diversity of legal forms available in sector (e.g. community interest company, cooperative, community benefit society, company limited by guarantee, etc.) allows for a certain degree of organisational experimentation with organisations combining these forms in different ways to meet their needs. Numbers found in the Co-operative UK database show a turnover of more than 24 million pounds for co-operatives in Bristol, accounting for 43 co-operatives with around 12,500 members (Co-op UK 2017). Another type of organisation in the more commercial side of the spectrum is the mission-led or purpose-driven enterprise, which are mainly – but not only – limited companies that seek to balance purpose and profit by embedding social and/or environmental goals in their core business. The B Corp is a popular framework that certifies this type of organisation. In Bristol and region in 2018 there are 8 B Corps (international certification for mission-led businesses), 6 Social Enterprise Mark organisations (national accreditation for social enterprises), and 12 social enterprises that are members of Social Enterprise UK (national membership following certain criteria).

In September 2013, Bristol was awarded as one of the UK's first Social Enterprise Cities by Social Enterprise UK (SEUK), the national membership body for social enterprises. The award is part of the organisation's Social Enterprise Places initiative which is aimed at building awareness across the country and helping grow the impact of social enterprises – currently, 20 regions have been awarded the title of Social Enterprise Place. The increase in the number and participation of social enterprises in local economies has been led in recent years mainly by the impact of austerity in public spending with social services and governmental funding for local charities. Consequently, local councils have been forced to contract out their services and in this process, existing workforces have sometimes won the new contract creating employee-owned organisations with a social mission. Others have arisen because of the strength of the networks and discourse within the city around sustainability. Here the City Council has been instrumental. On the environmental sustainability side, the city is also an important hotspot receiving the European Green Capital Award (EGCA) in 2015 (following on from Copenhagen in 2014). This status is awarded by the European Commission to one city each year and recognises and rewards local efforts to improve the environment, the economy, and the quality of life in cities. The EGCA is given to cities which are leading the way in environmentally friendly urban living and that can thus act as a role model to inspire other cities. The campaign in Bristol to win this award involved many organisations from different sectors including the social enterprise sector working closely with the City Council.

These changes have created a new economic base for the city building on existing skills but moving away from reliance on big international companies (which though still present, create vulnerabilities for local employees) towards smaller scale businesses and start-ups based on high levels of skills in digital and creative industries and drawing on a young educated workforce initially attracted by the two strong universities in the city and then looking for ways to settle in the area (Work Foundation 2006). In some ways, however, this does exacerbate problems of inequality as this economy is lop-sided and unequal. The city's current Labour Mayor, Marvin Rees, has already stated that 'there is another Bristol, one that tourists and even some of our citizens never see – the city of poverty and inequality' (Bristol City Council 2017b: 6). A significant number of areas in the city, 42 in total (mostly on the outside of the city in areas of large post-war council housing estates), are among the 10% most deprived in England. Moreover, 16% of its residents live in poverty (1 in 4 children and 1 in 5 elderly), and there is a gap in life expectancy of 9.6 years for men and 7 years for women between the most and least deprived areas (Bristol City Council 2017a).

Nevertheless, it is worth asking how the city moved from the situation of conflict that characterised the 1980s and early 1990s to the current state of dynamic growth even under conditions of austerity and uncertainty. Bassett points out that, in the early 1990s in Bristol, there was 'the rapid emergence of new forms of public-private partnerships in the city'. As described earlier, the Labour Group in the 1980s had 'maintained much of its traditional suspicion of the local business community' (Bassett 1996: 543). However, the failure of the council to win regeneration funds, the seeming vulnerability of the aircraft and defence industry (when the end of the Cold War led to reduced spending on weaponry and a loss of 23% of employment in this sector in the Bristol area), the inability of the council to make progress on infrastructure projects led to the emergence of new organisations aimed at overcoming some of these problems. Bassett described the formation of The Bristol Initiative (TBI) in 1991 as an example. Sponsored by the local Confederation of British Industry (CBI) employers, TBI reached out to involve the trade unions and the Labour Party and, building on developments in the creative sector, created a Bristol Cultural Partnership which became central to the effort to broaden the base of the city away from a reliance on aerospace and financial services (Griffiths et al. 1999). Another partnership was the Western Development Partnership (WDP) which brought together businesses, employers' organisations and local councils to apply for EU funds. A new revived Bristol Chamber of Commerce and Initiative also emerged in the early 1990s together with the Bristol Regeneration partnership. Bassett argues that these initiatives were led by a new and more active elite, 'mostly high-ranking executives in the regional offices of large firms in aerospace, financial services and privatized utilities' (Bassett 1996: 547). Such activities were also encouraged by the Blair government from 1997 with its focus on bringing together public and private actors to solve problems.

From the early 2000s, these partnerships became increasingly entangled with an emerging constituency within the professional middle-class population of Bristol that, building on earlier conservationist trends in the city, began to press more strongly for developing an environmentally sustainable city. Boddy et al. (2004) argued that 'the complex proliferation of partnerships and networks is weakly integrated and is lacking in collaborative capacity and strategic direction' (65). In our view, however, over the years since their research, these networks have become more established and whilst the network form per se means that these structures do not have the same capacities for quick authoritatively coordinated action as organisations, they nevertheless can become effective as the basis of an urban regime which is relatively inclusive. For example, Malpass et al. (2007), in their study of the spread of Fair Trade in Bristol, noted that whilst this was initially taken up by the local councils, 'the steering group quickly brought together a range of other activists and interests from around the city, including faith-based activists from Christian Aid, Traidcraft and Oxfam; ethical business interests representing local firms such as Café Unlimited (a fairtrade café) and Equop (an organic fair trade clothing company); and locally based national interests such as the Triodos Bank and the Co-operative; and representatives from school and university groups' (636). Interestingly, they also note that trade union representation was not part of this configuration of interest.

A key partnership that solidified the role of sustainability in the Bristol context was the Bristol Green Capital Partnership (BGCP). This was initially formed in 2007 with a mission of making Bristol a 'low-carbon city with a high quality of life' (Brownlee 2018). It was an outcome of a vision set by The Bristol Partnership – an outcome of Labour government to create Local Strategic Partnerships – which brought together the main public sector bodies, representatives of the business and voluntary sectors, creating a plan for the city called the Community Strategy 2003. It put forward a vision of Bristol becoming 'a green capital in Europe – creating sustainable communities and improving the quality of life' (Brownlee 2018). Based on this vision, a debate was organised in 2006 to discuss Bristol as a 'green capital' and, in 2007, Bristol City Council took the lead by bringing organisations across sectors together to form the foundations of BGCP. When the European Commission launched the European Green Capital Award in May 2008, Bristol City Council led a bid for the city to become Green Capital. The city was shortlisted in the first round but got no further and decided not to apply again until they felt more prepared to do so. A couple of years later under the Independent mayor, George Ferguson, well known in local and national circles for his commitment to sustainability, they applied and got selected in 2013 for the 2015 award. Bristol Green Capital Partnership became a Community Interest Company (CIC) in 2014 and another company was formed for the year, Bristol 2015 Ltd., to support the delivery of the award, with George Ferguson as a director. One year later the company was dissolved and BGCP continued to lead the sustainability agenda in the city, entering a new phase in January 2016 with funding from nine strategic partners of its Board of Directors and a new business model, which aims 'to enable, help deliver, and lead the efforts of organisations in Bristol to achieve the changes needed to realise an environmentally sustainable city' (Brownlee 2018).

In 2018, BGCP currently have 836 member organisations coming from different sectors (such as 56% private, 28% third sector, 11% voluntary, and 5% public sector). Among the nine key organisations supporting its activities are Bristol City Council, the two universities in the city, Business West (the leading private sector network), Triodos (which advertises itself as an ethical bank and states that 'By lending exclusively to organisations who put people and the planet before profits, our savers' money works to create a positive impact and real returns'), and Resource Futures (both B Corps), SusTrans, Centre for Sustainably Energy and Avon Wildlife Trust (three UK charities focused on mobility, energy, and wildlife, respectively). BGCP is recognised as 'the largest partnership of its kind in the world' and has in its network the main resource to drive change through the 'power of collective action'. As they describe it, 'Our unique network enables collaboration across public, private, and third sectors in and beyond Bristol, to realise the change needed to address the environmental sustainability challenges we face' (Bristol Green Capital Partnership 2018).

Social enterprises which clustered around BGCP described their social values mainly in terms of issues of sustainability rather than poverty and deprivation. Their business models were therefore often forward looking in terms of how to overcome issues of energy dependence on fossil fuels, how to encourage greater recycling, how to make the economy more local in order to avoid 'food miles' and dependence on outside corporates for key decision making. This perspective drew in younger people, often connected to the universities, building new hybrid social enterprises through innovative ideas linked both to technical expertise in fields such as computing, internet, web design, the management of local currency systems such as the Bristol Pound,[1] and also to reforming supply chains and production processes in food, coffee, craft beer, etc. It is also a narrative that has particular appeal to politicians as it can fit neatly into the vision of an open Bristol, pushing forward internationally and locally, and developing an environment that is encouraging to innovation, entrepreneurship, and mission-led businesses. It is relevant to note, however, that trade unions, although supportive of such moves, were generally not centrally involved.

In political terms, the changes in the city had led to new electoral outcomes and Labour domination of the council declined, with the growth of the Liberal Democrats resulting in a number of minority administrations during the 1990s and 2000s. Thus, at the same time that the city was creating more networks, building more businesses, and generally developing for itself a new identity, the City Council appeared to be a drag on this process (Sweeting et al. 2004). Not surprisingly, then, when offered the opportunity to have an elected executive mayor for the city, the electorate voted in favour. This organisational change seems to have created a stronger leadership inside the council (Hambleton and Sweeting 2014), though party conflicts remain. Under the Labour mayor, Marvin Rees, elected in 2016 and reelected in 2021, the council has played an increasing role in seeking to facilitate coordination and cooperation between the various actors and networks in the city by providing a common framework for activities built up after months of consultation. Known as the Bristol One-City Plan and published in January 2019, this sets out a vision for the city in 2050 by specifying six priority areas in turn linked to UN Global Goals for Sustainable Development. Each area is discussed in relation to what needs to be done and what are the challenges to achieving the vision.

If we discuss this in terms of our 'urban regimes' concept, this phase of the city's development has seen a change in the employment structure towards a more skilled and diversified labour force, a newly dynamic start-up and small firm sector associated with creative and digital industries (linked into global consumption chains) and with the social and green economy, the maintenance of a skilled manufacturing sector vulnerable to global trends in trade and technology and a financial and professional services sector associated with highly skilled qualified graduates. These changes have created an environment in which there are increasingly activist movements, organisations, and individuals seeking to combine business goals with a commitment to sustainability and social accountability. These objectives are increasingly managed not within a council dominated by a single party but through an extended and collaborative set of networks. In terms of our interest in trade unions, their influence has dwindled because of these changes though it has not disappeared. They are one group of actors – now increasingly dependent on public sector memberships with only a few pockets of significant private sector members (mainly aerospace). The urban regime has characteristics of post-Fordism, being decentralised and networked, with a focus on building the technology of the future as the basis for further economic development. The network and partnership model in the city has involved a series of experiments and institutional innovations that have in turn been successful in embedding more deeply these new forms. Inequalities persist within the city though the language in which this is discussed is increasingly in terms of creating an inclusive and diverse economy through increasing skill levels, dispersing technological resources, encouraging new businesses and social enterprises in deprived areas. An aspect of this has also been a growing detachment from central government since 2010, reflected in part by the squeeze on funding exercised under the UK austerity plans, making it futile for the council to think in terms of significant assistance in combatting the worst consequences of these policies by gaining extra funds from government. Instead this has been seen as an opportunity for the city to strengthen its own identity not just in the United Kingdom but in various global forums for cities in which Bristol is now heavily involved.

Conclusions

The objective of this chapter is to consider how urban regimes evolve, experiment, and innovate and the role of trade unions in these processes. In order to achieve this task, we argue that studies need to proceed through four steps. Firstly, it is necessary to understand the basic employment and industrial structure of an urban context. It is out of this that, secondly, a certain pattern of class and status groups emerge and become embedded in organisational forms and local governance regimes. These actors then, thirdly, influence the policies and actions that are taken regarding key aspects of local economic development. These influences can be exerted in a variety of ways that can be illuminated by drawing on theories of power developed by authors such as Lukes (2005) and Culpepper (2011, 2015). Such theories have been predominantly applied to the national context but they are also relevant in the local context so long as they are analysed – and this is our fourth point – in terms of the particular organisational structure which exists at the local level and the capacities embedded there arising from the delegation from the central government.

Crucially, our case study reveals how the actors change over time as the industrial structure itself changes. The business elite in the early days of our analysis of Bristol was primarily local, socially connected, and embedded in certain organisations such as the Merchant Venturers. By the 2010s, the business elite was very different, partly international through membership of multinational companies, and partly local but embedded in new industries and with technical skills rather than the old form of social and cultural capital that characterised Clement's 'local notables'. Some of the old elite survived and transferred their social capital into the new era but others, particularly small manufacturers of standard goods and owners of local retail outlets, were less prominent. Similarly, whereas trade unions had been central participants, particularly in the Fordist era of modernising the city and later in the conflicts over privatisation in the 1980s, by the 2000s they were relatively insignificant. Instead a range of new public/private partnership organisations had risen to prominence building a new identity for the city through their activities. Just as the actors had changed, so had the key institutions and sites in which decisions had taken place. Shifting from the privacy of the boardroom and the electoral bearpit of the council chamber, the 1990s had seen the beginnings of a process of networked governance and a slow gradual coordination of key actors around a new set of themes such as digital and creative industries, sustainability, and the green agenda.

More broadly, our approach emphasises that in order to understand the viability of institutional experimentation at the local level, we need to embed our approach in an understanding of the history, sociology, and politics of the context and how this has evolved in response to the dynamics of global capitalism and the transformations of national states as they, in turn, respond to the uncertainties of markets and geopolitics (e.g. Bristol's development cannot be understood without noting the role of the world wars and the Cold War on the development of its aerospace sector). In this way, we may be able to understand better the conditions of possibility for past innovations and crucially the capability for future institutional experimentation.

Note

1 The Bristol Pound is one of the largest local currencies in Europe with over 700 places in the City where it can be used. Its publicity situates it firmly as part of an alternative financial system; its latest 2018 Directory headlines one page with 'The financial system is broken – we can fix one part of it' and one of the articles is entitled 'Local Currencies are a Rebellious Act'. In part as a result of the growth of digital shopping and the collapse of the cash economy during the pandemic era, the Bristol Pound closed in 2020 and is aiming (at the time of writing, October 2021) to transform itself into Bristol Pay that will offer not just digital payment but other ways of keeping the economy local.

References

Almond, P. (2011) The sub-national embeddedness of international HRM. *Human Relations*, 64(4), 531–551.

Bakhshi, H., Davies, J., Freeman, A. & Higgs, P. (2015) The Geography of the UK's Creative and High-Tech Economies. London. Retrieved from https://www.nesta.org.uk/sites/default/files/summary_geography_uks_creative_high-tech_economies2015.pdf

Bassett, K. (1993) British port privatization and its impact on the port of Bristol. *Journal of Transport Geography*, 1(4), 255–267.

Bassett, K. (1996) Partnerships, business elites and urban politics: new forms of governance in an English city? *Urban Studies*, 33(3), 539–555.

Bassett, K. & Hoare, A. (1984) Bristol and the saga of Royal Portbury: a case study in local politics and municipal enterprise. *Political Geography Quarterly*, 3, 223–250.

Boddy, M., Basset, K., French, S., Griffiths, R., Lambert, C., Leyshon, A. et al. (2004) Competitiveness and cohesion in a prosperous city-region: the case of Bristol. In Boddy, M. & Parkinson, M. (eds.) City Matters: Competitiveness, Cohesion and Urban Governance. Bristol: Policy Press, pp. 51–69.

Boddy, M. & Lovering, J. (1986) High technology industry nexus in the Bristol sub-region: the aerospace/defence nexus. *Regional Studies*, 20(3), 217–231.

Boddy, M., Lovering, J. & Bassett, K. eds. (1986) Sunbelt City? Study of Economic Change in Britain's M4 Growth Corridor. Oxford: Oxford University Press.

Boddy, M. & Parkinson, M. (2004) City Matters: Competitiveness, Cohesion and Urban Governance. Bristol: Policy Press.

Bristol City Council (2017a) Bristol Economic Briefing. Retrieved from https://www.bristol.gov.uk/documents/20182/33191/Bristol+Economic+Briefing+September+2017/bc9009d0-ef38-f28f-22bc-0e5c6635eefd

Bristol City Council (2017b) Bristol Resilience Strategy. Retrieved 1 October 2019, from http://www.100resilientcities.org/wp-content/uploads/2017/07/Bristol_Strategy_PDF.compressed.pdf

Bristol Green Capital Partnership (2018) About Bristol Green Capital Partnership. Retrieved 1 October 2019, from http://bristolgreencapital.org/who-we-are/about-the-partnership/

Brownlee, E. (2018) History & Archive. Retrieved 1 October 2019, from http://bristolgreencapital.org/who-we-are/archive/

Centre for Economics and Business Research & Hampshire Trust Bank (2017) SME Growth Watch 2017–2018. Retrieved 1 October 2019, from https://www.htb.co.uk/news/sme-growth-watch

Clements, R. (1969) Local Notables and the City Council. London: Macmillan.

Co-op UK (2017) Co-operative data explorer. Retrieved 1 October 2109, from https://www.uk.coop/open-data/explorer

Culpepper, P. D. (2011) Quiet Politics and Business Power: Corporate Control in Europe and Japan. New York: Cambridge University Press.

Culpepper, P. D. (2015) Structural power and political science in the post-crisis era. *Business and Politics*. 17(3), 391–409.

Danford, A., Richrdson, M., Stewart, P., Tailby, S. & Upchurch, M. (2005) Partnership and the High Performance Workplace: Work and Employment Relations in the Aerospace Industry. London: Palgrave Macmillan.

Griffiths, R., Bassett, K. & Smith, I. (1999) Cultural Policy and the Cultural Economy in Bristol. *Local Economy*, November 1999, 4(3), 257–264.

Hambleton, R. & Sweeting, D. (2014) Innovation in urban political leadership: Reflections on the introduction of a directly elected mayor in Bristol, UK. *Public Money & Management*, 34(5), 315–322.

Hoare, A. (1997) Privatization comes to town: national policies and local responses – The Bristol case. *Regional Studies*, 31(3), 253–265.

Lukes, S. (2005). Power: A Radical View. 2nd ed. Basingstoke: Palgrave Macmillan.

Malpass, P. (1994) Policy making and local governance: how Bristol failed to secure city challenge funding (twice). *Policy and Politics*, 22(4), 301–312.

Malpass, A., Cloke, P., Barnett, C. & Clarke, N. (2007) Fairtrade urbanism? The politics of place beyond place in the Bristol fairtrade city campaign. *International Journal of Urban and Regional Research*, 31(3), 633–645.

Meegan, R., Kennett, P., Jones, G. & Croft, J. (2014) Global economic crisis, austerity and neoliberal urban governance in England. *Cambridge Journal of Regions, Economy and Society*, 7, 137–153.

ONS (2017) Business Register and Employment Survey 2016. Retrieved 1 October 2019, from https://www.ons.gov.uk/employmentandlabourmarket/peopleinwork/employmentandemployeetypes/bulletins/businessregisterandemploymentsurveybresprovisionalresults/provisionalresults2016revisedresults2015

Punter, J. (1992) Design control and the regeneration of docklands: the example of Bristol *Journal of Property Research*, 9(1), 49–78.

Punter, J. (1993) Development interests and the attack on planning: 'planning difficulties' in Bristol 1985–1990. *Environment & Planning A*, 25, 521–538.

Przeworski, A. & Wallerstein, I. (1988) Structural dependence of the state on capital. *The American Political Science Review*, 82(1), 11–29.

Social Enterprise Works (2013) Mapping the Social Enterprise Sector in the West of England. Bristol. Retrieved 1 October 2019, from https://s3-eu-west-1.amazonaws.com/so-welep-uploads2/files/Sector and Cross Cutting/Social Enterprise/WoE SE mapping report-1.pdf

Stone, C. (1989) Regime Politics: Governing Atlanta 1946–1988. Lawrence, KS: University Press of Kansas.

Stone, C. (1993) Urban regimes and the capacity to govern: a political economy approach, *Journal of Urban Affairs*, 15, 1–28.

Sweeting, D., Hambleton, R., Huxham, C., Stewart, M. & Vangen, S. (2004) Leadership and partnership in urban governance: evidence from London, Bristol and Glasgow in Boddy and Parkinson. In Boddy, M. & Parkinson, M. eds. City matters: competitiveness, cohesion and urban governance, Bristol, U.K: Policy Press, pp. 349–366.

Woods, E., Alexander, D., Labastida, R. R. & Watson, R. (2016) UK Smart Cities Index. London. Retrieved from http://www-file.huawei.com/-/media/CORPORATE/PDF/News/Huawei_Smart_Cities_Report_FINAL.pdf?la=en

Work Foundation (2006) Ideopolis: Knowledge City-Regions: Bristol Case Study. London: The Work Foundation.

3 Collective Bargaining and Regional Resilience: Recalibrating Labour Relations in the Great Lakes Region Automotive Industry

John Holmes

Introduction

Collective bargaining between companies and organised labour can play a pivotal role in influencing the resiliency of manufacturing within a region. This is especially true in the case of industries, such as the North American auto industry, in which production facilities are regionally concentrated and where bargaining is coordinated across companies. Employers, for example, can seek union concessions during bargaining to reset compensation and other aspects of the employment relationship that, if achieved, will enhance a region's competitive position relative to competing jurisdictions. Likewise, unions can make company commitments for renewed regional manufacturing investment a central bargaining demand. This chapter demonstrates how the outcomes of collective bargaining between 2000 and 2016 contributed to the continued resiliency of automotive manufacturing in the cross-border Great Lakes Region (GLR).[1] Historically, General Motors (GM), Ford and Chrysler (collectively referred to as the D(etroit)-3) dominated automaking across the GLR with all D-3 workers represented by two flagship unions – the UAW in the United States and Unifor (formerly the CAW and, prior to 1985, the UAW) in Canada.

Over the last two decades, investments by European and Asian-based automakers led to the emergence of lower-cost vehicle manufacturing regions in the US South and Mexico that challenged the long-term viability of the GLR industry (Yates and Holmes 2019). The GLR, however, has proven resilient and continues to dominate North American automotive manufacturing (Holmes 2022). We argue that a prime reason for this resiliency is the transformation of automotive labour relations that occurred in the region after 2000. The UAW and CAW/Unifor were forced to accept wage and benefit concessions to keep D-3 production costs competitive with Toyota and Honda's North American plants. Faced with a changing competitive landscape across the North American auto industry, their primary bargaining priority also shifted from economic gains to securing new investment for specific plants, a shift that represented a significant departure from past bargaining practice.

DOI: 10.4324/9781003001089-4

The CAW, for example, previously had argued that 'collective bargaining is not the terrain for dealing with new investment. Jobs were a political issue to be resolved at the level of the state and to attempt to deal with it in bargaining would … only lead to disaster' (Gindin and Rosenfeld 2016).

Our analysis focuses on the 2016 round of Unifor – D-3 contract negotiations in Canada. However, these negotiations must be viewed in the context of a labour relations landscape shaped by several previous rounds of bargaining in *both* Canada and the United States. We document how bargaining in both countries, by significantly resetting regional labour costs, played a decisive role in the continued resilience of the GLR automotive industry. However, resiliency came at a very real economic cost to workers and also severely tested the rank-and-file solidarity that traditionally existed within and across plants.

The GLR Automotive Industry

To provide context for the analysis of collective bargaining outcomes that follow, this section provides a brief overview of automotive production in the GLR, and the key structural elements of the North American automotive industrial relations system.

Automotive Production in the GLR

The GLR is a classic 'working region' (Clark 2013) in which automotive innovation and design functions and manufacturing co-exist and where their outputs are mutually reinforcing. North American automotive R&D and product engineering is highly concentrated in south-eastern Michigan (Hannigan et al. 2015; Holmes, 2022), while automotive manufacturing is spread throughout the GLR. Regional competitiveness factors such as the relative cost and quality of labour, energy, logistics, and other input costs strongly influence investment in automotive manufacturing (CAPC 2016). Given the strong multiplier effects associated with vehicle assembly, the capture and retention of assembly plant investment is critical to maintaining a regional automotive manufacturing footprint.

Overwhelmingly concentrated in southern Ontario, Canadian automotive manufacturing forms an integral and important segment of the Great Lakes automotive region (Holmes 2022). Five global automakers – Toyota, FCA, GM, Honda, and Ford – in 2018 built 2.0 million vehicles annually in southern Ontario; close to 90% of which are exported for sale in the United States. Suppliers, including many large global suppliers, export large volumes of Ontario-made automotive parts to US Great Lakes states and large volumes of parts are imported from those same states for assembly into Ontario-built vehicles.

This high degree of functional integration means that the fortunes of Ontario's automotive industry inextricably are tied to the overall vitality of the industry across the broader GLR. Thus, Ontario has a vested interest in the GLR's continued competitive position within the broader North American automotive industry but also must position itself to compete against states on the US side of the border for a share of new GLR auto investment (Holmes 2022).

Automotive industry development across the GLR has been uneven over time. During the 1990s, for example, automotive employment in Ontario grew by nearly 24% compared to just 9.6% in the US portion of the GLR due to several factors, but especially to the significant labour cost advantage enjoyed by Canadian plants (Rutherford and Holmes 2014). At the peak of employment in 2000, Michigan, Ohio, Indiana, and Ontario combined had 730,800 workers employed in automotive manufacturing but between 2000 and 2006, the heavily D-3-dependent region experienced a steady loss of employment as the D-3 lost market share to Asian and European automakers. Ontario's competitive position within the GLR also weakened as an appreciating Canadian dollar and 'transformational labour agreements [in the U.S.]' (CAPC 2013: 1) eroded its prior labour cost advantage.

Vehicle sales collapsed during the 2008–2009 global financial crisis, resulting in the bankruptcy-forced restructuring of both GM and Chrysler and consolidation within the supplier base (Stanford 2010). The restructured industry in the GLR rebounded in the wake of the 2008–2009 crisis, receiving 58% of the almost $US 148 billion of new North American investment announced by automakers in the ten years following the end of the 2009 recession (Swiecki 2020), and remains the dominant region for automotive production in North America.

Auto Industry Collective Bargaining in the United States and Canada

In the wake of the Great Depression, a distinctive labour relations system, built around the concept of the industrial union and a system of pattern and connective bargaining linking national and local plant level bargaining, developed in the automotive industry in the United States and Canada (Katz 1985; Holmes 2015). The *connective bargaining system* ensured uniformity in wages, benefits, and general contract provisions across plants within one company and *pattern bargaining* ensured similar uniformity across all D-3 plants (Holmes 1991). Prior to 1985, UAW labour contract expiry dates in Canada and the United States were synchronised with the pattern set by contracts negotiated first in the United States. For several decades, a uniform pattern of wages, benefits, and work rules existed across D-3 plants in the United States and Canada.

A fundamental shift occurred after 1980. As Japanese, and later Korean and European OEMs constructed mostly non-union vehicle assembly and component plants in North America, labour costs and employment relations diverged between these new plants and the unionised D-3 plants

(Katz 2008). Struggling to address their deteriorating competitive position, the D-3 sought concessions from the UAW

Disagreements over the issue of concessions between the UAW's Canadian wing and the union leadership in Detroit ultimately led Canadian autoworkers to leave the UAW and form the CAW in 1985 (Gindin 1989). By 1990, bargaining outcomes across the D-3 in the United States were no longer uniform as the UAW abandoned traditional annual base-wage increases in favour of lump-sum payments and profit sharing and 'modern operating agreements' (Hunter and Katz 2012). Traditional Fordist-style pattern bargaining has endured in Canada and played a critical role during 2016 contract negotiations. Nevertheless, UAW bargaining outcomes continued to exert a strong influence on automotive bargaining in Canada.

Restoring Regional Competitiveness: Concessionary Bargaining in the Great Lakes Auto Industry: 2000–2015

In 1999, with the D-3 coming off several years of record-breaking earnings, the UAW negotiated the richest contracts in the union's history. However, 1999 also marked a labour relations watershed in the Great Lakes auto industry. Rising oil prices caused a sharp decline in sales and a drop in D-3 market share. With global overcapacity, mounting competitive pressure from new, non-union Asian and European OEM plants in North America, and mounting financial losses, the D-3 entered an extended period of restructuring.

Total US automotive employment declined by 27% between 2000 and 2007. As D-3 union membership dwindled and the unions failed to organise Asian- and European-owned assembly plants, union bargaining power weakened (Katz 2008: 132). Between 2003 and 2015, the D-3 made repeated demands for union concessions to reduce all-in labour costs in both the United States and Canada. This unfolded in several phases, as indicated in Table 3.1. By the end of this period of concession bargaining, auto industry labour relations in the GLR had been recalibrated, labour costs reset, and D-3 plants in the region repositioned to compete for new investment.

It is important to recognise the decisive influence that the ascendency of financial capitalism and financialisation of the economy exerted on the industry during this period.[2] Firm strategies were increasingly shaped by 'their activities in capital markets rather than product markets, or for that matter labour markets' (Lippert et al. 2014: 24). During the 1990s, automotive firms in North America and Europe increasingly came to focus on shareholder value; a core doctrine of financialisation. As the D-3 continued to lose market share, many US automotive suppliers faltered, triggering a wave of financial investment company takeovers of suppliers that required injections of fresh capital to avoid impending bankruptcy (Lippert et al. 2014: 44).

Table 3.1 Summary of UAW and CAW Bargaining Outcomes 2005–2015

Year	*UAW (United States)*	*CAW (Canada)*
2005	2003–2007 UAW – D-3 Collective Agreement reopened: • large workforce reduction • health benefit concessions	2005 CAW – D3 Bargaining: • resisted concessions • modest base wage rate increases
2005	UAW – Delphi 'ultra' concessions: • 24 plants and 24,000 workers cut • all new hires made second tier with 50% lower wage	
2007	UAW – D-3 CA Bargaining: • two-tier wage and benefit structure for 'non-core' new-hires • VEBAs removed cost of employee and retiree medical benefits from company books • overall cost of a new-hire cut by 33%	
2008		2005–2008 CAW – D-3 Collective Agreement opened early: • freeze on base wages and COLA • lump sum • one-time 'bonus' • reduced pension benefit • new-hire grow-in system wage: 70% to 100% over 3 years
2009	GM/Chrysler Bankruptcy Restructuring • 2007–2011 UAW – D-3 CA reopened • Government forced lower labour cost to match Toyota • permanent second-tier wages extended to all new-hires • base wage rates frozen • COLA suspended • reduced paid-time off • Job Banks program suspended • hourly employment reduced 50% compared to 2005 • 12 assembly and power train plants closed • no strike allowed for 6 years	GM/Chrysler Bankruptcy Restructuring • 2008–2012 CAW – D-3 CA reopened • Government forced lower labour cost to match Toyota • base wage rates remain frozen • COLA suspended • limits on SUB program • reduced supplementary medical benefits • hourly employment reduced by 50% compared to 2005 • 3 assembly and power train plants closed
2011	UAW-D-3 Bargaining • base wage rates frozen • COLA suspended • new-hires: permanent two-tier remains • modest increase in new hire wage rate: top of Tier 2 $19.28/hour vs $28.50 Tier 1	

(*Continued*)

Table 3.1 (Continued)

Year	*UAW (United States)*	*CAW (Canada)*
2012		CAW – D-3 Bargaining • base wage rates frozen • COLA suspended • one time bonuses • new-hires: grow-in progression from 60% to 100% over 10 years; hybrid pension
2015	UAW-D-3 Bargaining • commitments for new investment • base wage rates: 3% increases in Yr.1 and Yr.3 • lump sums: 4% in Yr.2 and Yr.4 • Permanent second-tier replaced by grow-in progression over 8 years	

Source: Various UAW and CAW Bargaining Reports.

The Advent of Ultra-Concessionary Bargaining: 2003–2007

In late 2005, the UAW agreed to reopen its 2003 four-year agreements with the D-3. Threatened with widespread D-3 plant closures, the UAW agreed to health benefit concessions and large workforce reductions facilitated through voluntary severance or early retirement programs (Katz 2008). However, the pivotal moment in establishing the template for what Chaison (2012) labels 'ultra-concessionary bargaining' came with the concessions extracted from the UAW in 2005 by Delphi, the formerly GM-owned global automotive supplier. To save Delphi plants threatened with closure, the UAW already had agreed in 2003 to the introduction of tiered wages and benefits. As it entered bankruptcy restructuring in 2005, Delphi returned to the union demanding a cut of over 60% in the hourly wage rate for new workers, the elimination of COLA, and a reduction in benefits and paid vacations. An *Automotive News* editorial remarked that the UAW now found itself in a difficult situation:

> Whether the unions willingly negotiate or the bankruptcy court voids Delphi's labor agreements … wages and benefits will be cut, plants will close and workers will lose their jobs. It is inevitable … once the new competitive equilibrium is set during the Delphi reorganization it will become the standard for other suppliers and the bogey for the Big 3 [D-3] when they head into bargaining in 2007.
>
> (Lapham 2005)

The eventual UAW-Delphi agreement was central to the restructuring package shaped by the two largest Delphi shareholders, both financial hedge funds (Gilson 2012). It not only included the sale or closure of 24 Delphi plants in the United States with a loss of 24,000 jobs, but also established a wage rate of $14 an hour for new hires, and permitted Delphi to make *all* new hires either temporary or 'second-tier' workers.

D-3-UAW bargaining in 2007 proved to be a game changer. The D-3 pushed hard to extend Delphi-style concessions into the auto assembly sector. Under duress, the UAW accepted second-tier wages and benefits for 'non-core' new hires – those in sub-assembly, machining, and material handling. Starting wage rates for these workers were approximately 50% lower than those for existing workers and they were excluded from the defined benefit pension plan and health benefits enjoyed by 'traditional' workers. The union also agreed to the establishment of a *Voluntary Employee Beneficiary Association* (VEBA) effectively moving the cost obligation for employee and retiree medical benefits from the automakers' books onto the UAW. This instantly improved the credit ratings of the auto companies saving them billions of dollars in future quarterly interest payments (Cutcher-Gershenfeld et al. 2015). The concessions reduced the overall cost of a GM new hire to about one-third that of existing workers (*Ward's Automotive*, 22 October 2007) and GM's CEO commented that 'this agreement helps us close the fundamental competitive gaps [with non-union plants] that exist in our business' (*New York Times*, 27 September 2007).

In Canada, the CAW had resisted concessions and even achieved modest gains in base wage rates during bargaining in 2005, even though the rising value of the Canadian dollar was eroding its cost advantage.[3] Consequently, the 2007 UAW concessions narrowed the labour cost advantage enjoyed by Canadian plants and set the stage for the D-3 to pressure the CAW to grant similar concessions in the next round of bargaining scheduled for 2008. A full five months ahead of the expiry of the CAW 2005–2008 agreements, and perhaps cognizant of the impending global financial crisis, the CAW negotiated a new contract with Ford Canada that contained concessions and was quickly replicated at GM and Chrysler (Table 3.1). The CAW previously had pragmatically granted local concessions on work rules and outsourcing to enable Canadian plants to compete for new product mandates (Siemiatycki 2012). It was not until the 2008 agreements, however, that the CAW agreed to contingent compensation in lieu of annual increases in base wage rates. While resisting a *permanent* two-tier wage and benefit structure for new hires, as the UAW had, the CAW agreed to a 'New Hire Grow-in System' under which new hires would start at 70% of base wages and only attain 100% after three years.[4]

The 2008–2009 Bankruptcy Restructuring Crisis

Financialisation and the intrusion of the state into auto industry collective bargaining moved to centre stage in the industry during the 2008–2009 global financial crisis. As the crisis unfolded, automobile sales in the United States plummeted to a 40-year low and GM and Chrysler, already financially fragile following years of shrinking domestic sales, were forced to seek bankruptcy protection in the United States and government financial assistance.[5]

The outgoing Bush administration provided initial financial assistance but additional US federal assistance was made conditional on each company developing a restructuring plan to ensure its long-term viability. The newly installed Obama administration rejected GM's initial restructuring plan, which included significant new concessions by the UAW, and urged the automakers to make 'every effort to achieve labor cost parity with the [non-union] transplants' (USGAO 2009: 26). Following further negotiation, the final 2009 UAW-D-3 agreements contained extensive concessions and extended second-tier wages to *all new* hires (Table 3.1). GM and Chrysler were reborn as 'new' leaner but financially stronger companies.

While GM and Chrysler did not file for bankruptcy protection in Canada and the US Treasury Department orchestrated the bailouts, the Canadian federal and Ontario provincial governments contributed to the financial bailout packages and took equity holdings in both companies. To ensure a continued GM and Chrysler manufacturing footprint in Canada, Canadian governments provided roughly 20% of the $100 billion bailouts in return for the companies committing to maintain their current share of total North American production in Canada until 2016 (Stanford 2010).

Following the Obama administration's lead, Canadian financial aid was conditional on labour concessions beyond those already negotiated with the CAW, including further reductions in paid-time off, limits on the SUB program, reduced supplementary medical benefits, and changes in local plant operating rules to increase productivity (Table 3.1). Unlike the UAW, the CAW avoided the imposition of permanent two-tier wages for new hires and retained the right to strike in their next scheduled contract negotiations (Stanford 2010).

The crisis saw the D-3 and unions enter into new bargaining and financial arrangements. The UAW's message to GM workers urging ratification of the concessionary agreement reflected the extraordinary degree to which the state had intervened in bargaining:

> [after Obama's rejection of GM's restructuring plan] The Treasury's Auto Task Force moved into GM headquarters in an effort to find deeper and quicker changes to GM's U.S. footprint. The shocking plan that resulted, highlighted by the elimination of 16 existing U.S. facilities … levied severe and drastic cuts to the U.S. workforce and UAW membership. Faced with this dire situation and realizing that failure to meet the government requirements would surely mean the

> end of General Motors, your bargainers painstakingly put together modifications to the [2007] collective bargaining agreement to satisfy the Treasury Auto Task Force.
>
> (UAW 2009)

The governments of the United States, Canada, and Ontario became shareholders in GM and Chrysler for several years until they liquidated their shares. The UAW acted both as a negotiator with the federal government, representing workers being asked to make concessions as part of the bankruptcy restructuring and as a creditor holding considerable stock in all three companies as a result of the VEBA agreement (Cutcher-Gershenfeld et al. 2015).

Post-Crisis Bargaining: 2011–2015

Although auto sales had picked up, the UAW entered contract negotiations in 2011 with very modest goals. It was conscious of divided public sentiment over the taxpayer-funded bailouts and under the terms of the bailout agreements could not strike. The union won modest improvements in benefits and wages for entry-level workers but wage rates and COLA for 'legacy' workers remained frozen and the two-tier compensation structure for new hires was unchanged (Table 3.1). However, in 'selling' the agreement to their membership, the UAW leadership stressed their success in securing commitments for new investment at a number of plants.

Leading into 2012 bargaining in Canada, the D-3 launched a concerted media campaign emphasising that, with the Canadian dollar at par and growing numbers of lower-cost 'second-tier' workers in US plants, Canadian labour costs were now higher than in the United States. They publically threatened disinvestment if the cost gap with the United States was not addressed. A senior Unifor staffer later commented that:

> [in 2012] the automakers insisted that unless we followed the UAW two-tier system, we would absolutely not secure any new investment .... the assessment of the union's leadership and bargaining committees was that this was no idle threat .... the union's strategy was to ensure our compensation remained broadly comparable to the UAW so that Canada stayed in the ballpark for investment.
>
> (Murnighan 2016)

The new four-year agreements continued the freeze on base wages and pensions and the suspension of COLA (Table 3.1). Whilst rejecting the companies' demand for a 'permanent' two-tier structure for new hires, the CAW agreed to extend the 'temporary' grow-in period for new-hire wages and benefits from three to ten years and accepted a less attractive hybrid pension plan for new hires (Fowler 2013).

The 2016 Unifor-D-3 Contract Negotiations in Canada

The 2016 round of D-3-Unifor bargaining was of crucial significance for the future of automotive manufacturing in the Ontario segment of the GLR. Since 1999, there had been a net loss of five Canadian assembly plants and annual vehicle production had shrunk from over 3 million to just 2.28 million in 2015 (OICA 2018). Securing D-3 commitments for renewed investment into their Ontario operations was now the paramount issue for Unifor. OEM commitments made during the 2008–2009 bailouts to maintain their then Canadian manufacturing footprints until 2016 were expiring. GM Oshawa had no new vehicle programs scheduled beyond 2019, FCA Brampton needed a new paint shop as a necessary condition to secure future vehicle mandates, and Ford's Windsor engine production facilities were under threat. A failure to secure new investment and product mandates for these plants during bargaining would seriously jeopardise the long-term future of automotive manufacturing in Canada.

Context for Negotiations

i *Market Conditions*: coming off four years of sustained growth, the D-3 were operating at or near record profitability. With the D-3 not wishing to lose production in the event of a strike, Unifor appeared strategically well-positioned.

ii *Weakened Canadian Dollar*: a weaker dollar lowers the cost of manufacturing in Canada. In contrast to 2012, when it was near par with the US dollar, it now hovered in the mid US$0.70 range and with stable lower oil prices seemed unlikely to return to par during the life of a new agreement.

iii *Government*: both the Federal and Ontario governments were signalling a willingness to provide financial assistance to help secure new investment.

iv *2015 UAW-D-3 Negotiations*: the most recent UAW-D-3 agreements included commitments for new US plant investment, the first wage gains for legacy workers in nine years (companies were allowed expanded use of lower-paid temporary workers to offset these wage increases), and a modification of the two-tier system (Table 3.1). The permanent two-tier wage structure had become a source of friction within the union membership and a concern for management. The fact that workers working side-by-side in virtually every plant received different compensation for performing identical work was an affront to the long-cherished union principle of equal pay for equal work. The 2015 agreements replaced the *permanent* two-tier structure for new hires with a grow-in wage system (similar to that in Canadian plants) that enabled them to transition to 'traditional wages' after eight years. Nevertheless, workers were unhappy with the union's failure to achieve a return to a three-year grow-in for new hires and the UAW leadership encountered stiff challenges during ratification of the new agreements.[6]

v *Unifor Bargaining Objective*: the union entered negotiations with a strong mandate to make new investments and product mandates its key demand; a demand over which the membership was prepared to strike. However, there was also pressure from some segments within the membership to secure increases in compensation and reduce the grow-in period for new hires. Given market conditions, such wage improvements appeared to be a winnable demand.

vi *D-3 Bargaining Objective:* notwithstanding the 2015 UAW wage increases and the weakening of the Canadian dollar, Canadian production costs continued to be an issue for the D-3. With increased electricity costs, government-mandated payroll taxes, and a new carbon pricing system, Ontario was now perceived to be one of the higher cost vehicle manufacturing jurisdictions in the world. Moreover, with far more recent hiring occurring in US plants, the labour cost reductions afforded by the two-tier structure for new hires had worked to the competitive advantage of US plants. When coupled with the off-loading of pension and health costs to the VEBAs, this had significantly lowered all-in labour costs at US plants. Reducing the all-in labour cost differential between Canada and the United States was the core objective for GM and FCA. Signalling that they were looking to Unifor for concessions, they stated publically that there would be no announcements regarding the future of the Oshawa and Brampton assembly plants until after the conclusion of negotiations.

Bargaining Process and Outcomes

Unifor negotiated first with GM, then with FCA, and finally with Ford. At each, bargaining went down to the wire of the strike deadline but ultimately the Unifor Bargaining Committee unanimously recommended acceptance of 'a tentative framework agreement' to their membership.

i *GM Canada*: given its primary goal of securing new investment commitments for both Oshawa Assembly and the St. Catharines engine plant, Unifor selected GM as the target company for bargaining. After extended bargaining, a tentative 'Framework' agreement was approved by 64% of the union membership. The core elements of the new four-year collective agreement included commitments from GM to invest $400 million at Oshawa, to implement a new flexible module to allow the production of cars and pickup trucks on the same line, and $150 million at St. Catharines to extend the life of the current engine module and add an additional fuel-efficient engine variant (Unifor-GM Bargaining Report 2016). The agreement contained compensation increases for 'traditional' workers and the conversion of 700 temporary positions to permanent full-time job status. Although new hires would now receive full seniority rights, eligibility for benefits coverage, and paid vacation time, the contentious grow-in period for new hires remained at ten years and the new-hire hybrid pension plan, agreed to in 2012, was replaced by an even less attractive 'defined contribution' plan.[7]

ii *FCA*: Unifor bargained next with FCA and sought acceptance of the pattern agreement established at GM. Initially, FCA stated that it would resist the GM pattern since the improvements to the new-hire grow-in program would negatively impact FCA's cost structure. While GM had hired almost none, FCA and Ford had both hired significant numbers of new workers since 2012. While 'saving' Oshawa had been the most pressing issue for GM workers, for FCA workers improvements to the ten-year wage progression were the critical priority. At the very least, workers wanted the grow-in period reduced from ten to eight years to match the 2015 UAW agreement.

With the strike deadline looming, however, both parties agreed to accept the economic 'pattern' established at GM, including the retention of the ten-year grow-in structure. FCA committed $325 million to rebuild the paint shop at the Brampton Assembly plant and to assign a next generation product to Brampton subject to FCA and Unifor jointly pursuing and obtaining adequate government financial assistance in support of the investment (Unifor-Fiat Chrysler Bargaining Report 2016). FCA also committed $6.4 million to upgrade equipment at its Etobicoke Casting Plant and to the continued production of current products and the launch of a hybrid electric vehicle at its Windsor Assembly Plant that had recently received a $2.6 billion makeover. In recommending the agreement to the membership, which voted 70% in favour of acceptance, Unifor stressed that:

> The Unifor Master Bargaining Committee pursued with all three companies the idea of shortening the current 10-year wage progression understanding that Unifor members wanted to see improvements. In the eyes of U.S.-based CEOs, the 10-year progression was crucial for attracting new investment and new product in Canada (our number one priority in 2016 contract negotiations). On this point, the companies were unanimous and aggressive in rejecting any change to the progression length .... Therefore, to ensure the Committee met its investment objectives, attention turned to winning improvements to the progression so that members would receive higher and more consistent wage increases.
>
> (Unifor-Fiat Chrysler Bargaining Report 2016: 4)

and, in further justification:

> [in 2012] Our union rejected this [United States] permanent two-tier approach, and instead negotiated an alternative system that not only kept newly-hired workers on a path to full wages, but also helped secure investment and create thousands of new jobs.
>
> (Unifor-Fiat Chrysler Bargaining Report 2016: 4)

iii *Ford Canada:* the future of Ford's Windsor engine plant was in jeopardy unless the company committed to a new product mandate. Even before bargaining commenced, cracks appeared in the solidarity of Ford Canada workers. Faced with growing shopfloor opposition to the ten-year wage progression, the leadership of the largest Ford local (Local 707 at Oakville Assembly) publically stated that, if presented with the economic pattern already accepted at GM and FCA, they would vote against it.[8] A tense and very public spat developed between the leaderships of Local 707 and Local 200 representing workers at the Windsor engine facilities, for whom securing new investment was paramount. Leading up to the strike deadline, Ford was promising new investment for the Windsor engine plants but threatening to pull production out of Canada if the economic pattern was not accepted.

Shortly past the strike deadline, the Unifor Bargaining Team agreed to recommend acceptance of the tentative agreement, including the economic pattern. Ford committed $613 million to Windsor Engine to create a 'sole global manufacturing source … to supply next generation, high volume products planned for 2020 model year production' and $100 million to support production at Oakville Assembly. While 58% of the overall Ford membership voted in favour of the agreement, Oakville Assembly workers voted 55:45 to reject it, even though the local leadership had ultimately endorsed and recommended approval of the agreement.

Assessment of Outcomes

Emphasising that the union had achieved its prime bargaining objective, Unifor's National President boasted that:

> … Unifor has done more in the last three months to secure the industry's footprint in Canada and offer a brighter future for autoworkers, their families and their communities, than governments have in the last 10 years.
>
> (Dias 2016)

and the union's former chief economist wrote:

> After years of retrenchment, Canada's auto industry finally faces an optimistic future. Our labour and production costs are attractive.

> Our productivity and quality are unmatched. Government, the union, suppliers and the auto makers are showing that they can work together to stabilize, and hopefully rebuild, the Canadian footprint.
>
> (Stanford 2016)

How did the outcome of the 2016 bargaining round affect Ontario's relative competitive position with regard to vehicle production within the GLR? The D-3's success in retaining the ten-year new-hire grow-in period and achieving acceptance of a less costly pension plan for new hires served to keep labour costs in Ontario D-3 plants competitive with US sister plants in the GLR, especially when combined with a lower-valued Canadian dollar. In 2017, estimated average hourly vehicle manufacturing earnings were USD28.98 in Canada and USD29.08 in the United States compared to USD35.37 and USD27.83 respectively in 2014 (CAR 2019).

The response from many industry commentators was one of guarded optimism but others were highly critical of the new agreements, pointing to the conditional nature of the investment commitments should market conditions change, and the failure to address the corrosive effect on worker solidarity of the new-hire grow-in period.[9] The union's strategic focus on securing reinvestment for specific facilities at the expense of shortening the grow-in period had created real frictions within the union rank-and-file and exposed tensions within the union leadership.

In fact, the stabilised footprint proved short-lived. As part of a broader corporate restructuring, GM announced on 26 November 2018 that its Oshawa assembly plant would close by the end of 2019. Widespread anger erupted in Oshawa, with some workers engaging in wildcat walkouts and plant occupations and calling for the plant to be taken into public ownership (Labor Notes 2019). Unifor's National Office did not endorse the rank-and-file actions and instead mounted a high-profile PR campaign urging Canadians to boycott Mexican-built GM vehicles. The campaign was suspended after GM announced that some stamping operations involving around 300 jobs would remain at Oshawa. Sam Gindin, a former senior CAW official and a vigorous critic of Unifor bargaining strategy, observed:

> the Unifor leadership deserves credit for pushing GM off its original 'non-negotiable' declaration that a complete closure was a done deal. Yet it also shows the limits of its overall strategy. The concessions made during the last round of bargaining [2016] were to no avail but contributed to weakening workers' confidence to resist.
>
> (Gindin 2019)

Conclusion

Collective bargaining can play a significant role in influencing regional resilience by readjusting regional competitiveness in an established manufacturing industry. Automotive industry labour relations in the GLR were fundamentally recalibrated over the course of several rounds of bargaining between 2003 and 2016. Concessions made by the UAW and CAW/Unifor, including the introduction of tiered wages and benefits for newly hired workers and the freezing of base wage rates for 'traditional' workers, moderated D-3 labour costs in the region. While not entirely eliminated, the competitive gap between D-3 plants and the US and Canadian plants of foreign-owned OEMs narrowed and helped ensure the continued resilience of automotive manufacturing in the GLR.[10] The region received $62.2 billion in new automotive investment between 2009 and 2017; representing 52% of the North American total compared to the 21% and 17% received by Mexico and the US South respectively (CAR 2018). Likewise, Canadian bargaining was influenced by the need to keep labour costs at Ontario D-3 plants competitive with their US sister plants in the GLR.

Resilience, however, was only achieved at a very real cost to autoworkers. After 2010, the D-3 enjoyed record levels of vehicle sales and profitability in their North American operations but the ability of workers to capture and retain an enhanced share of value-added was severely constrained. Unions did not make concessions willingly. They made them in an effort to secure their members' jobs. Faced with a shifting competitive landscape and the ever-present threat of plant closings, the union's primary focus shifted to securing new investment commitments for specific plants. In some cases, such commitments proved only transitory, leading some to question this strategy. Furthermore, as new hiring shifted the balance between 'traditional' and 'new hire' workers within plants, the failure of the unions during bargaining to eliminate the tiered wage structure severely tested rank-and-file solidarity and the ability of the union leadership to secure ratification of new agreements.

Postscript

Since this chapter was first drafted (2018), a number of developments have again tested the resilience of GLR automotive manufacturing (Holmes 2022). A pall was cast over the industry by the Trump administration's protectionist stance that promised to undermine the continental integration of the industry. Trump threatened to impose tariffs on automotive products imported to the United States from Canada and Mexico and sought to renegotiate the NAFTA automotive rules to the advantage of the United States. Heightened recognition of the climate crisis, led OEMs to accelerate the transition from internal combustion engine vehicles to ones powered by electric motors (BEVs and PHEVs). This will involve the retooling or closure of existing assembly and powertrain plants and the opening of new plants. Then, in 2020, industry supply chains were disrupted by the global pandemic!

On balance, it is likely that both the 'new NAFTA' (aka the USMCA) and the transition to EVs will favour automotive manufacturing in the GLR (Holmes 2022). Not surprisingly, the securing of commitments for plant investments to build EVs became the primary focus of the next rounds of UAW-D-3 and Unifor-D-3 bargaining in 2019 and 2020 respectively. Both outcomes included significant levels of promised EV-related investment (and the reopening of GM Oshawa to build pickups) that augured well for the future of the region's automotive industry. In the United States, the new hire grow-in period for new hires was shortened from eight to four years. Together with base wage increases for 'traditional' workers and company failure to secure union concessions on health care costs, this resulted in a projected significant increase in labour costs over the life of the four-year UAW contract. In Canada, the grow-in period was only shortened from ten to eight years, which kept labour costs in Ontario plants competitive but added more fuel to rank-and-file anger over tiered wages. The next round of bargaining in both countries is scheduled for 2023.

Notes

1 The cross-border GLR comprises the states of Michigan, New York, Ohio, Indiana, Illinois, and Wisconsin and the province of Ontario.
2 Financialisation 'refers to the increasing importance of financial markets, financial motives, financial institutions, and financial elites in the operation of the economy and its governing institutions, both at the national and international level' (Epstein quoted in Palley 2007:1).
3 From a January 2002 low of USD0.625, the Canadian dollar rose steadily in value and by late 2007 stood slightly above par.
4 Previously, new hires started at 85% of the base wage rate and reached 100% after 18 months.
5 Ford avoided bankruptcy and the need for a federal bailout package. Nevertheless, it supported the unprecedented intervention by the US government to bailout its competitors knowing that the collapse of either GM or Chrysler would devastate the supplier base and potentially bring down the entire industry, including Ford (Cutcher-Gershenfeld et al. 2015).
6 The first tentative FCA agreement which maintained the permanent two-tier structure was voted down by a 2–1 margin. Subsequently, 77% voted in favour of a revised agreement containing the eight-year progression to traditional wages and more money for current workers. A similar agreement was ratified by 55% at GM, after initially being rejected by the skilled trades, and by the narrowest of margins – 51% – at Ford, only after appearing to be heading for certain defeat as several large locals voted it down by a 2–1 margin.
7 Changes to the schedule of wage increases did result in a slight improvement in a new hire's progression to a full wage.
8 Ford Oakville was not in jeopardy having received significant reinvestment in 2013 and building strongly selling vehicles. However, 40% of the Oakville workforce now consisted of 'new hires' adversely affected by the ten-year wage progression.
9 See Gindin and Rosenfeld (2016) and the debate between Gindin (2016) and Murnighan (2016).

10 In 2019, D-3 labour costs were estimated still to range between USD 5.00 and USD 13.00 per hour higher than US plants operated by foreign-owned competitors (CAR 2019).

References

CAPC (2013) *A Call for Action: II. A Report by the Manufacturing Competitiveness Committee of the Canadian Automotive Partnership Council.* Ottawa: CAPC.

CAPC (2016) CAPC Submission on a Canada Innovation Strategy, August 31, 2016. Retrieved from http://capcinfo.ca/en/CAPC-Innovation-en.html

CAR (2018) CAR Book of Deals 2017 Annual Review. *Center for Automotive Research.* Retrieved from https://www.cargroup.org/car-book-of-deals-2017-annual-review/

CAR (2019) The Issues in 2019 UAW-FCA, Ford, & GM Negotiations. *Center for Automotive Research.* Retrieved from https://www.cargroup.org/the-issues-in-2019-uaw-fca-ford-gm-negotiations/

Chaison, G. (2012) *The New Collective Bargaining.* New York: Springer.

Clark, J. (2013) *Working Regions: Reconnecting Innovation and Production in the Knowledge Economy.* New York: Routledge.

Cutcher-Gershenfeld, J. at al. (2015) Financialization, Collective Bargaining, and the Public Interest. In Weller, C. E. (ed.) *Inequality, Uncertainty, and Opportunity: The Varied and Growing Role of Finance in Labor Relations.* Labor and Employment Relations Association. pp. 31–56.

Dias, J. (2016) Canadian Auto Industry Is Back on the Right Path. Huffington Post 11/10/2016 https://www.huffingtonpost.ca/jerry-dias/canada-auto-negotiations_b_12888042.html

Fowler, T. (2013) Does fighting back still matter? The Canadian autoworkers, capitalist crisis and confrontation. *Capital & Class*, 36(3), p. 493–513.

Gilson, S. C. (2012) 'Restructuring at Delphi Corporation' Chapter 21 in S.C. *Gilson Creating Value through Corporate Restructuring: Case Studies in Bankruptcies, Buyouts, and Breakups.* Hoboken, New Jersey: Wiley, pp. 641–650.

Gindin, S. (1989) Breaking away: the formation of the Canadian Autoworkers Union. *Studies in Political Economy*, 29, 63–89.

Gindin, S. (2016) Misreading the Historical Moment: A Response to Murnighan's 'Unifor and Big Three Bargaining', Socialist Project E-Bulletin No. 1323 1 November 2016.

Gindin, S. (2019) GM Oshawa: Lowered Expectations, Unexplored Opportunities. Socialist Project E-Bulletin 29 March 2019.

Gindin, S. & Rosenfeld, H. (2016) Bargaining Over Corporate Investment: Innovation or Trap? Socialist Project E-Bulletin No. 1300 4 September 2016.

Hannigan, T. J., Cano-Kollmann, M. & Mudambi, R. (2015) Thriving innovation amidst manufacturing decline: the Detroit auto cluster and the resilience of local knowledge production. *Industrial and Corporate Change*, 24(3), 613–634.

Holmes, J. (1991) From Uniformity to Diversity: Changing Patterns of Wages and Work Practices in the North American Automobile Industry. In Blyton, P. & Morris, J. (eds.) *A Flexible Future? Prospects for Employment and Work Organization in the 1990s.* Berlin: De Gruyter, pp. 129–151.

Holmes, J. (1993) From Three Industries to One: Towards an Integrated North American Automobile Industry. In Molot, M. A. (ed.) *Driving Continentally: National Policies and the North American Auto Industry.* Ottawa: Carleton University Press, pp. 23–62.

Holmes, J. (2015) Labour Relations and Human Resource Management in the Automotive Industry: North American Perspectives. In Nieuwenhuis, P. & Wells, P. (eds.) *The Global Automotive Industry*. Chichester: John Wiley and Sons, pp. 118–138.

Holmes, J. (2022) New trade rules, technological disruption and COVID-19: Prospects for Ontario in the cross-border Great Lakes automotive industry. *International Journal of Automotive Technology and Management*, 22(1), 106–127.

Hunter, L. & Katz, H. (2012) The impact of globalization on human resource management and employment relations in the US automobile and banking industries. *International Journal of Human Resource Management*, 23(10), 1983–1998.

Katz, H. (1985) *Shifting Gears: Changing Labor Relations in the U.S. Automobile Industry*. Cambridge, MA: MIT Press.

Katz, H. (2008) Recent Developments in U.S. Auto Labor Relations: The Decline of the Big Three and the United Automotive Workers, Chapter 7. In Blanpain, R. & Lansbury, R. (eds.) *Globalization and Employment Relations in the Auto Assembly Industry*. The Netherlands: Kluwer Law International, pp. 131–142.

Labor Notes (2019) *Canada Interview with Tony Leah: Why We Occupied Our General Motors Factory in Oshawa*. Detroit: Labor Education and Research Project. Labor Notes, 11 January 2019.

Lapham, E. (2005) Delphi's Wage War Will Reshape U.S. Labour Market. *Automotive News*, 8 November 2005. Retrieved from https://www.autonews.com/article/20051114/SUB/511140759/comment-delphi-s-wage-war-will-reshape-u-s-labor-market

Lippert, I., Huzzard, T., Jurgens, U. & Lazonick, W. (2014) *Corporate Governance, Employee Voice, and Work Organization: Sustaining High-road Jobs in the Automotive Supply Industry*. Oxford: Oxford University Press.

Murnighan, B. (2016) Unifor and Big Three Bargaining: A Response to Gindin's 'Different Ways of Making History' The Bullet, Socialist Project E-Bulletin No. 1322 31 October 2016. http://www.socialistproject.ca/bullet/1322.php#continue

OICA (2018) 2017 Production Statistics. *Retrieved from International Organization of Motor Vehicle Manufacturers (OICA)*: http://www.oica.net/category/production-statistics/2017-statistics/

Palley, T. (2007) Financialization: What It Is and Why It Matters. Working Paper Series No. 153. *Political Economy Research Institute*. Amherst: University of Massachusetts.

Rutherford, T. & Holmes, J. (2014) Manufacturing resiliency: economic restructuring and automotive manufacturing in the Great Lakes Region. *Cambridge Journal of Regions, Economy and Society*, 7(3), 359–378.

Siemiatycki E. (2012) Forced to concede: permanent restructuring and labour's place in the North American auto industry. *Antipode*, 44(2), 453–473.

Stanford, J. (2010) The geography of auto globalization and the politics of auto bailouts. *Cambridge Journal of Regions, Economy and Society*, 3(3), 363–405.

Stanford, J. (2016) The end of Australia's auto industry offers cautionary tales for Canada. Globe and Mail 21 November 2016. B4.

Swiecki, B. (2020) *State of the Automotive Industry, 2020 Post-Election Automotive Outlook Webinar*. Ann Arbor: Center for Automotive Research.

UAW (2009) UAW General Motors Modifications to the 2007 Agreement and Addendum to the VEBA Agreement, A Message to UAW Members at GM, May 2009. Detroit: UAW Solidarity House.

Unifor-General Motors Bargaining Report (2016) Highlights of the Tentative Agreement between Unifor and General Motors. October 13 2016. Toronto: CAW.

United States Government Accountability Office (USGAO) (2009) Summary of Government Efforts and Automakers' Restructuring to Date, Report to Congressional Committees, GA-09-553, 2009.

Yates, C. & Holmes, J. (2019) *The Future of the Canadian Automotive Industry*. Ottawa: Canadian Centre for Policy Alternatives.

Part II

Institutional Experimentation

4 Reflections on Labour Strategy in Urban and Regional Governance

Ian MacDonald and Thorben Wieditz

Labour unions have for decades been engaged in the governance and economic restructuring of urban regions across North America. Despite declining bargaining power and labour market coverage, unions still represent the largest membership-based organisations within urban regions and they remain the only ones to foreground working-class interests in urban and regional governance. This engagement has only become more important with the decline of collective bargaining and the ongoing shift of union membership from industry to the urban services economy. As labour organisations adopt more social unionism-type union renewal strategies that link the workplace demands of their members to the multiple interests and identities they hold as residents and citizens, they have developed capacities that allow them to shape urban policy and regulatory decision making. Union actors are learning how to use these urban capacities to shore up bargaining relationships with employers, defend union employment levels, ease union accreditation of new bargaining units, and, more ambitiously, begin confronting the rise of platform capitalism. This extension of union repertoires into the arena of urban governance carries variable implications for an urban working class beyond a union membership.

That there is very little written on the role of unions in urban regions is likely the result of the question having slipped through disciplinary boundaries. Neither political science nor urban studies have considered how unions (when unions are considered at all) relate to urban and regional governance insofar as they are particular institutions of the working class. In the case of industrial relations, there has been as yet little reflection on how our understanding of union capacities and strategic decision making might differ in an urban context, nor has there been much recognition of the complexity of union participation in urban alliances beyond the union-community coalitions associated with union renewal. Of course, geographers would say that space complexifies class analysis, and a certain amount of complexity is useful if it clarifies strategic questions facing our labour movements. We aim to show in this chapter that it is necessary to contextualise union capacities and strategic decision making within an urban political economy framework in order to understand the relevance

DOI: 10.4324/9781003001089-6

of unions to urban governance, as well as to clearly identify the limits and contradictions of unions engaging in this role.

We begin by situating unions as place-bound working-class institutions that have an interest in defending what Harvey refers to as the 'structured coherence' of their urban region (Harvey 2001 [1985], p. 329). Rather than relating union strategic decision making to the firm only, we discuss how unions manoeuver within the shifting alliances of class actors that govern urban regions. Contextualising union actors within this urban political economy framework is important if we are to understand the variety of issues that unions in both the private and public sectors must consider. A firm-centred political economy understates the range of issues that unions must address insofar as they are institutions of the working class and not just organisational vehicles for collective bargaining. Unions in North America are incentivised and constrained to defend workplace-based collective bargaining under the Wagner Act model. But in a challenging environment characterised by the loss of 'good jobs' with deindustrialisation and the rise of new business models in the service economy, unions must also become involved in attempts to shape labour markets, public services, and housing markets in order to buttress collective bargaining and respond to the multiple interests of their members insofar as they are also working-class residents.

In a second section, we propose to extend the literature on union capacities through the prism of urban political economy. Five capacities – the capacity to assemble productive territories, to balance production with social reproduction, to grant legitimacy to growth regimes, to connect planning to everyday life, and to mobilise urban electorates – define what is unique to unions insofar as they are urban political-economic actors. We develop these capacities analytically, through a comparison with other actors in the territorial alliances that govern North American urban regions, and empirically, through references to cases of union campaigns across various economic sectors. These campaigns are typically advanced by unions forming or joining cross-class territorial alliances and they rarely challenge the dominant accumulation strategies favoured by more dominant actors.

In a third, concluding section, we point to the limits of these strategies and seek to understand how these limits are the product of constrained decision making. Our approach identifies common ground between unions and other class actors, class fractions, and the local state, and this is important if we are to understand how it is possible for unions to advance their priorities in urban and regional governance in their present weakened state. A critical theory of unions in urban and regional governance ought also to identify the constraints that accompany these strategies, which are both structural and highly contextual in nature, while also arguing that different decisions might result in better outcomes for the labour movement.

The empirical material in this chapter draws on the authors' participation in urban labour campaigns and past research in Toronto and New York. Wieditz has worked on campaigns with a focus on urban planning and policy for the Toronto Labour Council, UNITE-HERE, and Unifor (Wieditz 2017b, 2017c, 2017d). Both authors were involved in a multi-year collaborative research project concerned with understanding how unions in Toronto and New York were negotiating urban change as a result of the ways they pursued their institutional interests within broader sectoral economic development strategies (MacDonald 2017; Wieditz 2017). Four sectors (hospitality, film, green energy and manufacturing, and child care) were selected on the grounds of their importance to urban growth regimes and to unions as well-organised sections of local labour markets. The work established a framework for thinking about unions as urban actors, highlighting both the potential and the limits of renewing union power through engagement in urban politics and planning. The politics of linking workplace demands and identities to urban working-class life in policymaking and planning disputes is extraordinarily complex and there is nothing automatically progressive in this. In a number of cases we have seen unions becoming entangled in contradictions that are directly related to the fact that their strategies are designed to work within neoliberal capitalism.

Unions and Urban Political Economy

An urban region is usefully conceptualised in political-economic terms as a space that displays a certain coherence between different moments in the circuit of capitalist value relating to production, distribution, exchange, and consumption. David Harvey refers to this as the 'territorial and regional coherence' (2006 [1982], p. 416) of urban regions, comprising four dimensions. To begin with, the structured coherence to production, distribution, exchange, and consumption materialises in a regional space within which socially necessary turnover time is not being exceeded by the time and cost of movement. Secondly, central to such a regional space is a relatively coherent labour market defined by its commuter range, that is, by the time and cost of the daily movement of labour power. Thirdly, it is undergirded by a state space, by a formal territory towards which state policies are directed to regulate capital-labour relations, including policies that regulate the labour process, labour organising, workers' standard of living through welfare provision, and so on. Lastly, a region's structured coherence also represents an informal territory, one that is invested with meaning and identity by non-state actors. Such regional structured coherence, Harvey insists, is 'actively produced rather than passively received as a concession to "nature" or "history"' (Harvey 2006 [1982]: 416).

The need to maintain a region's structured coherence in the face of a maelstrom of undermining forces provides the material basis for regional class and factional alliances (1989, 2001 [1985], 2006 [1982]). This can be explained by the fact that former rounds of long-term capital investments into forms of spatial organisation for production and consumption entailing 'everything from industrial parks, ports and airports, transport and communications nets to sewage and water systems, housing, hospitals, schools' (Harvey 2003: 111), are tied to specific sets of actors with a vested interest in protecting the longevity of such physical assets. Most committed to defending existing investments in urban infrastructure from localised and place-specific devaluation are alliances of land and property owners, renters, developers, builders, the local state as well as finance capitalists who have a stake in mortgages. Production capital, which cannot easily move, may also support such property-led alliances as may those factions of labour which have, through past struggles, managed to gain relatively strong positions and which rely, for its own reproduction, on the kind of infrastructural investments such alliances aim to defend.

Capital is internally divided along any number of axes – industrial versus financial, leading versus declining sectors, and even narrower distinctions between firms – because they differ in terms of their relative commitment to place and because they compete with one another over how to position their region within the world economy – i.e. what local growth strategy to pursue and how to prioritise competing claims on land and public resources in pursuit of these strategies (Jessop 1997). Individual capitals often find themselves competing over the same parcels of land or local markets. Labour cannot be indifferent to these contests, because different growth strategies and business models associated with different firms will have varying distributional implications for labour in terms of wages, employment levels, the quality of employment, public spending, and regulations that bear on the livelihoods of their members. Individual unions are able to exert influence in these contests by exploiting divisions between competing territorial alliances, or narrower firm-level contests, and by lending their sometimes considerable political capacities to resolve these contests within the local state in ways that align with labour's priorities.

Unions are driven to join and even to initiate these alliances because they are among the most place-bound of governance actors. While labour markets extend across national, and to a much lesser extent, global economies, firm-level commitments to internal labour markets, investments in firm-specific skills and collectively bargained pensions, and other workplace benefits, bind unionised workers to workplaces. Of equal importance, family and neighbourhood connections figure centrally to working-class social reproduction (Peck 1996). Furthermore, unions have institutional interests in the structured coherence of a particular locality that go beyond the livelihood concerns of their members. Industrial relations regimes play an important role in shaping union preferences in this respect. In a North American context defined by the severely eroded but still dominant Wagner Act model of exclusive workplace-centred union accreditation and collective bargaining, local unions have much stronger incentives to defend particular workplaces than in more encompassing regimes. Unionisation, for instance, involves the investment of considerable resources in organising and first-contract campaigns that are recouped over a long period of time in terms of incremental contract gains and dues payments. Union decline in North America is associated with industrial and regional restructuring owing to the difficulty of organising greenfield plants and transitioning into new sectors (Jackson and Schetagne 2004). Unions for this reason come to see themselves as superintending regional geographies and specific workplaces in which they have already achieved recognition and bargaining power. In the context of weak employment protections and, absent union representation, including low and uneven social security coverage, in the United States, the tight link between health care coverage and union employment, union members are much more likely than in Europe to look to their organisations to protect their jobs.

Labour's commitment to place is prior to the investment decisions of firms and the locational tournaments that multinational companies employ to extract benefits from local communities. Investment in fixed capital is episodic, and the ownership of local productive assets cycles more and more rapidly under financialised capitalism. Unions have long-term stakes in specific regional assemblages of physical plants, skilled labour pools, supplier firm ecosystems, and the supportive public infrastructures necessary to 'ground' further rounds of capital accumulation. Superintending the legacies of previous rounds of accumulation is important because they take a long time to form and are at risk from the short-termist calculations of capitalist fractions, especially commercial and real estate capital, which can regard these legacies as barriers to profit-making (Nugent 2017).

Furthermore, it cannot be said that unions are concerned with winning new investment in general since they are often in the position of opposing certain kinds of investment that are inimical to their interests. For instance, unions must oppose investment that undermines union labour markets and bargaining relations with established firms. We see examples of this when industrial unions mobilise to defend industrial-zoned land threatened with conversion to what is euphemistically referred to as its 'highest and best (i.e. most profitable) use', or when public-sector unions campaign against private sector developments that undermine the tax base while imposing strain on public services such as casinos (Tufts 2017). Condo and mall redevelopment of industrial-zoned land, for example, may be the most profitable use for a developer, while it displaces industrial labour and may represent a socially sub-optimal choice when comparative employment levels, wage structures, and the sustainability of the local tax base are taken into consideration.

In North American labour movements, power is concentrated at the local level, with national organisations and peak-level federations concerned primarily with political affairs and the management of inter-union conflict. Uniquely among local governance actors, the labour movement's federated structure parallels the federal structure of the state. Unions are thus able to scale up local priorities to sub-national and national office-holders. Indeed, the priorities of local unions tend to override political decisions at higher levels. It is likewise with local and regional labour councils, which rely on voluntary membership and dues payments from affiliated locals. Typically, these local councils are dominated by the building trades, which have the most at stake in urban policy and planning: urban infrastructure spending and development-friendly planning decisions are responsible for maintaining a flow of projects that keep their members at work. As an exasperated former president of the New York labour council once put it to one of the authors, 'If it were proposed to build a pyramid in Central Park, the only question from the steamfitters union would be, "Does it have steam?"'.

In this context, union interventions in urban and regional spaces are rationalised by the need to defend or create 'good jobs', understood as employment that pays a wage sufficient to live decently in place, accompanied by the security that allows you to plan a future, and the opportunity to express voice and some measure of control at work. Across large North American cities, unions have wagered that they can produce good jobs, and even good green jobs, by shaping firm investment and employment practices through the regulatory framework in which firms must operate. Good job strategies range from attempts at blocking or strictly regulating fractions of capital or particular business models that undermine union standards, leverage campaigns which seek to force particular employers or developers to improve employment and labour relations practices, and steering policies designed to shift urban regional economies away from low road growth trajectories. Campaigns to defend or produce good jobs can move from blocking to leverage to steering based on a variety of contextual factors, including union power resources and political opportunities that may open or close in specific cases, as well as more strategic and political calculations in terms of reactive versus proactive or particularist versus class-oriented commitments.

Union Capacities within Urban Regions

Unions exercise institutional capacities that are ultimately founded on power resources that are specific to workers in a capitalist society. Workers exercise power by acting in solidarity through their associations and by virtue of their strategic position within production. Wright's (2000) concepts of 'associational power' and 'structural power' effectively convey this idea. Capacities, by which we mean 'sets of aptitudes, competencies, abilities, social skills and know-how' (Lévesque and Murray 2010: 321) are more specific to unions as institutions and are consciously developed and deployed by union actors. While they can be described in general terms, union capacities are particular to the political economies in which they are actuated (ibid.).

Large urban regions in general, and the global city in particular, can be conceptualised as a capitalist structure of production, distribution, and realisation that conditions new opportunities for deploying union capacities. For instance, workers who are residentially located in the path of state-led attempts to realise profits in land speculation can exercise a form of urban structural power by negotiating enhanced workplace rights as their union develops the capacity to intervene in the planning process (MacDonald 2011). The struggles of unionised workers involved in the production, what Harvey calls the 'built environment for production', are likewise exploiting vulnerabilities in capitalist valorisation that are specific to urban regional spaces (Harvey 1978, p. 106). Even low income and marginalised workers can exercise considerable associational power by virtue of their electoral and street mobilisation within political spaces that are highly sensitive to political and economic elites. Below we develop a more systematic way of thinking about union capacities in the context of capitalist urbanisation.

Capacity to Assemble Productive Territories

Reproducing labour relations in place requires that all of the moments of the production process be brought together in a territorial assemblage. This involves ensuring that land is reserved for productive uses at competitive rents, supportive infrastructure is in place, labour is available at different skill levels, local or export markets are identified or created, and investors commit capital in the expectation of at least average profit rates. Unions with long-term commitments to a particular sector cannot assume that all of these moments will always come together given the centripetal tendencies noted above. The work of assembling and defending territorial assemblages involves labour in complex cross-class territorial alliances, and it often devolves to labour to lead these alliances. This can involve simply blocking a changed land use or new investment or land use planning tools that reserve land for employment purposes or specific industrial uses. Good green jobs strategies are more ambitious still as they see unions taking effective responsibility for all of the moments of production, including creating markets for green industries and securing policy support and financing from national governments and global climate treaties.

The 'site fights' that the United Food and Commercial Workers (UFCW) has waged against Walmart in major metropolitan areas are well-known examples of new investment blocking strategies (Sites 2007). Labour mobilises public opinion and community opposition to the city granting a permit or financial incentive to a developer which intends on landing the low-wage retailer as an anchor tenant. Opposition is raised on labour standards grounds in public mobilisation, but as these are not eligible criteria in urban planning decisions – cities are constitutionally pre-empted from regulating labour relations – effective opposition hinges on quality of life issues and impact on local businesses. Labour must form broad neighbourhood coalitions to win these fights, which, depending on the neighbourhood and who is included in the coalitions, can vary considerably in their class nature. For example, a campaign waged by film unions in a rapidly gentrifying neighbourhood in Toronto found effective opposition to Walmart among the local gentry, concerned to defend a gentrifying commercial streetscape, as well as among film studio owners, concerned with the contagion effects of big-box retail development on area ground rent. This was the primary concern of local film industry workers, who alerted their union to the likelihood that the development would displace film industry jobs (Wieditz 2017). A high-wage union sector was defended and a low-wage employer was blocked in a way that affirmed gentrification.

These blocking campaigns are easier to win if supportive policy frameworks have been established beforehand. In Toronto, concerns that the condo boom would completely undermine the city's productive base led the Toronto and York Region Labour Council, after many 'site fights', to mount a campaign to comprehensively protect the city's 'employment lands' (Lehrer and Wieditz 2009; Wieditz 2017). In a good example of a successful blocking strategy, unions helped push through legislation that prevents owners of productive assets in designated areas of the city from converting their properties to uses, such as residential, that threaten well paid and unionised blue-collar jobs.

Campaigns to defend employment lands can oppose labour to industrial capital seeking to disinvest or can lead to 'productivist' alliances between labour and industrial capital that is committed to a particular site. In some cases, industrial capital will even take the lead in these site fights, as in Nestlé Canada's labour-supported anti-condo campaign in Toronto's West end ('More condos mean fewer good jobs') (Alamenciak 2012). More commonly, labour takes the initiative in forming productivist alliances with industrial capital, small businesses, the local state, and sometimes homeowner or tenants associations.

In a recent labour-led campaign to regulate Toronto's growing short-term rental market, Unite HERE has built coalitions with tenants' rights and grassroots organisations of low- and moderate-income families to create municipal regulations to govern short-term rental companies like Airbnb and individual short-term rental hosts alike (Wieditz 2017b). This campaign evolved into a cross-class coalition that not only included labour and tenants' rights activists, but also middle-class homeowners, ratepayers' associations, and even one hotelier. It was this broad political spectrum represented by what came to be known as Fairbnb Canada that made this coalition successful. Fairbnb campaigned not only on housing affordability and availability (Wieditz 2017c, 2017d), perhaps the most significant problem facing low- and moderate-income residents in Toronto, but also on nuisance and party house issues that enraged neighbours across Toronto's residential neighbourhoods and condo towers. In December 2017, after an 18 month-long campaign, Toronto's City Council approved one of the strictest rules governing Airbnb and other short-term rental companies in North America (Rieti 2017). In many ways, it was labour which took up the initiative to regulate this emerging market even before other employers in the hotel industry pushed their national association to turn short-term rental regulation into one of their main policies and lobbying planks (http://new.hotelassociation.ca/home/advocacy/).

'Good green job' strategies to steer capital into 'green' sectors that are unionised and pay decent wages all the while remediating ecological damage have required much stronger forms of regulation and more significant public incentives. The territorial alliances required to make these work can be very complex and tax labour's political capacities. Consider the complexity of the following example. Across the New York metropolitan area, the Laborers International Union (LIUNA) has been involved in campaigns to shore up its position in the labour market by creating good jobs, and paths to entry into those jobs for low-income people who have traditionally been excluded from the building trades, by inducing the growth of residential retrofitting work. The union applied an organising model in partnering with community-based organisations (CBOs) which would function as programme service providers for the direct consumers. The key elements of the strategy included the formation of new locals and establishment of special rate agreements, working with worker centres to target the workforce, partnerships with programme service providers, which hire from their network of contractors and do the outreach to homeowners, and workforce development in partnership with CBOs to ensure entry of community residents into the unionised workforce. Financing was partly secured through Obama-era recovery funds and credits from international carbon markets. All of this for jobs paying between $14 and 18$/hr. (Figueroa 2017).

Such campaigns hinge on creating the conditions for profit-making in a 'green' industry, and union-scale employment, while working with social justice movements and mobilising marginalised and low-income residents to secure the necessary political support. The difficulties that confront these strategies multiply at the local level, with scalar tensions appearing between local and national union bodies, organisational culture differences between unions, environmental, and community-based organisations, conflicting financial incentives facing property owners and renters, and differences in policy preferences between financial capital, industrial capital, and commercial real estate. All of this increases the coordination burden on unions, and this partly explains why these strategies have not been more successful in terms of generating good green jobs, let alone in reducing GHG emissions.

Capacity to Balance Production and Social Reproduction

While unions share a concern for defending productive assets and territorial assemblages with the local state and the more place-bound fractions of capital, unions are the only governance actors, beyond the local state, to consider the importance of balancing production with social reproduction. This is owing to the dual character of wage labour: the value of the collectively bargained wage is relative to the price level of wage goods and levels of collective consumption available in the local or regional labour market. In more concrete terms, what is gained at the bargaining table can be lost by a decision to de-regulate housing markets, hike transit fares, increase taxes, or impose user fees for public services. Growth interests systematically privilege the most profitable uses of urban land with scant consideration for impacts on collective consumption and the ability of workers to raise families in place, which represent to individual capitals costs and sometimes barriers to development. And yet the articulation between production and social reproduction is key to the coherence of urban and regional economies. While unions also privilege the workplace (thewhich represent to individual capitals workplace represents the state-sanctioned basis of their organisational power and legitimacy), they are constrained in their promotion of employment and workplace-based interests by the residential or broader social implications of any growth strategy for their members, and for their social legitimacy as working-class actors.

Labour is internally divided on where to draw the line between these two priorities. Decision making is highly contextual, is typically gendered, and the decisions that result are not necessarily politically 'progressive' in the sense of promoting collective over individual consumption. High-wage industrial unions with a largely male, home-owning membership base residentially located in exurban or suburban areas will make different calculations on how to weigh employment versus collective consumption than a union representing low-wage, mostly female and immigrant renters in the city. Service sector unions are particularly attuned to the implications of urban planning and policy decisions for their members as working-class residents of the city (Tufts 2009). Large general unions that have come to represent workers in both the declining industrial sectors and the rising service sectors, as is the case when industrial unions move into the city, will have to confront tensions around these questions internally through deliberation and member education. What are at root pragmatic livelihood concerns take on a political and even ideological character when articulated in terms of labour strategy. Public sector unions with members working in the 'social state' should find these tensions easier to mediate. But this requires a strategic vision on the part of labour activists who understand how bargaining power can be built in the process of linking the workplace demands of their members to raising the level and quality of public services (Gindin and Hurley 2010). Expanding access to collective consumption would also be more effective in decarbonising our economies than subsidising profit-led 'green' industry.

Because expanding collective consumption is not profitable, it is much less likely that public-sector unions will be able to engage cross-class alliances. They do try, however, by framing expanded social services in terms of steering regional economies along 'high road' trajectories. Campaigns by unions representing child care workers in US cities are good examples. Unions have attempted to forge alliances with regional employers and business associations using the argument that the provision of affordable, quality child care increases female labour market participation rates and has been related to better educational outcomes and workplace productivity, both of which are determinants of inward investment and economic growth (Warner 2006). Advancing child care policy in an economic competitiveness frame exploits a rhetorical contradiction of urban competitiveness strategies: urban regimes claim to favour growth policies but the powerful economic actors that comprise them are more concerned with firm-level profits and cutting social costs. Neoliberal policy advisers and austerity-minded local governments favour a low cost and differentiated child care system, good enough to sustain local labour supply. When we take a close look at US labour strategies in this sector, we find that successful outcomes owe more to the political power of 'feminized' unions and their mobilisation of low-income residents through a gendered and racial justice frame, with cross-class alliances playing a supportive and discursive role (Black 2017; Schaller et al. 2017).

Capacity to Grant Social Legitimacy to Growth Strategies

Growth regimes claim to speak on behalf of local economies and foreground in their public discourse arguments that are designed to appeal to wage-earners. Thus arguments touting the benefits of profit-led accumulation strategies commonly emphasise the generation of local employment and the need to defend the local tax base to support public services. Yet growth regimes are led by capitalist class fractions, typically including large local firms, real estate developers, and property owners, and they face considerable legitimacy deficits when public debates turn on working-class concerns. Unions are the only actors which legitimately speak for a working-class public in planning and public policy debates. They may face their own legitimacy deficits when speaking to political and social issues perceived as too far removed from the workplace, but no one questions their legitimacy when, in business-union mode, union leaders in the private sector speak in defence of the jobs of their members, or even of employment creation more generally. Unions parlay this legitimacy, granting social license to elite-led projects, in exchange for commitments to 'good job' creation or institutional compromises that may secure their role as labour market intermediaries. In the public sector, unions may prefer to have community allies and public service recipients speak to their concerns, while effacing their own involvement in campaigns to defend public sector jobs from austerity drives (Black 2017).

These kinds of bargains imply labour fragmentation. Capitals in different sectors will make their own claims regarding 'good jobs' and local benefits, and unions that successfully wager their legitimacy on one sector will find themselves opposed to unions which have made the same calculations in another, competing sector, as Tufts (2017) describes in his account of how the Toronto casino debate split labour into pro- and anti-gaming factions. In this case, fragmentations occur along public sector/private sector lines, as the public is called upon to subsidise the generation of private-sector employment through tax abatements which impose costs on the public. But conflicts occur within the private sector as well, especially between industrial and service sector capitalist fractions (Nugent 2017a, 2017b).

Lending legitimacy to profit-led growth strategies is not costless for labour. Unions that have staked out 'social union' identities are particularly exposed when project-level deal-making returns negative social outcomes for local residents with little in the way of 'good job' creation, or when the resulting 'good jobs' are unbalanced in terms of union/non-union workers and fail to address equity demands in highly racialised urban spaces and labour markets (Figueroa 2017). Unions representing high-wage, high-skill workers in footloose industries are vulnerable to these critiques (Figueroa and Gray 2017). Blocking investments can also cost unions social legitimacy. Walmart's lawyers are adept at pointing out that unions are *de facto* aligned with elitists who cringe at the prospect of a Walmart opening in their community, while claiming to defend the consumption interests of low-wage workers (Wieditz 2017). Labour needs a realistic development model for working-class residents who are structurally dependent on low prices and low-wage retail employment.

Capacity to Connect Planning to Everyday Life

Among the political actors involved in growth regime politics, unions are uniquely positioned to consider workers' everyday lives and are therefore armed with legitimacy to speak on behalf of wage-earners in ways that all other growth regime actors are not. Everyday life, as Lefebvre (1947) reminds us, has to be understood in its totality, which includes experiences at work, at home, as well as those we make during our daily routines between the two. More progressive unions have developed social union programmes that go beyond the administration of workplace grievances and engage in important questions of social reproduction that matter to their members and their members' communities, ranging from economic development to childcare, transit, policing, and housing. Improving the totality of workers' lives, in other words, requires labour strategies that deal with matters outside the workplace and are typically the preserve of urban politics, municipal service delivery, and planning.

Unions use this legitimacy to weaponise the everyday life experiences of their members in strategies to shape urban policy and planning regulation, flows of capital into reproductive infrastructure, initiatives to end the over-policing of their members' communities, etc. At a very pragmatic level, unions that are successful in directing investments into, say, affordable housing, transit or public childcare, underwrite their members' social wage, often with dramatic results. On a more abstract level, union involvement in the politics of planning and development also ultimately counters the very trends that tend to undermine the structured coherence of urban regions. When the reproduction of labour in a particular place, for instance, is challenged by rising costs of housing and poor transit, union-led campaigns to establish co-op housing and free transit passes contribute greatly towards establishing the material support upon which an urban region's structured coherence is built.

Using everyday life experiences as a weapon in the class struggle allows unions, drawing on Lefebvre (1991 [1974]), to challenge abstract notions of space conceived by planners, architects, investors, etc., who render spatial conceptions for the sole purpose of increasing the turnaround time of capital for their clients. Labour's spatial strategies promise to shape everyday life for workers in beneficial ways. Because everyday life is expressed in and through spatial practice, the very material support that enables such practice is what undergirds a region's structured coherence: road and transit networks, residential neighbourhoods, child care centres, employment districts, etc.

Unions employ a range of tactics to engage in such non-workplace struggles, but what these tactics have in common is that they successfully link urban and regional development processes to the lived experiences of workers. Without the commitment of unions to social unionism, the voices of workers would not be heard at town halls, council meetings, or during judicial proceedings. Without labour strategies that aim at more socially just urban environments, the everyday life concerns of workers would not find their way into actual urban policy or new developments. Yet, unions have shown time and time again that their involvement in struggles over the nature and form of built environments, the articulation of urban policy or investment flows into public infrastructure can make a real difference in the everyday life of workers.

Limits and Possibilities

We see two limits or dilemmas in unions developing the urban capacities sketched above. One is more conjunctural and varies by context, having to do with the way union engagement in cross-class urban alliances tends to fragment local labour movements. The other is more long term and structural. In becoming responsible for the structured coherence of 'their' urban region, unions are taking responsibility for the local reproduction of capitalism in its neoliberal phase, an inherently self-limiting role which, in any event, exhausts their capacities.

We have argued that union institutional goals in urban governance are specific to their concerns to reproduce bargaining relationships, defend employment levels in unionised labour markets, and sometimes to represent their members' interests insofar as they are working-class residents, public service users, and recipients of social spending. These goals cannot be achieved by unions acting in isolation or as a labour bloc. Urban politics is the politics of territorial alliance formation and territorial compromise (Schmid 2004). As we have seen, the 'geometry' of labour-inclusive territorial alliances is complex, always shifting with context, and rarely resolves itself along class lines.

This orientation explains why local union interventions in urban and regional governance are as likely to fragment as to unite the working class across different spheres of social life. A spectrum of class actors, from middle-class homeowners to small business owners and large employers, will have concerns in sector regulation or site-specific planning that overlap with differently situated labour organisations. The politically effective coalition in any one instance will incorporate the broadest array of consequential partners, and compromises are inevitable on issues that are deemed peripheral to the agreed-upon basis of unity. The alliance between hotel sector unions and homeowner and tenant associations formed to regulate Airbnb, for instance, will have positive implications for workers' housing when hospitality employment is preserved by preventing small investors from transforming affordable rental housing into short-term tourist rentals that undercut unionised hotels (Tufts 2017b; Wieditz 2017b). The same coalition in a different context – negotiating neutrality card check agreements with the developers of new-build hotels in exchange for labour's political support through the planning process, for instance – may have the contrary effect if the development in question touches off land speculation (MacDonald 2011).

Revived and empowered labour centrals might be in a position to mitigate these tensions if they built power horizontally across different locals and challenged their particularism with class politics. Labour councils are sometimes able to overcome these fragmentations by leading encompassing campaigns that address working-class interests in urban space, such as campaigns against cuts to public services and planning policies to defend industrial land for unionised employment. By virtue of strong leadership, labour councils are capable of building a measure of autonomy from local labour unions through a committed activist base and social movement alliances. But as it stands, labour's fragmentation hinders the work of local labour councils, and their effectiveness across North America remains weak and uneven. A local left rooted in the trade unions could lean against fragmentation and insist on the importance of linking sector regulation to issues of collective consumption and a jobs-rich, public sector-led green transition. Labour's fragmentation is very much symptomatic of the absence of such a left.

Our discussion of union capacities has shown how unions are most motivated and are uniquely situated among urban governance actors to defend the structured coherence of their regions. In the face of 'disruptive' capital, unions are 'responsible'. They are responsible not only in the Fordist sense of the term (i.e. not questioning the legitimacy that ownership affords over the control and organisation of labour power) but responsible now also for bringing the different moments of the production process together (land, labour, capital, infrastructure), balancing production with social reproduction, and securing the social legitimacy of urban and regional accumulation strategies. This assumption of responsibility could be considered positive insofar as it is necessary to protect members' abilities to live decently in place. It could also be considered positive, and even necessary, in the sense that the local and regional reproduction of capitalism requires non-capitalist actors – not motivated by profit – to see to the long-term coherence of a given territory.

This is typically considered a function of the state. The state plays a particularly important role in ensuring the longevity of a region's structured coherence and its ability to compete internationally. The local state is normally captive of capitalist class fractions that have the most at stake in urban planning and infrastructure development. But regional class and factional alliances acting in and through the state can use the state powers to influence regional dynamics through its policies and actions in ways that provide firmer shape to such regional class and factional alliances. In support of such regional forces, the state can impose relatively firm political and administrative boundaries to undergird otherwise porous and unstable urban regions. If the structured coherence is threatened, the state can impose a variety of powers, such as land use regulation, land expropriation, land use planning, and, finally, actual investment, particularly in transport and communications, education, and research, 'to counter incoherency and periodic speculative fevers land markets are periodically heir to' (Harvey 2006 [1982]: 371). In the last instance, 'the state becomes the central institution through which interregional conflicts are worked out, and the base from which each regional alliance seeks its "spatial fix"' (Harvey 2006 [1982]: 449).

Local labour unions continue to play a crucial role in articulating the interests of their members, across a broad array of everyday life concerns, from the workplace to urban politics and policy development and enforcement. This is particularly important in a late neoliberal context in which the capacities of the state have been hollowed out and public policy is more and more subject to the short-termist logics of financial capital and their local avatars. We have shown how, in their concern for the regional reproduction of capitalist social relations, unions are thinking like states and acting like states. Indeed, we should think of unions as part of the local state in the inclusive, Gramscian sense. The point is worth emphasising because this is not how unions are perceived in the dominant neoliberal discourse (as rent seekers or barriers to competitive regionalism), or indeed in much of the scholarly literature (as concerned with distributional issues in alliance with community organisations, or with winning new rounds of investment). Our critical account has also highlighted where we see the limits and contradictions of this state-like responsibility: in particular the gap between labour's assumed responsibility and their actual capacities, and the tendency towards fragmentation that accompanies cross-class territorial alliances. Our discussion has revealed why the 'social union' perspective in the labour renewal literature ought to be more careful in celebrating this extended form of labour action, whether in terms of participation in planning and public policy-making or community coalitions, when what we are dealing with is a more entrepreneurial and particularist labour politics that is as likely to fragment urban working classes as it is to unite them around a common vision of a socially just urban region.

There is a weakness attached to being overly responsible. The responsible actor with the fewest exit options and the most to lose is the weakest party in any negotiation. To bolster its bargaining power, labour needs to re-locate its disruptiveness and its irresponsibility. Mapping urban and regional territories in terms of capital fixes and circuits of capital is useful in identifying where labour disruption would have maximum effect. Moody (2017) locates this in capital's secondary circuits (warehousing, transportation hubs) while McAlevey (2016) makes a persuasive case for a focus on the tertiary circuits (education, health care). Closer to Lefebvre, Greenberg and Lewis (2017) argue that the city or urban region should be conceived strategically in terms of value flows between different waged and non-waged labour processes. Slowing down and blocking capital flows in an 'urban strike' (Kipfer 1998) is the most radical thing that labour could do to exercise power in a moment of crisis. Labour does not have the capacity or legitimacy to pull this off. But in a moment of crisis there needs to be an understanding of where to go. The patient building up of workplace and political capacities that we have detailed in this chapter could, in a moment of crisis, switch from reproducing capitalist social relations to challenging them.

References

Alamenciak, T. (2012) Condos and the chocolate factory: Nestlé Canada wages campaign against development. *Toronto Star*. (22 September). https://www.thestar.com/news/gta/2012/09/27/condos_and_the_chocolate_factory_nestl_canada_wages_campaign_against_development.html

Black, S. (2017) Labor in the Caring City. In MacDonald, I. T. (ed.) *Unions and the City: Negotiating Urban Change*. Ithaca: Cornell ILR Press, pp. 167–170.

Figueroa, M. (2017) Building a Green New York: Construction Unions and Community Alliances. In MacDonald, I. T. (ed.) *Unions and the City: Negotiating Urban Change*. Ithaca: Cornell ILR Press, pp. 125–145.

Figueroa, M. & Gray, L. (2017) New York Film Production Unions Enter the Political Arena in Search of Tax Subsidies. In MacDonald, I. T. (ed.) *Unions and the City: Negotiating Urban Change*. Ithaca: Cornell ILR Press, pp. 79–101.

Gindin, S. & M. Hurley. (2010) The Public Sector: searching for a focus. *The Bullet*. (15 May). Accessed on 7 September 2018 at https://socialistproject.ca/2010/05/b354/.

Greenberg, M. & Lewis, P. (eds.). (2017) *The City Is the Factory: New Solidarities and Spatial Strategies in an Urban Age*. Ithica, NY: Cornell University Press.

Harvey, D. (2001 [1985]) The Geopolitics of Capitalism. In Harvey, D. (rd.) *Spaces of Capital*. Edinburgh: Taylor & Francis, pp. 312–344.

Harvey, D. (2003) *The New Imperialism*. Oxford; New York: Oxford Press.

Harvey, D. (2006 [1982]) *Limits to Capital*. London, New York: Verso.

Jackson, A. & Schetagne, S. (2004) Solidarity forever? – An analysis of changes in union density. *Just Labour*, 4: 53–82.

Jessop, B. (1997) A neo-Gramscian approach to the regulation of urban regimes: accumulation strategies, hegemonic projects, and governance. *Reconstructing Urban Regime Theory: Regulating Urban Politics in a Global Economy*, 5, 1–74.

Kipfer, S. (1998) Urban Politics in the 1990s: Notes on Toronto. In Inura (ed.) *Possible Urban Worlds*. Zurich: ETH, pp. 172–179.

Lefebvre, H. (1947) *Critique of Everyday Life* (Vol. 1). New York: Verso.

Lefebvre, H. (1991 [1974]) *The Production of Space*. New York, Blackwell Publishing.

Lehrer, U., & Wieditz, T. (2009) Condominium development and gentrification: The relationship between policies. *Journal of Urban Research*, 18(1), 140–161.

Lévesque, C. & Murray, G. (2002) Local versus global: activating local union power in the global economy. *Labor Studies Journal*, 27(3), 39–65.

Lévesque, C., & Murray, G. (2010) Understanding union power: resources and capabilities for renewing union capacity. *Transfer: European Review of Labour and Research*, 16, 333–350. 10.1177/1024258910373867

MacDonald, I. T. (2011) Bargaining for Rights in Luxury City: The Strategic Dilemmas of Organized Labor's Urban Turn. *Labor Studies Journal*, 36(2), 197–220.

MacDonald, I. T. (2014) Beyond the Labour of Sisyphus: Unions and the City. Panitch, L., Albo, G. & Chibber, V. (eds.) *Socialist Register: Registering Class*. London: Merlin Press, pp. 247–265.

MacDonald, I. T. (2017) *Unions and the City: Negotiating Urban Change*. Ithaca: Cornell ILR Press.

MacDonald, I. T. (2017b) Labor Strategy and the Politics of Elite Division in Midtown Manhattan. In MacDonald, I. T. (ed.) *Unions and the City: Negotiating Urban Change*. Ithaca: Cornell ILR Press.

McAlevey, J. (2016) *No Shortcuts: Organizing for Power in the New Gilded Age*. New York, NY: Oxford University Press.

Moody, K. (2017) *On New Terrain: How Capital Is Reshaping the Battleground of Class War*. Chicago: Haymarket Books.

Nugent, J. (2017a) Struggling for Good Green Jobs in Toronto's De-industrializing Suburbs. In MacDonald, I. T. (ed.) *Unions and the City: Negotiating Urban Change*.

Ithaca, NY: Cornell University Press, pp. 146–166. https://doi.org/10.7591/9781501712692-013

Nugent, J. (2017b) The right to build the city: can community benefits agreements bring employment equity to the construction sector? *Labour/Le Travail*, 2017, 80, 81–114.

Peck, J. (1996) *Workplace: The Social Regulation of Labor Markets*. New York: The Guilford Press.

Rieti, J. (2017) Toronto tackles long-term rental supply with new Airbnb rules: Short-term rental rules limit people to hosting only at their primary residence. *CBC News* (8 December). Retrieved from https://www.cbc.ca/news/canada/toronto/council-airbnb-vote-1.4437321

Schaller, S. F., Wagner, K. C. & Warner, M. E. (2017) Creating a City for Workers: Union Strategies on Child Care in NYC. In MacDonald, I. T. (ed.) *Unions and the City: Negotiating Urban Change*. Ithaca, NY: Cornell University Press, pp. 171–188. https://doi.org/10.7591/9781501712692-015

Schmid, C. (2004) A New Paradigm of Urban Development for Zurich. *The Contested Metropolis: Six Cities at the Beginning of the 21st Century*. Basel: Birkhauser, pp. 237–246.

Sites, W. (2007) Beyond trenches and grassroots? Reflections on urban mobilization, fragmentation, and the anti-Wal-Mart campaign in Chicago. *Environment and Planning A*, 39(11), 2632–2651.

Tufts, S. (2009) Hospitality unionism and labour market adjustment: toward Schumpeterian unionism? *Geoforum*, 40(6), 980–990.

Tufts, S. (2017) Organized Labour and Casino Politics in Toronto. In MacDonald, I. T. (Ed.) *Unions and the City: Negotiating Urban Change*. Ithaca: Cornell ILR Press.

Tufts, S. (2017b) Unions and the Gig-Economy: The Case of AirBnB. Accessed on 7 September 2018 at https://socialistproject.ca/2017/11/b1508/

Warner, M. E. (2006) Putting child care in the regional economy: empirical and conceptual challenges and economic development prospects. *Community Development*, 37(2), 7–22.

Wieditz, T. (2017) Film Unions' Struggle to Defend Studio Space in Toronto. In MacDonald, I. T. (ed.) *Unions and the City: Negotiating Urban Change*. Ithaca, NY: Cornell University Press, pp. 102–120. https://doi.org/10.7591/9781501712692-010

Wieditz, T. (2017b) On Responding to Airbnb. Retrieved from https://www.acto.ca/on-responding-to-airbnb/

Wieditz, T. (2017c) Could Airbnb Turn Toronto's Most Affordable Rental Housing Stock into Ghost Hotel Suites? Retrieved from http://fairbnb.ca/wp-content/uploads/2017/11/Fairbnb_Report-on-Secondary-Suites_final.pdf

Wieditz, T. (2017d) Squeezed Out: Airbnb's Commercialization of Home-sharing in Toronto. *Policy report prepared for* FAIRBNB.CA *coalition*. Accessed on 7 September 2018 at http://fairbnb.ca/reports/

Wright, E. O. (2000) Working-class power, capitalist-class interests, and class compromise. *American Journal of Sociology*, 105(4), 957–1002.

5 Institutional Experimentation in the Montreal Taxi Industry: What Role for the State and Collective Action?

Urwana Coiquaud and Lucie Morissette

Passenger transportation via the taxi industry long carried the image of a sclerotic and antiquated sector unable to respond to the many challenges it faced. Yet, its future looked promising, with a growth in demand due to the combined effect of population ageing and urban sprawl.

The arrival of Uber, however, provoked a small revolution with its innovative approach to the provision of transportation by taxi, made possible by a digital application connecting drivers with passengers. With Uber, using the personal vehicle of a 'partner', the provision of transportation is fully automated and the whole process is carried out in real-time, from booking the taxi to paying the fare, including the determination and modulation of thc cost of thc farc. This incursion could have benefited the entire industry, except that it took place in disregard of the actors and regulations in force (Coiquaud et al. 2018). Backed by technological innovation, Uber argued that it was not bound by the regulatory framework in effect, including the permit system. Thus, Uber gave itself an illegal competitive advantage, exacerbating the poor economic situation of traditional taxi drivers (D'Amour 1981; Coiquaud 2009).

The Montreal taxi industry has thus been at the heart of institutional experimentation and change, brought about by various actors over the years (Kristensen and Morgan 2012). This chapter will seek to understand how, through experimentation, the state and collective actors endeavoured to structure this industry in the territory of Montreal. While the government often took the lead in regulating the sector by ensuring safety and the control of supply and prices, collective associations, including the unions, used various means to enrich the regulations and improve taxi drivers' working conditions. This process of sedimentation (Mahoney and Thelen 2009) refers to a series of changes aimed at strengthening the institutionalisation and homogenisation of a domain, ensuring the resilience of its regulations. These changes are referred to as non-divergent changes (Battilana et al. 2009). However, with Uber's arrival, this institutional architecture was threatened. Hence, unions and taxi driver associations

DOI: 10.4324/9781003001089-7

revitalised their collective action to strive against the unfair competition from Uber. This pressure forced the state to react, albeit belatedly and with some hesitation. It took the path of regulatory experimentation, granting privileged status to Uber, while also encouraging the deployment of a new business model of transportation by taxi (Téo Taxi), which was financially supported by the unions.

Framework of Analysis

The arrival of an institutional entrepreneur, such as Uber, can introduce a series of divergent changes aimed at dismantling current institutions (Battilana et al. 2009). It will do so by proposing a new, innovative business model, taking on the features of a bricolage, borrowing ideas, and repertoires of action from different institutional fields (e.g. finance, technology, economics) in order to induce change (Crouch 2005).

The success of an institutional entrepreneur will be based on two dimensions: the characteristics of the targeted sphere of action and its social position (Battilana et al. 2009). First, an economic or political crisis or a technological innovation can facilitate the entry of an institutional entrepreneur into an industry, especially if the latter is marked by uncertainty, being weakly institutionalised and driven by a heterogeneity of actors. Second, the institutional entrepreneur's capacity to act will be based on a network, resources (financial, social capital, etc.), and socially constructed legitimacy. The vision and discourse underlying the entrepreneur's innovation project will also mobilise actors around the idea that change is better than the institutional status quo, providing solutions to existing problems.

However, the institutional entrepreneur remains dependent on the regulations and institutional arrangements in force. Indeed, '… these institutions sometimes translate seemingly common trends into wholly different problems in divergent national contexts' (Thelen 2018: 923). These arrangements will thus have an effect on the regional actors' veto to oppose change, on their mobilisation, their ability to form coalitions (between interest groups, politicians, and consumers) and the narrative they mobilise to frame the conflict.

This analytical framework will be used to decipher the singular response of actors in the Montreal taxi industry following the arrival of Uber (Thelen 2018). The conflict with this multinational company thus emerged in the City of Montreal around the issue of equity and moved onto the provincial political scene. Although the associations representing the traditional industry vigorously sought to defend the existing institutions by exercising their veto, the government instead took the path of adaptation and experimentation, promoting the deployment of new business models driven by entrepreneurs, namely Uber and Téo Taxi.

Methodology

Before specifying the methodological approach adopted for this study (2), a presentation of the Montreal taxi industry will clarify its importance and distinctive characteristics (1).

The Montreal Taxi Industry

In Montreal, there are 4,522 taxi owner's permits, 6,000 taxi drivers, 265 fleet managers, and 17 service intermediaries. This represents 24 million trips a year and an annual turnover of $500 million (BTM 2018). The average value of permits in the City dropped from $190,958 in 2014 to $101,068 in 2018 (Commission des transports du Québec 2018).

Passenger transportation by taxi is organised around different actors. The driver, who provides the transportation service, can own or rent a vehicle or be an employee. The connection between a request for transportation by taxi and the provision of service is made by a service intermediary; through any means, including digital platforms, these companies provide advertising and distribution services to holders of taxi owner's or taxi driver's permits. The permit is linked, with some exceptions, to a vehicle, but also to a territory set out by regulation, called an 'agglomeration'. Public authorities regulate this industry by determining the rules for granting permits and the number of permits as well as the modes of service delivery, geographical areas of practice and prices. Moreover, the regulatory framework operates at multiple levels, involving both the provincial government and municipalities, who share the regulatory prerogatives.

Research Methodology

For the purposes of this study, we conducted a content analysis of various documentary sources dating from the 1960s to February 2019 (Krippendorff 2018). This methodology was used to examine the historical trends at the regulatory and institutional levels, and in collective action. More specifically, we analysed the bills and parliamentary proceedings pertaining to the regulation of this industry. These sources are known to help trace the positions, interests, and beliefs of different actors over time (Sabatier and Jenkins-Smith 1993). Other sources of information (reports, newspaper articles, professional, and scientific publications) were used to fill in the context of the regulatory and institutional changes examined, as well as the action of representative associations. This method has been used by other researchers to investigate the impact of Uber on national systems (see, in particular, Thelen 2018).

For the analysis, we chose a grid of mixed codings (deductive and inductive). Our analytical process was based on two waves of coding.

The first involved reconstructing the significant events. Thus, two periods were identified: (1) the beginnings of the industry's institutionalisation and (2) the period marked by the arrival of the institutional entrepreneurs Uber and Téo Taxi, characterised by institutional experimentation. The second wave of coding brought out (1) the actors' collective action; (2) the government's priorities regarding the taxi industry; and (3) the characteristics of institutional change.

The development of the institutional framework and collective action in the Montreal taxi industry will be presented in the next section.

Presentation of Results

After a period of laissez-faire contested by several short-lived collective action movements, the state laid the institutional foundations on which original union action was to be based (1), a founding framework that was subsequently weakened by Uber's arrival (2).

1 Birth and institutionalisation of an industry

In the early 20th century, the Montreal taxi industry experienced many conflicts due to the lax application of the few existing standards. One of the first strikes broke out in the 1930s, organised by small-scale taxi owners and drivers (Tucker 2017). Other strikes and attempts at unionisation followed in the 1950s (D'Amour 1981: 8), but it was in the 1960s that collective action forced the government to act.

At that time, Montreal was the theatre of major conflicts concerning Murray Hill, a taxi company that was given the monopoly to operate some lucrative sites, such as the airport, pertaining to the federal government (D'Amour 1981: 11). These protests reached a peak in 1968 when more than 7,000 drivers formed the Taxi Liberation Movement to oppose Murray Hill's privileges and demand a better quality of life (Cyr 2018). The Government of Quebec responded by commissioning a report on the industry. The finding was not very glowing: an overabundance of permits; long hours of work and inadequate income for drivers; poor mechanical condition of vehicles; carelessness of drivers in their fight over customers; and a lack of consistency in taxi industry regulations (Bossé 1970). The government, therefore, had no choice but to put an end to the prevailing unbridled liberalism.

The first step in this direction was the adoption, in 1973, of a law regulating the industry. It created the *Commission des transports du Québec* (Quebec Transportation Commission, CTQ), responsible for determining the agglomerations, safety rules and customer service rules, and setting fares for trips. At the request of industry actors, new bodies, called the Taxi Leagues, were created, bringing together permit owners and service associations (D'Amour 1981).

In the 1980s, local actors began to take charge. A new group was formed in 1982, the *Association haïtienne des travailleurs du taxi* (the Haitian taxi drivers' association, AHTT), which made the fight against racial discrimination in Montreal its main battleground. The AHTT subsequently became a key player in the industry. The Montreal Taxi League, for its part, being concerned about the number of permits in circulation, set up a voluntary buy-back plan in 1987. This led to a 25% reduction in the agglomeration's permits. This measure, combined with an economic recovery, helped to improve the working conditions of taxi drivers (Trudel 1988).

The City of Montreal took advantage of a new law[1] to increase its powers over the taxi industry (Trudel 1992). Thus, in 1987, the Montreal Taxi Bureau (BTM) and the Taxi Industry Advisory Panel were created to maintain the dialogue between the various actors (Després 2005). The BTM's mission was to develop the taxi industry, oversee this service, improve drivers' skills, and ensure the safety of users and drivers.

In the early 1990s, the governments and industry actors sought to further institutionalise and regulate the industry to facilitate social and economic development. In 1989, an attempt to unionise[2] tenant drivers was undertaken by the United Steelworkers, affiliated with the FTQ,[3] the largest labour federation in Quebec. However, this endeavour failed because drivers were not recognised as employees of taxi permit owners, but rather as self-employed workers (Coiquaud 2009). This paved the way for another innovative model of representation, as will be seen below.

Later on, in 1995, taxi companies and co-operatives came together to form a single interlocutor with the government through the *Comité provincial de concertation et de développement de l'industrie du taxi* (provincial committee for consultation and development of the taxi industry, CPCDIT) (CPCDIT 2016a). Then, the legislator adopted a law to modernise the industry by creating new representative bodies. Thus, the *Association professionnelle des chauffeurs de taxis* (professional association to represent taxi drivers, APCT) replaced the Taxi Leagues which, aside from the permit buy-back project, had failed to defend the drivers' interests. The United Steelworkers, which had been claiming a 'right to representation for taxi drivers' for ten years (FTQ 2000), saw this development in a positive light: 'This is a great victory for taxi drivers who have been trying for a long time to form an association to defend their rights' (FTQ 2000; trans). They relied on the APCT to provide members with products such as group insurance and legal services (Desrosiers 2002). Claiming to have put the unionisation of drivers behind them, the Steelworkers said they were ready to work to improve the drivers' lot by promoting this new mode of representation. In addition, the *Forum des intervenants de l'industrie du taxi* (Forum of the parties involved in the taxi industry) was created to encourage dialogue among the industry actors, including the *Comité consultatif des titulaires de permis de propriétaire de taxi* (Advisory committee of holders of taxi owner's permits) and advise the Minister on any questions regarding the business practices of owners.

These representative bodies were created under a project to modernise the industry, which led to the adoption, in June 2001,[4] of the *Act respecting transportation services by taxi* (ATST). This Act aims to provide the industry with the means to take charge of its own development, improve the quality of services offered and increase the safety of users.[5] It also aims to improve the control of supply and of the number of permits. It stipulates that no person may offer or provide in Quebec, remunerated passenger transportation services without a taxi owner's permit,[6] in order to counter 'disguised taxi' practices. The government granted, by order, a quota of taxi owner's permits per agglomeration, and new permits were not renewable, to avoid fuelling the secondary market and inflation in the cost of permits.

The success of this reform was, however, mitigated, starting with the APCT, the ineffectiveness of which was denounced by the Steelworkers, who sought to sign a service agreement with the new Association: 'We met the leaders of the Professional Association. We were about as welcome as a horde of ants at a picnic. Their anti-unionism blinds them to the point of forgetting the interests of taxi drivers' (FTQ 2003; trans.). In response, the *Regroupement professionnel des chauffeurs de taxi Métallos* (Professional association of Steelworkers taxi drivers, RTAM) was created to provide services[7] to drivers. The RTAM also provided funding for the purchase of permits at affordable rates through the creation of FinTaxi (Guay 2002), founded in 2002 by the Steelworkers and the FTQ Solidarity Fund (FSFTQ). The FSFTQ, the financial arm of the FTQ, with net assets of nearly $15 billion,[8] stands as a unique union innovation, giving the FTQ significant economic and, to some extent, political influence.

In addition to the difficulties of coordinating actors to ensure their representation in the early 2000s, a report (Després 2005) also noted shortcomings in the industry regarding its quality of service and its ability to develop new markets (for example, adapted transportation). Several of this report's recommendations were taken up when the Act was amended in 2009, including the CTQ's control over the setting of quotas for owners' permits and determination of the agglomerations, along with a strengthening of the rules around illegal taxi transportation.

Thus, after a period of laissez-faire and crisis, the government acted as an institutional builder by organising supply management and the control of permits, prices, and the conditions of entry into the occupation. At the same time, the Montreal taxi industry actors sought to organise their own representation, with varying success. The union, for its part, although failing to play its traditional role, innovated by developing a new union 'business model' through the creation of RTAM and Fintaxi, both aimed at providing drivers with services and funding. However, the conditions of success for the industry were sorely lacking. As explained by Trudel (1995: 11): 'The future of taxi service depends on its ability to adapt to the transportation needs of various clienteles [...] if taxis do not fill the vacant space, others will.' Indeed, Uber took the initiative to fill this space.

2 Faced with Uber and Téo Taxi: the industry put to the test

The arrival of new players forced the industry actors and government to act. In the fall of 2014, Uber began operating in Montreal. Through its digital platform, the multinational company allowed individuals, without a taxi driver's or taxi owner's permit, to provide transportation services for a fee. For a while, it was able to evade the applicable regulations, claiming that it was merely a technological service supporting the 'sharing' economy and playing the role of digital intermediary.[9] In response, the representative associations organised protests (1). In the meantime, another business model, Téo Taxi (French acronym for Optimized Green Transportation), sought to establish itself using a social and environmental responsibility approach, supported by the government and the unions (2).

Uber: From Contesting to Experimentation

Despite Uber's illegal establishment in Montreal (non-payment of taxes, drivers without training or permits), the government was slow to act against it. It took mobilisation on the part of the representative associations for the government to react. In 2015, the crackdown on Uber's operations intensified: in addition to demonstrations staged by drivers, the BTM expanded its staff to fight against illegal transportation, seizing more than 400 vehicles, and the Taxi Industry Advisory Panel asked the Minister of Transport to suspend the permits of illegal drivers.

In the meantime, the *Act respecting transportation services by taxi*[10] was amended. The Minister of Transport could now authorise any person or body that was a holder of a permit to implement pilot projects designed to experiment or innovate in the industry, in compliance with standards and rules prescribed by the Minister that differed from the regulations in force. In other words, the Minister could entrust a third party with the power to operate in a regulated sector for a purpose determined and assessed by the government, without being bound by the full constraints of the existing regulatory framework. The path was thus open for Uber and Téo Taxi.

In February 2016, the government scheduled the hearings of a parliamentary committee. The Minister of Transport announced that technological innovation could not be avoided and that supply management may have come to an end. He aspired to review the regulatory framework to preserve a 'fair, competitive and innovative business environment and eliminate tax evasion' (MT 2016; trans.). In April 2016, the RTAM launched a 'Save Quebec from Uber' media campaign in response to a 'Save Uber Quebec' campaign launched by Uber. The multinational company threatened to leave the province if it did not obtain the advantages it demanded, namely exclusion from the existing regulatory framework.

In May 2016, a bill was tabled. The FTQ and the RTAM were satisfied because this bill forced Uber to comply with the industry rather than the other way around. The FTQ President stated: 'The taxi workers won because they chose to stand in solidarity against injustice and a multinational company that did not respect the laws of Quebec. They defended our laws and the citizens of Quebec'[11] (trans.). It must be said that the RTAM had been keeping the pressure on since the beginning of the year.[12] In November 2015, more than 350 taxi drivers took to the road, driving towards Parliament on the highway at low speed. In February 2016, 800 drivers attempted to block access to the international airport and, a few days later, 500 taxis occupied downtown Montreal. In January 2016, a historic gathering brought together nearly 1,000 taxi drivers and taxi owners.

In contrast, activists and the youth wing of the Liberal Party, in power at the time, were in favour of maintaining Uber in the market and denounced the bill, which would impose on Uber's occasional drivers 'a series of obligations and fees (…), [that] would spell the end of the company's activities in Quebec' (Croteau 2016; trans.).

The Minister of Transport, under pressure, proposed to amend Bill 100, 'delaying its coming into force by three months, thus providing time to negotiate the terms of a pilot project with Uber' (Dutrisac 2016; trans.). To this end, he obtained the agreement of Uber and the CPCDIT (Comité de concertation et de développement de l'industrie du taxi). In the latter's view, postponing the application of the legislation was a less risky compromise than postponing its adoption. However, the RTAM denounced this amendment, stating that it 'would consecrate the existence of two permit regimes, one for taxi drivers and the other for Uber drivers' (Agence QMI 2016; trans.). It withdrew its support for the bill, which was nevertheless adopted in June 2016 under a gag order, allowing the government to recover Uber's unpaid sales and income taxes.[13]

This law included several provisions to accommodate Uber. It specified which remunerated passenger transportation services were not subject to the ATST. The definition of in-service intermediary was broadened to include requests for taxi transportation services using a digital platform, as was the case with Uber. While the CTQ retained the prerogative to issue permits, it lost to the government the prerogative to set the maximum number of taxi owner's permits and determine the agglomerations. Thus, the government took control of supply management and liberalised the definition of taxi transportation service intermediary. It created the possibility of developing pilot projects, whose content and rules were not necessarily in line with those in effect, but could be negotiated between the government and the project owners.

The pilot project with Uber was adopted on 8 September 2016,[14] amended in 2017, and then extended until October 2018.[15] The government set out in the agreement its statement of principles, including fair competition, no impact on the stability of the value of permits, the improvement of user services and user safety, transparency in fare setting, the integration of new technologies, and maintaining a single regime for the taxi industry. To meet the requirements of the pilot project, Uber obtained the status of taxi transportation service intermediary.[16] This agreement thus allowed Uber to emerge from illegality with a tailor-made regime. As feared by the RTAM, this project created a two-tier regime, one for Uber and the other for traditional industry drivers. Several requirements were lightened for the former: no obligation for drivers to obtain a permit, limited training and criminal background checks controlled by Uber or subcontracted to a firm.

The RTAM, dissatisfied with the agreement, formed a Common Front with other industry players such as the AHTT, the CCDIT, the Quebec Taxi Intermediaries' Association (RITQ), and the Montreal Taxi Owners' Association (RPTM). They took legal action to force Uber[17] to comply with the regulatory framework in effect and oblige the government to suspend the agreement,[18] challenge Uber's legality, and cancel the pilot project.[19] All these proceedings were doomed to failure.[20] Finally, the RTAM's President, Mr Jean-Paul, acting on the Common Front's behalf, obtained authorisation from the Court to institute a class action[21] to offset the pilot project's negative impact on taxi drivers' income and the value of taxi owner's permits.[22] In the meantime, the government announced that compensation would be awarded to owners for the loss of value of their permits. However, this amount only compensated for 56% of the loss estimated by the agglomerations (Marin 2018).

Some industry spokespersons[23] loudly proclaimed that the compensation offered by the government, at taxpayers' expense, actually represented a way to allow Uber to operate in the province. At the same time, the government extended the pilot project, while tightening some rules for Uber drivers (criminal background checks, 35-hour mandatory training).

Social Innovation – the Case of Téo Taxi

In 2015, another entrepreneur emerged in the Montreal taxi industry. Although this company also used a digital platform, its business model differed from that of Uber. Going by the name of Téo Taxi, it provided transportation services by means of a fleet consisting only of electric vehicles, and its drivers, who were employees, enjoyed good working conditions, including an hourly wage above the minimum wage.

Téo Taxi's arrival was well received by the industry actors because of its innovative nature and compliance with the existing regulatory framework.

The pilot project negotiated between the government and the company provided for Téo Taxi to continue its activities while complying with the existing permit system by renting out taxi owner's permits. In addition, drivers had to hold a taxi driver's permit and to have completed the training required under the Act.

Although Téo Taxi was born out of the vision of an entrepreneur, its existence was the work of collective entrepreneurship. Several institutional investors financially supported this vision of a modernised and electrified industry, including the FTQ Solidarity Fund and Fondaction, the financial arm of the Confederation of National Trade Unions (CSN), the second-largest labour body in Quebec. The other investors were the *Caisse de dépôt et de placement du Québec,* which manages the pension fund of state employees, and *Investissement Québec,* a government organisation aimed at supporting economic development in Quebec, as well as *XPND Croissance,* a private investment fund. Together, they invested more than $35 million in Taxelco, the parent company of Téo Taxi and two other taxi companies (Hochelaga and Diamond) (Dufour 2017).

Téo Taxi worked with actors in the traditional industry to encourage its modernisation and lobby the government. It participated in a common front with the CPCDIT and the Montreal Taxi Owners' Association (RPTM) to better compete with Uber. They demanded a permit rental system at an hourly rate and the possibility for taxi-owning companies to provide their own 35-hour training program to new drivers (Agence QMI 2017). The government responded favourably to the latter's request, authorising a two-year pilot project[24] (Bellerose 2017).

However, in 2017, Téo Taxi began to experience difficulties. In June, the company claimed to be a victim of its own success and demanded authorisation to rent a greater number of permits than allowed under the initial pilot project, a request that the government granted. However, its growth was hampered by the reality on the ground, i.e. the cumbersome regulatory framework and technological challenges (Goudreault 2017). In addition, management problems led to the unionisation of the company's 400 drivers in October 2018 (Halin 2018).

This union venture was short-lived, however, since the company declared bankruptcy in early 2019. There was no profitability due to regulatory inequity, as Téo Taxi had to comply with the permit system and could not adjust prices to demand as was authorised for Uber (Larocque 2019).

Between Contesting, Innovation, and Experimentation

Uber and Téo Taxi were both able to emerge as institutional entrepreneurs by offering new business models backed by a technological revolution.

As a peripheral actor in the industry, Uber managed to carve out a place for itself by legitimising its action based on an innovation that offered solutions to recurring problems in the industry, particularly regarding the quality of service. Through its resources, it mobilised governments and forced them to accept the idea of adopting a parallel regime to the existing one. Its social capital allowed it to set up in the City of Montreal, despite demonstrations and protests staged by the collective actors. It represented real divergent change. While the pilot projects, a source of institutional experimentation, were temporary, they instilled a gradual but definite transformation. The layering of regulatory frameworks left little doubt regarding the coming transformation. In response, the RTAM and AHTT organised opposition to denounce Uber, but without much success. Faced with developing uncertainty regarding the 'post-pilot-project' phase, and with the new government announcing a major overhaul of regulations in the taxi industry, the two organisations merged to form a common front.

Thus, despite opposition from the traditional actors, a two-tier regime could not be avoided. The hope that the FTQ, in particular, had placed in Téo Taxi to promote social and ecological innovation and supplant the Uber model was short-lived. It was as if the state saw in Uber's arrival a pretext to transform an industry that was struggling to renew itself. Once introduced, the pilot projects would serve as a transformational vector to carve out a place for the multinational company and induce the industry to become more flexible and modernised.

Discussion

Our analysis of this case of institutional experimentation in the Montreal taxi industry brought out the importance of the actors' role in transforming this industry in Montreal. While the state played a leading role in proposing a regulatory model acquired through the effect of sedimentation over decades (Mahoney and Thelen 2009), the union demonstrated great resilience in its action.

In the first phase, the union attempted to organise the taxi drivers, but came up against a legal system that denied drivers employee status. In the second phase, rather than withdrawing from this industry, it took the path of experimentation, creating an association of self-employed taxi drivers (RTAM), dedicated to providing these workers with services and funding. The RTAM thus established itself as one of the players in this industry, advocating for strengthening regulations and maintaining anti-competitive measures by controlling entries and market prices and imposing public interest provisions aimed at protecting customers and the drivers themselves (Harding et al. 2016). This strategy was, moreover, favoured by the state, which took the initiative to regulate the industry since no industry representative had the capacity to merge the diverse interests involved (tenant or owner drivers; service companies).

Then, Uber's arrival in the Montreal taxi industry caused significant disruption, shaking the existing regulatory structure constructed through sedimentation and arbitration between the numerous interests involved. This structure was deconstructed to benefit Uber's business model, and ended up espousing its broad lines, that is, moving away from or limiting regulations aimed at controlling prices, permits, safety, and consumer protection. Uber should have been made to comply with the existing regulations, had it not been for the ambivalence of the state and the industry's unpopularity with consumers. As a determined and arrogant institutional entrepreneur, this multinational company was able to capitalise on the surprise effect and deploy its political force, supported by the network of consumers behind it, to limit and guide the new regulations to its advantage (Battilana 2009). It also systematically weathered the debates against it in the judicial arena. This strategy resulted in a deregulation policy that gained ground through the non-application of the regulations in force and their 'corrosion' through the adoption of 'pilot projects' for the sole owners of these projects. The subsequent regulations branched off from those laid down in the pre-Uber period, creating a tailor-made regime largely based on the model proposed by Uber.

In response to the threat of Uber, the union entered a third phase of action. First, it continued fighting against Uber through the RTAM, uniting with other associations, including the AHTT. Second, through the FTQ Solidarity Fund and Fondaction, it supported an innovative business model, that of Téo Taxi, which was socially acceptable as it complied with the existing regulatory framework. However, these actions failed to preserve the institutional legacy of the Montreal taxi industry. How can this failure be explained?

The magnitude of Uber's strike force on the political, legislative, and judicial scenes weakened the representative actors of the traditional industry, who sought concrete support from the state, but to no avail. These actors, who were initially fragmented, subsequently joined forces to exercise their veto, but belatedly (Mahoney and Thelen 2009). Moreover, they received little support from the judiciary or the government, with the latter being torn between the desire to modernise this industry and that to preserve equity among the actors. The state eventually gave in and deregulated the market (see Table 5.1).

This second period thus revealed a confrontation between the different forms of experimentation brought about by the actors, of which Uber came out a winner. It should be noted that, despite its regulatory power, the state abdicated from its role as the guarantor of supply, safety, and equity in the industry, letting itself be seduced by the promises of technological innovation (Zuboff 2019). Surprisingly, Téo Taxi, which promoted a model driven by technology and social responsibility was not afforded the same regulatory flexibility even though it was supported by the state economic bodies alongside trade unions and traditional industry actors. We consider that Uber has been promoted by the state as it seems to be a quick fix to the modernisation of the industry. But at the same

Table 5.1 Confrontation between Forms of Institutional Experimentation in the Montreal Taxi Industry

	Traditional industry	*Uber*	*Téo Taxi*
Models of capitalism and business models	Regulatory capitalism based on the control of supply, prices, and safety	Libertarian capitalism based on the rejection of state interventionism, individual freedom, and technological innovation	Renewed regulatory capitalism based on social, environmental, and technological innovation
Type of institutional experimentation	Uniform regulations for all actors	Regulatory experimentation allowing for the coexistence of parallel regimes	
Discourse	Equity	Consumer demand	Sustainable and socially responsible development
Union action	Attempt to unionise and form an association of self-employed workers	Strategy centred on fighting, mobilisation, and building solidarity	Funding a new business model: employees, then unionisation

time, it overlooked the risks of deregulation. We will see in a few years if history repeats, knowing that regulation has always been at the core of this industry that is vulnerable to an open market.

It must be concluded from these forms of institutional experimentation that, while the situation could evolve in the future, the divergent change underway does not appear to be moving towards better working conditions for the taxi industry, or even positive change for consumers.

Notes

1 *Act respecting transportation by taxi*, 1983, RSQ c. T-11.1.
2 A first attempt at unionisation had failed in 1974.
3 *Union des chauffeurs de taxis, Métallurgistes unis d'Amérique, local 9217* c. *Taxi Cartier inc.*, D.T.E. 89T937 (C.T.), AZ-89144049.
4 *Act respecting transportation services by taxi*, 2001, c. 15, s. 88; after consolidation: Q.R.S., c. S-6.01 See also: *Taxi Transportation Regulation*, RSQR c. S-6.01, r 3.
5 Assemblée nationale du Québec, Journal des débats parlementaires – Bill n°163, *An Act respecting transportation services by taxi*, introduced during the 36th Legislature, 1st session, online: http://www.assnat.qc.ca/fr/travaux-parlementaires/projets-loi/projet-loi-163-36-1.html; the Act introduces requirements to ensure the quality and safety of services, including renewed mandatory training, the mechanical inspection of vehicles, and the installation of taximeters. Moreover, the intermediaries' activities and presence are regulated: service associations (co-operatives) or taxi companies are required to hold a taxi transportation service intermediary's permit.

6 *Act respecting transportation services by taxi*, RSQR c. S-6.01, s. 4, 24 and 32, (hereinafter: 'ATST').
7 Including a group insurance plan and access to legal aid.
8 The FSFTQ is a capital fund fuelled by the retirement savings of Quebecers. Its mission is to grow the economy by creating, maintaining, and protecting jobs through investments in small and medium-sized enterprises. The FSFTQ's investment in a company is conditional on compliance with some social criteria, such as the creation of sustainable employment and respect for labour laws.
9 These claims were undermined by the Court: 'One cannot claim that one's business is beyond the reach of the law on the basis that one is operating in violation of the clear and unambiguous terms of this law' (trans.), in *Uber Canada inc.* c. *Agence du revenu du Québec* 2016 QCCS 2158 (CanLII), par. 205 (leave to appeal refused, 2016 QCCA 1303 (CanLII)).
10 *An Act to amend various legislative provisions mainly concerning shared transportation*, SQ 2015, c. 16, s. 11 http://www.assnat.qc.ca/fr/travaux-parlementaires/commissions/cte-41-1/journal-debats/CTE-150604.html#_Toc443379166
11 https://ftq.qc.ca/communiques/modifications-a-la-loi-sur-le-transport-par-taxi/
12 https://www.metallos.org/enjeux/taxis-et-limousines/
13 https://ici.radio-canada.ca/nouvelle/786828/taxi-uber-loi-baillon-couillard-khadir-chauffeurs
14 Order number 2016-16 by the Minister of Transport, Sustainable Mobility and Transport Electrification, dated 30 September 2016; https://www.ctq.gouv.qc.ca/fileadmin/documents/publications/Arrete_Ministeriel_UBER.pdf
15 https://www.ctq.gouv.qc.ca/fileadmin/documents/secteurs/taxi/Arrete_Projet_pilote_taxi_-_29_septembre_2017.pdf; https://www.transports.gouv.qc.ca/fr/entreprises-partenaires/entreprises-taxi/Pages/projets-pilotes-taxi.aspx
16 Order-in-Council 919–2016.
17 Regroupement des travailleurs autonomes Métallos, section locale 9840 c. Uber Technologies inc., 2016 QCCS 4626
18 Regroupement des travailleurs autonomes Métallos, section locale 9840 c. Québec (Procureure générale), 2016 QCCS 4491 (CanLII) (application for an interlocutory provisional injunction ordering the Minister to suspend the implementation of the Agreement with Uber Canada inc.).
19 Rejected by the Superior Court on 5 October 2017. *Regroupement des travailleurs autonomes Métallos, section locale 9840* c. *Uber Technologies inc.*, 2017 QCCS 4447 (CanLII).
20 On this last proceeding, the decision is being appealed.
21 Jean-Paul c. Uber Technologies Inc., 2017 QCCS 164 (CanLII).
22 In Montreal, between January 2014 and June 2017, the value of permits decreased from $192,694 to $118,375, respectively; https://www.transports.gouv.qc.ca/fr/entreprises-partenaires/entreprises-taxi/Documents/rapport-ministre.pdf (consulted on 13 October 2018).
23 http://maxcommradio.com/presse/quebec-va-compenser-lindustrie-du-taxi
24 Order number 2017-08 by the Minister of Transport, Sustainable Mobility and Transport Electrification, dated 24 August 2017, Gazette officielle du Québec, 6 September 2017, 149th year, No. 36.

References

Agence QMI (2016) Projet de loi sur le taxi: les Métallos réclament le retrait de l'amendement 'Uber'. Le *journal de Montréal*, June 9, 2016. https://www.journaldemontreal.com/2016/06/09/projet-de-loi-sur-le-taxi-les-metallos-reclament-le-retrait-de-lamendement-uber (consulted 12 January 2019).

Agence QMI (2017) L'industrie du taxi veut une modernisation. Le *journal de Montréal, Actualités*, August 18, 2017, p. 20.

Battilana, J., Leca, B. & Boxenbaum, E. (2009) How actors change institutions: towards a theory of institutional entrepreneurship. *Academy of Management*, 3(1), 65–107.

Bellerose, P. (2017) Québec crée une classe de taxi. *Journal de Montréal, Actualités*, September 15, p. 21.

Bossé, A. (1970) *Rapport sur les problèmes de l'industrie du taxi dans la région métropolitaine de Montréal*; soumis à l'honorable Premier ministre du Québec, par M. Alfred Bossé, député de Dorion, Montréal: non publié, p. 55.

Bureau du taxi (BTM) (2010) Faits marquants du BTR. *Le Journal Taxi*, 12(4), 13–14.

Bureau du taxi (BTM) (2018) Trousse média 2018. Montréal: BTM.

Coiquaud, U. (2009) Le difficile encadrement juridique des travailleurs autonomes en situation précaire: Le cas des chauffeurs locataires de taxi. *Relations industrielles*, 64(1), 95–111.

Coiquaud, U., Sanni Yaya, M. & Morissette, L. (2018) Regulation of the Uber transportation platform by local governments in Canada. Noguellou, R. & Renders, D. (ed.) *Uber and Taxis Comparative Law Studies*, Brussels, Bruyant, pp. 93–110.

Comité provincial de concertation et de développement de l'industrie du taxi (CPCDIT) (2016a) Mot du président. http://www.cpcdit.ca/a-propos/mot-du-president/ (consulted on 10 October 2018)

Comité provincial de concertation et de développement de l'industrie du taxi (CPCDIT) (2016b) Les gestes d'Uber parlent plus fort que ses paroles. http://www.cpcdit.ca/revue-de-presse/communiques-cpcdit/ (consulted on 15 April 2019).

Commission des transports du Québec (2018) Transfert de permis de propriétaire de taxi – estimation des valeurs trimestrielles. Documents transmis dans le cadre d'une demande d'accès à l'information. https://www.ctq.gouv.qc.ca/diffusion_de_linformation/decisions_et_documents_transmis_dans_le_cadre_dune_demande_dacces.html (consulted on 15 April 2019).

Croteau, M. (2016) Uber: au tour des jeunes libéraux de forcer la main de Québec. La Presse.ca, le 12 mai, https://www.lapresse.ca/actualites/politique/politique-quebecoise/201605/12/01–4980795-uber-au-tour-des-jeunes-liberaux-de-forcer-la-main-de-quebec.php (consulted on 15 January 2019).

Crouch, C. (2005) *Capitalist Diversity and Change: Recombinant Governance and Institutional entrepreneurs*, New York: OUP Oxford.

Cyr, M.-A. (2018) Le mouvement de libération du taxi. *Nouveau projet 13*, 10, printemps-été 2018, pp. 38–39.

D'Amour, M. (1981) Les plaies du taxi. 31 (nov.) *Vie ouvrière*, 11, 26–31.

Després, M. (2005) Rapport sur la Loi concernant les services de transport par taxi. Québec: Gouvernement du Québec, Bibliothèque nationale, p. 65 file:///C:/Users/00011281/Downloads/2270-20051102.pdf

Desrosiers, É. (2002) La FTQ débarque dans le taxi. *Le Devoir*, Actualité, Wednesday, August 14, p. A1.

Dufour, R. (2017) Téo Taxi 4,5 millions pour passer l'été, La Presse+, 2 juin 2017, section Affaires, http://plus.lapresse.ca/screens/f3528762-050c-4e81-b066-b7c7ac7580ab__7C___0.html (consulted on 19 January 2019).

Dutrisac, R. (2016) Jacques Daoust accorde trois mois à Uber pour négocier un projet-pilote, Actualités, Wednesday June 8, p. A3.

Fédération des travailleurs et travailleuses du Québec (FTQ) (2000) Taxi: La FTQ invite les dissidents à se rallier au sein d'une vraie association professionnelle. https://ftq.qc.ca/communiques/taxi-la-ftq-invite-les-dissidents-a-se-rallier-au-sein-dune-vraie-association-professionnelle/ (consulted on 19 April 2019).
Fédération des travailleurs et travailleuses du Québec (FTQ) (2003) Devant l'inertie de l'association professionnelle des chauffeurs de taxi du Québec – La FTQ et les métallos démarrent le regroupement des chauffeurs de taxi métallos (FTQ). https://ftq.qc.ca/actualites/devant-linertie-de-lassociation-professionnelle-des-chauffeurs-de-taxi-du-quebec-la-ftq-et-les-metallos-demarrent-le-regroupement-des-chauffeurs-de-taxi-metallos-ftq/ (consulted on 19 April 2019).
Goudreault, Z. (2017) Téo Taxi répond à la demande grandissante. *Journal de Montréal*, Actualités, 13 November, p. 16.
Guay, M. (2002) Le monde syndical monte à bord du taxi. *La Presse*, Affaires, Wednesday 14 August, p. D3.
Halin, F. (2018) Transport: La grogne s'installe chez Téo Taxi. *Journal de Montréal*, Argent, Wednesday 16 May, p. 27.
Harding, S., Kandlikar, M. & Gulati, S. (2016) Taxi apps, regulation, and the market for taxi journeys. *Transportation Research Part A*, 88, 15–25.
Krippendorff, K. (2018) Content Analysis. An Introduction to Its Methodology. Fourth Edition. Sage Publishing, p. 472.
Kristensen, P. H. & Morgan, G. (2012) From institutional change to experimentalist institutions. *Industrial Relations*, 51(S1), 413–437.
Larocque, S. (2019) Un plan d'affaires qui faisait fausse route. *Le Journal de Montréal*, Argent, January 30, p. 23.
Mahoney, J. & Thelen, K. (2009) *Explaining Institutional Change*. New York: Cambridge University Press, p. 236.
Marin, S. (2018) Jusqu'à 46 700$ d'indemnité par permis de taxi. *Le Devoir*, Économie, Saturday, August 18, p. A6.
Ministère des transports, de la mobilité durable et de l'électrification des transports (MT) (2016) Document d'information sur le transport rémunéré de personnes par automobile. Québec: ministère des Transports, p. 12.
Presse canadienne (2019) Des chauffeurs de taxi se regroupent sous une association. La Presse.ca, 24 février, https://www.lapresse.ca/affaires/economie/transports/201902/24/01-5215948-des-chauffeurs-de-taxi-se-regroupent-sous-une-association.php (consulted on April 19, 2019).
Sabatier, P. A. & Jenkins-Smith, H. C. (1993) *Policy change and learning*. Boulder: Westview.
Thelen, K. (2009) Institutional change in advanced political economies. *British Journal of Industrial Relations*, 47(3), 471–489.
Thelen, K. (2018) Regulating Uber: the politics of the platform economy in Europe and the United States. *Perspectives on Politics*, 16(4), 938–953.
Trudel, M. (1988) L'offre et la demande dans l'industrie du taxi au Québec -Évaluation du plan de rachat de permis de taxi dans l'agglomération de Montréal, Direction générale du transport terrestre des personnes et des marchandises, ministère des Transports, Études et recherches en transport, Montréal: ministère des Transports, p. 136.
Trudel, M. (1992) Le taxi: une ressource omniprésente pour le transport des personnes à mobilité réduite. Le développement intégré des transports dans un projet de société, 27ème congrès de l'AQTR. Sherbrooke: Ministère des transports du Québec, 12–15 April.

Trudel, M. (1995) The Fundamentals of Taxi Regulation and the Quebec Experience, Presentation to the 7th Congress of the European Taxi Confederation, Donostia-San Sebastian, Espagne, February 1995.

Tucker, E. (2017) Uber and the unmaking and remaking of taxi capitalisms: technology, law and resistance in historical perspective. In Annual Meeting of the Canadian Association of Work and Labour Studies, May 31st–June 2nd. pp. 357–392.

Zuboff, S. (2019) *The Age of Surveillance Capitalism*. New York: Public Affairs.

Part III

Comparative Studies of Experimentation

6 Marginalising Manufacturing: The Politics of Downgrading in the UK Apparel Industry

Nikolaus Hammer and Lucy Brill

Economic restructuring concomitantly reshapes the regional and functional division of labour as economic activities are necessarily embedded in specific localities as well as global production networks (GPNs). Restructuring, therefore, not only puts regions in competition with other regions, it also puts them in competition over specific roles in the production of goods and services. Processes of competition, development, and contestation are intertwined in complex ways across the functional division of labour as well as space and scale (as foreshadowed in Peck and Theodore's (2007) 'variegated capitalism'). These issues have been addressed in a rich and varied literature investigating the intersection of institutional and value chain analyses (Bair and Mahutga 2012), the articulation and disarticulation of social relations in capitalist dynamics (Bair and Werner 2011; Werner 2015), or the types of regional strategic coupling with GPNs in Coe and Yeung's (2015) formulation of GPN2.0.

The renewed growth of UK apparel manufacturing over the last ten years – of 110% in real turnover and 61% in real gross value added (aGVA) between 2008 and 2016 – also throws up key questions regarding the linkages between value chain dynamics that focus on the networks between different actors in the functional division of labour, and economic and social processes that are territorially embedded at regional level. It seemed to suggest – after the phasing out of the multifibre agreement in 2005 and its import quotas, after the financial crisis of 2008, followed by years of austerity – that lead firms and manufacturers had developed a competitive business model that could provide an alternative to the cheap labour cost advantages of SE Asian producers. Fast fashion (Taplin 2014), by contrast, relied on the proximity and responsiveness of production to UK consumer markets. However, by accentuating those aspects of the business model that were to do with speed-to-market and price – most visible in online-only fashion retailers – fast fashion profoundly reshaped the regional and functional division of labour. On the one hand, it brought the UK into competition with nearby regions that could offer skills, low prices, and speed-to-market, that is, with parts of Eastern Europe, Turkey, and the North African rim. On the other hand,

DOI: 10.4324/9781003001089-9

the emergence of a new type of lead firm not only changed the speed at which orders were to be fulfilled, it also led to much smaller volumes being ordered more often, which had the overall effect of increasing uncertainty and competition amongst manufacturers.

While this episode clearly brought success in terms of key headline figures, a deeper analysis needs to look into how any benefits of the emergence of fast fashion were distributed: the role of firm strategies and other actors in the production network, the nature of new inter-firm networks, the distribution of capabilities within the production network, within and across regions, as well as how the fast fashion production network is strategically coupled with specific regions.

The aim of this chapter is to assess the economic and social impact of fast fashion production in key producer regions in the United Kingdom and to analyse the role capital, labour, and policy actors have played in this. Our evidence from the national industry level, as well as from key regional production hubs, shows that the industry, certainly as far as it is integrated into fast fashion, has experienced significant economic and social downgrading at the same time as it achieved significant growth (Hammer and Plugor 2016; HWW 2019). In order to gain a better understanding of how the fast fashion value chain is linked into particular producer regions, we also investigate the politics of restructuring, of industry collective actors and policymakers. The chapter is organised into four main sections.

The following section differentiates restructuring across regions and industrial sub-sectors. It shows that growth was driven by a very specific dynamic that concentrated production in a few hubs that were characterised by the entrepreneurial capabilities, adverse labour market prospects, and the gender division of labour within the, initially dominant, British Asian workforce. The differentiated sub-sectoral structures and growth trajectories offer a starting point to understand the de-coupling and re-coupling the industry has experienced.

The second section provides quantitative and qualitative evidence of economic and social downgrading. It argues that the dynamics around the emergence of a fast-fashion production network, in fact, constitute significant structural ruptures: while offshoring de-coupled the industry from the major producer hubs in the United Kingdom (underscored by Marks and Spencer's decision in the late 1980s to source from abroad, as well as the break-up of Coats Viyella in the late 1990s (Lane and Probert 2009)), the emergence of fast fashion re-coupled apparel manufacturing under very different conditions, that is, small, transactionally dependent manufacturers that relied on precarious, informal employment, and wage theft.

In the third section, we investigate the extent to which this process of de-coupling and re-coupling is reflected and driven by collective actors within the industry and industrial policy. By way of conclusion, we argue that the emergence of fast fashion was accompanied, first by economic and social downgrading, which was, second, accompanied by a widening of the 'representation gap' within the industry: between small(er) manufacturers and lead firms as well as capital and labour. The weakening of industrial relations as well as labour standards enforcement effectively keeps unproductive firms in business and undermines compliant ones. Initiatives to develop the industry do carry regional imprints of the respective subsectoral structures but tend to be driven from the top: in many cases by the peak retailer body (the British Retail Consortium), lead firms (Manchester), and manufacturers (Leicester). What is common amongst these initiatives is that they neither impact the social relations at the workplace, nor the relations between manufacturers and lead firms.

The fourth section reflects on a possible turning point in the wake of the COVID-19 pandemic. Following an exposé by Labour Behind the Label (LBL 2020) on continued wage theft and the violation of rules on social distancing and furlough in the early months of the pandemic, the industry has come together to start negotiating on a comprehensive binding agreement for the industry. While this episode clearly presents opportunities, protracted negotiations might well veer towards path-dependent rather than transformational outcomes.

Growth in UK apparel manufacturing across regions and subsectors

UK apparel manufacturing has experienced an upturn in growth, of 110% in real turnover and 61% in real aGVA, between 2008 and 2016. A closer look into this development (see Table 6.1), however, suggests that this growth was driven by a specific segment of the industry. The share of enterprises, for example, did not change significantly across regions in the period 2010-19, with London, the East Midlands and the North West accounting for 31%, 16.5% and 10% respectively of all enterprises in the apparel manufacturing sector. What did change significantly during this period, however, was the growing share of the 'manufacture of other outerwear' which rose by 30% (an additional 490 enterprises) to 53% of all wearing apparel (the only other rise was in the 'manufacture of workwear' by 95 enterprises or 36%). This dynamic in the 'manufacture of other outerwear' is also confirmed by the growth in firms in *all* turnover bands (except in the lowest band, below £50,000) between 2010–2019. While the share in the 'manufacture of other wearing apparel and accessories' declined by 5% during that period, it still remained the second largest subsector with 1090 local units.

Growth in these subsectors, the manufacture of other outerwear and the manufacture of other wearing apparel, was preceded by the foundering of mid-market apparel which worked with longer fashion cycles. While Robinson and Hsieh (2016) show how reshoring can constitute a viable

Table 6.1 Enterprise Structure across Sub-Sectors and Regions

	Number of enterprises 2019	*Main regions*	*Percentage change 2010–19*	*Percentage of micro businesses (0–9), 2019*
Manufacture of leather clothes	55	London (55%)	0	91
Manufacture of workwear	360	North West (15%), East Midlands (14%)	36	81
Manufacture of other outerwear	2,110	London (37%), East Midlands (16%)	30	85
Manufacture of underwear	140	London (36%), East Midlands (14%)	−18	86
Manufacture of other wearing apparel and accessories	1,090	London (28%), East Midlands (17%)	−5	87
Manufacture of articles of fur	10	London (50%)	0	50
Manufacture of knitted and crocheted hosiery	45	East Midlands (33%), North West (22%)	−36	67
Manufacture of other knitted and crocheted apparel	145	North West (31%), East Midlands (28%)	−26	62

Source: ONS UK Business Counts.

value capture strategy for a luxury fashion brand, this chapter argues that much of the renewed growth was underpinned by the rise of fast fashion in the UK, often renewing fashion ranges on a weekly basis. Froud et al. (2018: 1657-8) usefully expand on this:

> These developments have been associated with the collapse of a long-established mid-market segment of apparel retailing where higher prices were charged for better quality clothes. The landmark move by mid-market retailer Marks and Spencer away from UK sourcing in the late 1980s (Toms and Zhang 2016) forced the exit of large UK-based apparel producers. Twenty-five years later, Marks and Spencer, which did not make the shift to global fashion-led retail brand like H&M or Inditex, is also under pressure from new fashion retailers who are making life very difficult for small survivor producers as the mid-market is eroded. Between 2010 and 2014, the UK clothing market grew by 10% overall, while the value segment increased by 25% (Verdict Retail 2015); strikingly, online retail of textiles, clothing and footwear has grown threefold from 2010 to 2015 (ONS).

This development was driven by the entry of new types of retailers – supermarkets, discount retailers, and online retailers – into the fashion industry which put a premium on low-value fashion that could respond very quickly to cultural or marketing developments. Online retailers, in particular, implemented lean supply chain and retailing strategies that relied on relatively small batch production that could be adapted and re-ordered as soon as goods were selling well through the online portal (Sullivan 2017). Such 'speed-to-market' strategies proved effective as they drastically reduced the size of discounted stock and allowed gains in market share through the close link to consumer culture (Hammer et al. 2015; Taplin 2014). This development was also driven by the entry of South Asian entrepreneurs who took advantage of the lower entry barriers in this industry. The industry, however, was re-coupled in a way that increased the power imbalances along the value chain, exemplified by the very large share of micro businesses across all sub-sectors (see Table 6.1).

At the level of production, fast fashion increased the pressure on manufacturers. The nature of quick response strategies resulted in a very large number of relatively small orders, which made it difficult for manufacturers to use their factories to capacity. In consequence, manufacturing in a quick response context tends to rely on workforces that accept (or have to accept) a high flexibility in working hours and incomes: female ethnic minority workers who manage to juggle their care responsibilities with the demands of informal employment that does not include a set number of working hours or schedule. Quick response models constitute a built-in pressure on prices as lead firms have considerable market power and as virtually *all* manufacturers need to accept orders to fill their capacity, virtually *all* the time. These dynamics of fast fashion suggest considerable pressures on manufacturers through competition in their product markets as well as through the power of lead firms, pressures that seem to make it difficult for manufacturers to upgrade. It is difficult, however, to read trajectories of economic upgrading off existing quantitative statistics and it is therefore necessary to complement this information through qualitative research. Another reason for this is that fast fashion has overlaid an earlier development of the 1970s when production was outsourced to rural areas to take advantage of lower wages and more captive workforces (Phizacklea 1990; see e.g. New Economy 2016). As a consequence, production is often distributed across small local clusters that are difficult to capture through regional statistics. A number of studies exist that have investigated different segments of the market at different times and in different regions.

London has remained the region with the highest share of enterprises and turnover, 31% and 27%, respectively (2017). As its manufacturing industry is specifically affected by the high rents as well as the continuing demand from smaller, more niche, designers, the research into trajectories of economic upgrading by Evans and Smith (2006) is even more relevant. Their research, based on a quarter of active London clothing manufacturers in 2004, revealed a dominant trajectory of factory closures and job losses amongst the cut-make-trim (CMT) units that predominantly employed workers from the ethnic minority communities of East and North London. Evans and Smith (2006) did identify experiences of economic upgrading in the form of original design manufacturing, however, they remained marginal in the light of closures. The UK apparel industry suffered under the competition from global sourcing as well as near-sourcing from the European periphery that was to become more important as fast fashion and online lead firms entered the market. Resulting from these trends, the 2000s showed that 'the industry in London is no longer able to sustain larger scale production of lower quality, lower price-point garments' (Evans and Smith 2006: 2256). The revival experienced in London is likely to be more focused on design-intensive segments of the industry than fast fashion.

As exposés such as *Fashion's dirty secrets* (2010) and *Britain's cheap clothes* (2017) as well as Hammer et al. (2015) have shown, the East Midlands, which have a tradition of apparel manufacturing and ethnic communities who have the apparel-related entrepreneurial and worker skills, have become a core hub for fast fashion, together with the North West and the West Midlands. Fieldwork from 2014 in the East Midlands has shown a considerable number of (the larger) manufacturers supplying UK high-street retailers, particularly in the low but also the medium quality and price segments. However, rather than being able to use this integration into the fast fashion value chain as a platform to expand and upgrade, manufacturers generally reported what Palpacuer and Parisotto (2003: 107) called 'transactional dependence': manufacturers were clear that lead firms' ability to dictate prices, small volume orders, very intermittent orders without forward planning, as well as retrospective changes in terms and conditions (Greenfield and Butler 2018) posed great risks for investments that might not be recouped through sufficiently high and continuous orders. This (daily to weekly) time dimension is, in addition, underlaid by a seasonal dimension as Brill (2017: 2) documents through her fieldwork in Greater Manchester:

> its getting harder … the industry has always been seasonal, but the quiet time is getting longer … we're still not open now and it's well into August.[1]

In such a context, manufacturers have to balance between two different business models and judge to what extent they can accept large orders at low/no margins in order to cover overheads or to hold out for smaller orders with reasonable margins. Either way, it was clear that any gains within quick-response manufacturing were not shared across the supply chain (Hammer et al. 2015). In fact, the way to deal with such transactional dependence in the fast fashion value chain has been to accept all orders a manufacturer can get from a high-street brand or intermediary, and to then outsource production should the factory be over capacity. In many cases, so manufacturers claim regarding their competitors, those 2nd or 3rd tier manufacturers operate in a grey area regarding their responsibilities in terms of incorporation, taxation, certification as well as work and employment standards. According to those data, (unauthorised), subcontracting is crucial in order to absorb the risks that have been passed onto manufacturers by lead firms.

The growth of UK apparel manufacturing has often been subsumed under the broad label of 'reshoring', assuming that, as key operational and cost factors change in favour of the UK (Prime Minister's Office 2014), this would more or less mechanically trigger a movement to the status quo ante. By contrast, we mobilise the concepts of value capture trajectories and strategic coupling, as developed in Coe and Yeung's (2015) account of the GPNs perspective into GPN2.0. Resulting from the varied and contingent operationalisation of political-economic dynamics and challenges into actor strategies, GPN2.0 is able to analyse 'different value capture trajectories that can result when a firm in a particular locality connects into a global production network' (Coe and Yeung 2019: 780). Value capture trajectories can reflect the varying tensions within firm strategies: for example, there is no automatic relation between moving to higher value-added tasks and functions and higher value capture, the ability to retain value. Individual firms may well 'trade down' while upgrading (Gibbon and Ponte 2005; Tokatli 2013), or they may only be able to maintain existing levels of value capture. In an aggregated perspective, where one or more sets of distinct value capture trajectories intersect – or 'couple' – with particular regions, they are central in defining regional economic development.

The concept of strategic coupling has a longer history but has been adopted widely and assumes a central place within the GPN framework. Coe and Yeung (2015: 171) define it as follows:

> Once a firm has established reasonably stable transactional relationships with other actors in a global production network, …, we characterize this as the firm having strategically coupled with the wider production system. This notion highlights the intentionality of the connections from the perspective of the actors involved and the fact that the relationships involved are time-place specific rather than generic and deterministic connections that can be read off from broad notions of governance within particular industries or production networks.

GPN2.0 can therefore analyse the articulation of vertical production networks and horizontal territorial relationships, their specific forms and evolution, how they are connected, disconnected, and re-connected: the way particular value capture trajectories and regional actors and institutions intersect constitute specific forms of strategic coupling. Before we elaborate on economic and social upgrading, we can say that the observed growth in UK apparel manufacturing had very little to do with 'reshoring', in the sense of a return to formerly established industry structures. On the contrary, significant parts of apparel manufacturing were de-coupled in the 1980–90s as lead firms developed their international sourcing networks. The last decade has seen new types of lead firms develop new business models and value capture strategies, based on online retailing, quick response manufacturing, and near-sourcing in the low-value segment. This has re-coupled some regions into key apparel value chains, as considerably smaller establishments that are even more transactionally dependent on lead firms, and whose original equipment manufacturing (OEM) capabilities were severely limited. The following section demonstrates how regions are differentially re-coupled on the basis of their specific sub-sectoral mix, as well as their entrepreneurial capabilities and workforce compositions.

Economic and Social Downgrading within United Kingdom Wearing Apparel Manufacturing

Recent interventions have aimed to address gaps within GVC analysis in integrating labour. Newsome and colleagues (2015) emphasise the status of labour as agent and creator of value in the labour process, while Barrientos et al. (2011: 322) see a 'disjuncture in the literature between a "firm focus" that treats labour as a factor of production, and a "rights focus" on the conditions and entitlements of workers'. The latter, then, analyses labour both as a factor of production and as socially embedded in order to investigate the relationship between the quantity and quality of employment in more detail. While economic upgrading distinguishes between process, product, functional, and chain upgrading, the concept of social upgrading is framed by the ILO's Decent Work Agenda, focuses on improvements in the 'employment, standards and rights at work, social protection and social dialogue', and is operationalised through work and employment standards as well as enabling rights (ibid.: 324):

> Measurable standards are those aspects of worker well-being that are more easily observable and quantifiable, including type of employment (regular or irregular), wage level, social protection and working hours. They can also include data on sex and unionization, such as the percentage of female supervisors or the percentage of union members in the workforce. However, measurable standards are often the outcome of complex bargaining processes, framed by the enabling rights of workers.

A great deal of the interest in upgrading is related to the ability to contrast and measure economic and social aspects of upgrading (or downgrading), which in itself is a descriptive task. Milberg and Winkler (2011) explore analytical links between the two measures, for example, aiming to assess the extent to which competitiveness is raised through the lowering of factor inputs (including labour costs) or increases in productivity. Lerche's (2012) concern is more with the focus of the ILO's Decent Work agenda as he fears that the emphasis on a social floor is pushing back central questions as to problems and power imbalances at work. Further caution must be exercised with regard to the firm-centrism of the GVC approach: analysis must not sideline the context in which firms and labour operate in as well as the specific forms they assume in response. Froud et al. (2017), for example, emphasise the conditions, or ecology, that allow firms to develop specific capabilities.

As regards economic upgrading in UK apparel manufacturing, Hammer and Plugor (2016) have shown how factory gate prices (PPI) in UK apparel manufacturing exhibited only marginal growth of 17% between 1997 and 2015 (in comparison, the PPI in manufacturing rose by 41%), at the same time as the consumer price index (CPI) for clothing fell by a cumulative 51%. Competition between lead firms clearly has been very intense, particularly as new business models emerged, and qualitative evidence shows that these pressures were passed on to manufacturers who also had to accommodate above-average wage increases as a large part of their wages were driven by developments in the National Minimum Wage. A rise of the PPI in the context of a declining CPI can be due to a range of factors. First, manufacturers might have shifted to a higher share of high-end clothing, an explanation that does not hold for the industry more broadly. Second, investment in technology might have raised productivity; this seems implausible though as capital expenditure in wearing apparel fell faster than in manufacturing precisely in the period 1999–2007 when the former's PPI growth was significantly below the latter's. Third, the PPI in wearing apparel might have been lower than in manufacturing due to cheaper input costs; this explanation might hold for material inputs, however, the 5–6% growth rates in real hourly pay would certainly weigh in such a labour-intensive industry.

Table 6.2 confirms these conclusions as it shows, comparing the two periods 1998–2007 and 2008–2016, how more turnover was needed to produce the same aGVA, which is at odds with economic upgrading. At the same time, the changing ratio between turnover and employment costs leaves the possibility that growth was achieved through increases in productivity. The implications of growth for social upgrading, however, need to be investigated in more detail.

Table 6.3 suggests that social upgrading was not straightforward. There are two issues to consider here. First, as regards the substance of social upgrading, statistics suggest that the considerable growth in turnover and aGVA did not necessarily translate into higher employment, nor did productivity increases result in a parallel rise in employment costs. Furthermore, while all parameters develop in parallel during the decline from 1998 to 2007, we can observe significant regional differences in the way employees and employment costs account for the growth in turnover and aGVA, suggesting a divergence in the way different subsectors develop at regional level.

Table 6.2 Turnover, Gross Value Added, and Employment Costs, 1998–2016

	aGVA/Turnover		*Turnover/Employment Costs*	
	1998–2007	*2008–2016*	*1998–2007*	*2008–2016*
North East	0.34	0.36*	4.51	5.53*
North West	0.35	0.30*	4.91	6.31*
Yorkshire and the Humber	0.37	0.33	4.38	5.4
East Midlands	0.37	0.28	4.65	6.57
West Midlands	0.38	0.29	4.6	6.81
East	0.38	0.29	4.67	7.14
London	0.36	0.28	5.24	7.05
South East	0.42	0.3	4.21	6.47
South West	0.39	0.34	5.25	5.92
UK	0.36	0.3	4.76	6.3

Source: Annual Business Survey, Regional Results.

Note: * data for 2008–2014.

Even if social upgrading did not keep up with the pace of economic growth, would it be possible to argue for marginal social upgrading since employment has grown, wages have grown at above-average rates, especially for female operators in the lowest decile, essentially mirroring the development of the National Minimum Wage? At this point, the analytic aims of Milberg and Winkler (2011) become crucial, as it does make a difference what the underlying sources of productivity are. In this case, the productivity growth of 16% (2008–2016) needs further investigation.

First, qualitative data already alluded to above, point to serious issues regarding working time and wages which results in significant wage theft and underpins the intensification of work, the elimination of unproductive spaces in the labour process, and an informalisation and precarisation of labour (Warren 2005; Hammer and Plugor 2019). Second, there is also a measurement issue as official statistics do not account for all the hours worked (or the employees, or the employment costs) and it is likely that measures based on official data significantly overestimate productivity. It also has to be said that minimum wage legislation, led by the research and recommendations of the Low Pay Commission, has enormously benefited low paid machinists in the apparel industry. Unfortunately, for too many, these benefits only existed on paper, as wages are notoriously difficult to enforce in the industry, particularly in the absence of trade unions or other forms of worker representation. These measurement problems further undermine any arguments that might have supported the notion of social upgrading.

Contemporary fast fashion has intensified the capital circuit and entrenched the dependence of manufacturers on a small range of buyers (see also Evans and Smith 2006). As lead firms have established social

Table 6.3 The Manufacture of Wearing Apparel in the UK, 1998–2016

	UK		*East Midlands*		*North West*	
	1998–2007	*2008–2016*	*1998–2007*	*2008–2016*	*1998–2007*	*2008–2016*
Real Turnover	−60	110.2	−56.9	97.9	−59.9	66.1
Real aGVA	−64.5	60.9	−63.8	58.4	−61.2	*
Real Emp Costs	−64.8	42.1	−60.3	54.4	−63.7	3.5
Employees (a)	−79.4	8.4	−77.2	63.3	−79.7	−57.1
Productivity growth (b)	14.1	16.2	11.4	17.2	13.5	14.1

Source: ABI regional (ONS), BRES, ASHE.

(a) UK data for Great Britain.

(b) NW Productivity for 2008–2013 only.

compliance standards and audit practices, manufacturers have established parallel worlds of employment: workers are effectively on zero-hours contracts as they only work when there are orders, are formally paid at minimum wage rates for part of their working time, but work much longer than recorded on their wage slip[2]. For workers and for purposes of wage 'negotiations' between workers and employers, this resulted in going wage rates of 3 pounds per hour in Leicester (Hammer and Plugor 2019), which has also been confirmed by Brill (2017) for Manchester:

> We're paid £4 an hour now that we're experienced workers – when you start out you only get £2.50–£3/hour[3]

It is difficult to detect economic upgrading for the majority of manufacturers in the industry as there is a shift to lower value-added production and a transactional dependence that results in items being produced below cost (see O'Connor 2018). Unauthorised subcontracting, the intensification of work and wage theft might well result in higher employment and high productivity growth in official statistics, but have to be seen as a clear example of social downgrading as it undermines and violates virtually all work and employment regulations. This reshaping of value capture strategies constituted a key characteristic of the way the industry re-coupled into particular regions, specifically those sub-sectors that are connected into fast fashion. In Froud et al.'s (2018: 1653) words:

> In effect, the apparel sector was redefined as a workshop, not factory activity, and this is, interestingly, a distinctively British path of adjustment. In Germany, for example, an 80% reduction in the number of clothing manufacturers from 1980 to 2001 was accompanied by an increase in average firm size from 76 to 99 employees. (Adler 2004)

Marginalising Apparel Manufacturing in Greater Manchester and Leicester: Two Political Projects

Apparel manufacturing in both Greater Manchester (GM) and Leicester had significant enough importance for them to see high-profile political interventions and initiatives. Neither region could stop the slide of economic and social downgrading in core subsectors, yet, the different industrial and sub-sectoral compositions and the associated political dynamics resulted in different trajectories which can loosely be described as broad economic downgrading (GM) and downgrading into a workshop (Leicester) (Froud et al. 2018), associated with corresponding degrees of social downgrading.

Greater Manchester's regional industry structure is more diverse and, with considerable textiles *and* apparel manufacturing sectors, has a perspective onto a larger part of the value chain (New Economy 2016). A key feature of restructuring in Greater Manchester is the existence of a historical textiles manufacturing sector that is fairly diverse and has, to some extent, been able to implement process and product upgrading strategies. In contrast, apparel manufacturing in Leicester consists overwhelmingly of micro, small-, and (rarely) medium-sized businesses that were founded by ethnic minority entrepreneurs as the established production was closed and offshored.

Across both regions, a great part of apparel manufacturing, certainly those firms established in the last three decades, suffer from a significant representation problem: their size and business models set them apart from established industry organisations that championed longstanding relational forms of coordination between manufacturers and lead firms. Incidentally, this also applies to a new type of lead firm, such as discounters and online-only retailers, who are not represented in industry bodies at their level. In fact, until very recently, the institutions of representation within the industry were those of the 1970s, which by now have become a hollow shell. Interestingly, it was only in 2018 that the British Retail Consortium took the lead in formulating and arguing a Sector Deal in the context of the Conservative government's industrial strategy. This industrial representation gap is much less severe within textiles manufacturing, even though this sector has suffered considerably from the closure of research, training, and education facilities (e.g. within Colleges and Higher Education).

It is argued here that the political coalition between lead firms, politics, and manufacturers explains the politics and strategies in Manchester. Since 2012, Greater Manchester has hosted the Alliance Project, which in 2014 produced an upbeat assessment of the sector's potential for future growth and then secured substantial regional growth funding to help to realise this potential (Alliance Project 2015). Importantly, this project covers both textiles manufacturing *and* apparel manufacturing and often communicates data encompassing both sectors. Under the N Brown Textile Growth Programme, £27m has been invested in 340 textile manufacturers across the North and Midlands of England, matched by £123m from the private sector. A short summary report on this project (Alliance Project 2017) shows an increase in exports from the sector, rising from £5.7 billion to £9.1 billion, which is not strong enough to reverse the steadily growing trade deficit in the sector (up from £13 billion in 2012 to £15.4 billion). To date, the extensive research and learning that has been completed in the course of this project, including an evaluation of the grants made, has not yet been published.[4]

The report highlights the diversity of GM textile manufacturing, with companies' products ranging from designer clothes and fast fashion, to technical textiles, workwear and bedding and homewares, alongside the production of yarn and cloth. It also flags up what the Alliance project sees as the key challenges facing the sector, namely the lack of large manufacturers with significant capacity to invest in the sector and the challenge of finding sufficient skilled labour.

A more critical report from the University of Manchester (Froud et al. 2017) gives a more nuanced analysis of the UK textiles industry, highlighting the significant challenges facing subsectors such as garment manufacturing as well as greater potential for growth in particular product areas (carpets, woollens, and worsteds). The central importance of branding and marketing in the fashion industry, amplified by the rise of fast fashion and e-tailing, has created a significant asymmetry in company size between the local manufacturers (typically employing between 10 and 20 people), and the much larger retailers on whom they often depend for orders. A key message coming out of this research emphasised the absence of any leadership and collective voice for manufacturers, rather than the wider fashion industry, whose umbrella bodies tend to prioritise the needs of the designers and retailers.

While activities within the Alliance project have been very intense and widespread, it is clear that the core aims have been driven by local lead firms, that is, fashion-, design-, and technology-intensive firms and the subsequent investments focused on linkages, capabilities, and skills in their respective supply chains. This approach has been developed by a coalition of lead firms, local politicians, and core first-tier manufacturers that are linked through relational interactions and, by implication, have less of an interest in questioning existing power imbalances within their value chain strands. Consequently, while the Alliance Project made considerable progress in building a political coalition to further industrial interests, and has gained a good deal of publicity, it has written most apparel manufacturers out of the political economy in Greater Manchester in what might well have been a one-off initiative.

By contrast, Leicester has historically been a location for large and important manufacturers rather than lead firms (the NEXT headquarters on the outskirts of Leicester constituting an exception). Channel Four's investigative programme *Fashion's Dirty Secrets* (2010), together with concerns from lead firms' ethical trade managers and social auditors, triggered a large community and stakeholder meeting in 2013 that sought to develop a programme to restrain unauthorised subcontracting and what were seen as widespread violations of work and employment rights. After the extent of these problems were confirmed through research commissioned by the Ethical Trading Initiative (Hammer et al. 2015), the ETI took steps to design a bundle of initiatives to tackle non-compliance with work and employment regulations. However, the implementation of these initiatives was hampered, again, by a reliance on lead firms. Even though work and employment issues constituted the core of those initiatives and even though unions and NGOs made their voices heard within the ETI project group, the implementation was to be designed and carried out by lead firms themselves.

Equally, while manufacturers were consulted in the process, they were not involved in the design phase. This resulted in a dual approach: while a handful of manufacturers were considered to be compliant with work and employment regulations (at the same time as they were thought to be expensive), the majority of manufacturers were considered off-limits, that is not sufficiently trustworthy and reliable to source from. This dualism also reflected a split within the local manufacturer base as to the appropriate political and business strategies to go forward. A further important component in the politics of this political project was that the local authority's involvement (the city hall and the local enterprise partnership) remained relatively low key. Initial scepticism as to the existence of the problem gave way to the facilitation of ETI initiatives. It was only later, as a parliamentary committee (Joint Committee on Human Rights 2017) visited Leicester on a fact-finding mission, that the local enterprise partnership put bottom-up advice and support for local manufacturers in place.[5] Subsequently, Leicester was declared a pilot case by the new Director of Labour Market Enforcement (2018) to develop closer cooperation between enforcement bodies and has also come under closer scrutiny by the Gangmaster and Labour Abuse Authority (GLAA). A large part of the efforts here was channelled into a tug of war over how active top-down enforcement activities should be (see e.g. the very cautious approach by the local authority (Davies et al. 2020) and the strategy laid out by the Director of Labour Market Enforcement (2018)). In a sense, the political project in Leicester has shifted from a dynamic led by a multi-stakeholder platform on labour standards to one led by statutory bodies, focused more narrowly on enforcement.

In spite of these different political coalitions, as well as the actual content of their respective initiatives, both projects share a blind spot as regards the underlying power dynamics of the apparel value chain. The industrial strategy and an approach to employment standards enforcement as policing assisted in re-coupling apparel manufacturing as an even more transactionally dependent industry than the one that was de-coupled. It also instituted the informal economy and wage theft as the industry norm within fast fashion production. Froud et al. (2018) emphasise the importance of national institutional conditions: in the absence of effective labour market regulation and enforcement of factory and workshop legislation, textiles and garment producers under pressure will generally take the low road.

Thus, while the respective projects in Manchester and Leicester will result in isolated capacity building and labour rights enforcement, they are not designed to use work and employment rights as a lever for economic upgrading (see also Ram et al. 2019), to build them into the industrial strategy as beneficial constraints. Consequently, productive and compliant manufacturers will keep being undercut, thereby institutionalising the path of economic and social downgrading.

From the Lockdown to New Public-private Beginnings?

The COVID-19 pandemic and associated national lockdown in Spring 2020 posed great difficulties for the industry: retail stores were closed, international supply chains were interrupted or re-designed to support hospitals' demands, and workers whose wages were cash-in-hand received insufficient income support. In fact, this situation also opened up opportunities for fast fashion brands with local supply chains, with Boohoo having become the main player in Leicester, which continued to place orders with factories. An exposé by Labour Behind the Label (LBL 2020) confirmed that sourcing and production in Leicester continued throughout the lockdown, entailing the disregard of positive COVID-19 cases, containment measures, and furlough fraud on top of what was already a problematic scorecard for the industry.

Boohoo responded resolutely through a review of its supply chain monitoring and compliance processes and commissioned a report that absolved the company of any legal liability while, at the same time, detailing an abundance of failures in Boohoo's social auditing and purchasing practices. The introductory summary of this report by Alison Levitt QC (2020: 6; emphasis added), for example, concludes that

1. There is no evidence that the company itself or its officers have committed any *criminal offences*;
2. I am satisfied that the allegations about poor working conditions and low rates of pay in many Leicester factories are not merely well-founded but *substantially true*;
3. Boohoo's monitoring of its Leicester supply chain was *inadequate* and this was attributable to *weak corporate governance*.

The aftermath of the exposé by LBL and further investigations by The Guardian (Bland 2020) saw increased enforcement and compliance activity without affecting the underlying governance of the industry, a dynamic that is in line with the political cycle of labour exploitation and rights abuses in the industry. For example, enforcement agencies such as the GLAA, HSE (Health and Safety Executive), and HMRC (HM Revenue and Customs) took a more active role, and Boohoo itself, after a review of its approximately 200 suppliers, cut ties with 64 of them (Martin 2020).

Most importantly, though, LBL, trade unions, and other civil society actors created sufficient pressure that eventually led to the formation of a comprehensive industry forum. Discussions took a protocol – the Apparel and General Merchandise Public Private Protocol (GLAA n.d.) – that had been drawn up by key public and private stakeholders in 2018 as a starting point, with a view to developing an 'enforceable agreement with accountable commitments signed by stakeholders' (ibid.). Under consideration were detailed provisions regarding standards and monitoring mechanisms; rules governing disputes, sanctions, and remediation; as well as institutions to support a programme of work on a day-to-day basis. Negotiations on this agreement have been protracted and are still not finalised at the time of writing.

Not wanting to wait for the end of these protracted negotiations, key lead firms and civil society actors have pressed ahead with two initiatives in the second half of 2021, in some respect exposing complex divisions not only between but also amongst stakeholders. A select number of lead firms signed a workplace access agreement with the Midlands TUC that provided supply chain transparency and opened the door for trade unions to support workers. Further, a key community centre was funded by brands and trade unions to employ two outreach workers to support the multi-ethnic garment worker communities in the area.

It is too early to assess the outcomes of these ongoing initiatives, however, it is noteworthy that, in contrast to past efforts, they do include a focus on worker engagement through union access and community engagement. It is also important to recognise that, whilst both initiatives formally stand on their own, they are also firmly embedded in the wider context of an emerging form of hybrid, public-private governance of employment standards.

Conclusions

This chapter showed that the growth in UK apparel manufacturing over the last decade has occurred in the context of economic and social downgrading. On the economic side, the emergence of fast fashion has further entrenched the transactional dependency of manufacturers on lead firms, built-in incentives for manufacturers to meet order fluctuations through subcontracting, further reduced the capabilities of small manufacturers to upgrade, and decreased the diversity of the sector towards a dominance of the manufacture of other outerwear. On the social side, the dual pressures of quick response business models and the permissive enforcement environment have led to wage theft and violations of work and employment regulations as industry standards.

It is argued that recent growth dynamics cannot be explained through value chain analysis or societal/regional analyses as both the functional division of labour as well as the social and institutional context they map on played central roles in determining where what kind of sub-sectoral industrial restructuring occurred. Industrial policy is paradoxical in a number of ways. On the one hand, central government considers apparel manufacturing as a sunset industry (Evans and Smith 2006); regional industrial development actors might well agree with this judgement but often find themselves part of political coalitions or political binds that involve them in major restructuring plans (Manchester) and/or passive support through permissive enforcement (Leicester). On the other hand, policy actors depend on the 'visible' downstream end of the value chain, that is, large and powerful lead firms and brands, and inevitably structure regional industrial policy measures in favour of these lead firms or major first-tier suppliers. Such measures include supply-side interventions, business-to-business networking, capital grants, or, to a lesser extent, support for training.

Such policy approaches are biased, however, and ultimately contribute to the unsustainability of current practices: neither do they address the power imbalances between lead firms and manufacturers, nor do they acknowledge the power imbalance between capital and labour at the workplace. In this context, subcontracting and informalisation are likely to remain key in manufacturer strategies and further institutionalise economic and social downgrading. Given the importance of a local manufacturer base for a large number of UK-based global fashion brands, it remains to be seen whether social downgrading proves dysfunctional for the value chain overall, or whether industry stakeholders can develop a more sustainable footing through an enforceable agreement to govern employment standards.

Notes

1 Interview with knitwear manufacturer, 22 August 2017.
2 These practices have a long tradition in the industry, as documented in a 1983 *Report on the Clothing Industry and Public Sector Investment in East London* (NUTGW & Hackney TUSG 1983, 6–7; cited in Phizacklea 1990, 79).
3 Interview with garment machinist, 20 September 2017.
4 The Alliance Project (2017, 8) refers to an external evaluation as well as a series of other studies on various aspects of the industry.
5 The tension between regional industrial policymakers and manufacturers became evident in a consultation on what form support to the industry should take: whereas the former favoured a city centre one-stop steel and glass space to enable B2B networking (buyers, designers, manufacturers), the latter argued for support based in the manufacturer and worker communities to focus on skills training of machine operators.

References

Adler, U. (2004) Structural change: the dominant feature in the economic development of the German textile and clothing industries. *Journal of Fashion Marketing and Management*, 8(3), 300–319.

Alliance Project (2015) *Repatriation of UK Textiles Manufacture*. Manchester: Greater Manchester Combined Authority.

Alliance Project (2017) Realising the growth potential of UK Fashion and Textile Manufacturing: The Alliance Project and NBrown – National Textiles Growth Programme. http://www.ltma.co.uk/wp-content/uploads/2017/05/The-Final-Alliance-Project-Report-Oct-2012-to-May-2017.pdf

Bair, J. & Mahutga, M. (2012) Varieties of Offshoring? Spatial Fragmentation and the Organization of Production in Twenty-First Century Capitalism. In Morgan, G. & Whitley, R. (eds.) *Capitalisms and Capitalism in the Twenty-First Century*. Oxford: Oxford University Press, pp. 270–297.

Bair, J. & Werner, M. (2011) Commodity chains and the uneven geographies of global capitalism: a disarticulations perspective. *Environment and Planning A: Economy and Space*, 43(5), 988–997.

Barrientos, S., Gereffi, G. & Rossi, A. (2011) Economic and social upgrading in global production networks: a new paradigm for a changing world. *International Labour Review*, 150(3&4), 319–340.

Bland, A. (2020) Leicester factory put lives at risk during lockdown, claims garment worker, *The Guardian* 11 July 2020, https://www.theguardian.com/uk-news/2020/jul/11/leicester-factory-put-lives-at-risk-during-coronavirus-lockdown-claims-garment-worker

Brill, L. (2017) Greater Manchester Textile & Garment Workers' Research Project, Phase 1 report. *Unpublished Research Report*. Leeds: Homeworkers Worldwide.

Britain's cheap clothes (2017) by Hadland, K. & Ahmad, T., Dispatches. First broadcast 23 January 2017. London: Channel 4.

Coe, N. & Yeung, H. (2015) *Global Production Networks. Theorising Economic Development in an Interconnected World*. Oxford: Oxford University Press.

Coe, N. & Yeung, H. (2019) Global production networks: mapping recent conceptual developments. *Journal of Economic Geography*, 19(4), 775–801.

Davies, D., Bua, A., Cortina Oriol, M. & Thompson, E. (2020) Why is austerity governable? A Gramscian urban regime analysis of Leicester, UK. *Journal of Urban Affairs*, 42(1), 56–74.

Director of Labour Market Enforcement (2018) United Kingdom Labour Market Enforcement Strategy 2018/19 (HMSO)

Evans, Y. & Smith, C. (2006) Surviving at the margins? Deindustrialisation, the creative industries, and upgrading in London's garment sector. *Environment and Planning A*, 38, 2253–2269.

Fashion's dirty secrets (2010) by Jones, J. & Ahmad, T., Dispatches. First broadcast 2010 [DVD] London: Channel 4.

Froud, J., Hayes, S., Wei, H. & Williams, K. (2017) *Coming Back? Capability and Precarity in UK Textiles and Apparel*. CRESC, University of Manchester.

Froud, J., Hayes, S., Wei, H. & Williams, K. (2018) Capabilities and habitat in industrial renewal: the case of UK textiles. *Cambridge Journal of Economics*, 42(6), 1643–1669.

Gibbon, P. & Ponte, S. (2005) *Trading Down: Africa, Value Chains, and the Global Economy*. Philadelphia: Temple University Press.

GLAA (Gangmasters and Labour Abuse Authority) (n.d.) Apparel and General Merchandise Public Private Protocol, https://www.gla.gov.uk/i-am-a/i-use-workers/apparel-and-general-merchandise-public-private-protocol/

Greenfield, P. & Butler, S. (2018) Arcadia's poor sales blamed for squeeze on suppliers, https://www.theguardian.com/business/2018/jan/17/arcadia-poor-sales-blamed-for-squeeze-on-suppliers

Hammer, N. & Plugor, R. (2016) Near-sourcing UK apparel: value chain restructuring, productivity and the informal economy. *Industrial Relations Journal*, 47(5–6), 402–416.

Hammer, N. & Plugor, R. (2019) Disconnecting labour? The labour process in the UK fast fashion value chain. *Work, Employment and Society*, 33(6), 913–928.

Hammer, N., Plugor, R., Nolan, P. & Clark, I. (2015) *A New Industry on a Skewed Playing Field: Supply Chain Relations and Working Conditions in UK Garment Manufacturing*. Leicester, London: University of Leicester/CSWEF, Ethical Trading Initiative.

HWW (2019) *The Greater Manchester Textile and Garment Industry: A Scoping Study*. Leeds: Homeworkers Worldwide, http://www.homeworkersww.org.uk/assets/uploads/files/HWW-GM-textiles-manufacturing-FINAL.pdf

Joint Committee on Human Rights (2017) *Human Rights and Business 2017: Promoting responsibility and ensuring accountability. Sixth Report of Session 2016–17*. House of Lords and House of Commons.

Lane, C. & Probert, J. (2009) *National Capitalisms, Global Production Networks. Fashioning the Value Chains in the UK, USA, and Germany*. Oxford: OUP.

LBL (Labour Behind the Label) (2020) *Boohoo & COVID-19: The People behind the Profit*. Bristol: Labour Behind the Label, https://labourbehindthelabel.net/wp-content/uploads/2020/06/LBL-Boohoo-WEB.pdf

Lerche, J. (2012) Labour regulations and labour standards in India: decent work? *Global Labour Journal*, 3(1), 16–39.

Levitt, A. (2020) Independent Review into the boohoo Group PLC's Leicester supply chain, 24 September 2020, https://www.boohooplc.com/sites/boohoo-corp/files/final-report-open-version-24.9.2020.pdf

Martin, D. (2020) Boohoo cuts ties with 64 Leicester suppliers with plans for its own 'huge' city factory. Leicester Mercury 24 December 2020, https://www.leicestermercury.co.uk/news/leicester-news/boohoo-cuts-ties-64-leicester-4826559

Milberg, W. & Winkler, D. (2011) Economic and social upgrading in global production networks: problems of theory and measurement. *International Labour Review*, 3&4(150), 341–365.

New Economy (2016) Deep Dive: 02 Manufacturing. *Final Report*. Greater Manchester Combined Authority.

Newsome, K., Taylor, P., Bair, J. & Rainnie, A. (eds.) (2015) *Putting Labour in its Place. Labour Process Analysis and Global Value Chains*. London: Palgrave.

O'Connor, S. (2018) Dark factories: labour exploitation in Britain's garment industry. *Financial Times*, 17 May 2018.

Palpacuer, F. & Parisotto, A. (2003) Global production and local jobs: can global enterprise networks be used as levers for local development. *Global Networks*, 3(2), 97–120.

Peck, J. & Theodore, N. (2007) Variegated capitalism. *Progress in Human Geography*, 31(6), 731–772.

Phizacklea A. (1990) *Unpacking the Fashion Industry. Gender, Racism, and Class in Production*. London: Routledge.

Prime Minister's Office (2014) Businesses are coming back, https://www.gov.uk/govern-ment/publications/businesses-are-coming-back/businesses-are-coming-back (Accessed 29 April 2016).

Ram, M., Edwards, P., Meardi, G., Jones, T. & Doldor, S. (2019) The Roots of Informal Responses to Regulatory Change: Non-compliant Small Firms and the National Living Wage. *British Journal of Management*, 31(4), 856–871, DOI:10.1111/1467-8551.12363

Robinson, P. K. & Hsieh, L. (2016) Reshoring: a strategic renewal of luxury clothing chains. *Operations Management Research*, 9(3), 89–101.

Sullivan, C. (2017) Boohoo business model pushes fast fashion to step up a gear, Financial Times, 22 May 2017, available at https://www.ft.com/content/f1a24648-3a19-11e7-ac89-b01cc67cfeec

Taplin, I. M. (2014) Global commodity chains and fast fashion: how the apparel industry continues to re-invent itself. *Competition and Change*, 18(3), 246–264.

Tokatli, N. (2013) Toward a better understanding of the apparel industry: a critique of the upgrading literature. *Journal of Economic Geography*, 13(6), 993–1011.

Toms, S. & Zhang, Q. (2016) Marks & Spencer and the decline of the British textile industry. *Business History Review*, 90, 3–31.

Verdict Retail. (2015) UK Value Clothing Market in the UK, available at http://www.verdictretail.com/uk-value-clothing-market-benefits-from-3-8-million-more-value-seeking-shoppers/, date last accessed May 2016.

Warren C. (2005) Coming Undone: The Implications of Garment Industry Subcontracting for UK Workers. In Hale, A. & Wills, J. (eds) *Threads of Labour. Garment Industry Supply Chains from the Workers' Perspective*. Oxford: Blackwell, pp. 133–160.

Werner, M. (2015) *Global Displacements: The Making of Uneven Development in the Caribbean*. Oxford, UK: Wiley Blackwell.

7 Power Dynamics, Regional Governance Institutions, and the Quality of Work: A Comparison of Baja California and Queretaro Aerospace Clusters

Christian Lévesque, Redi Gomis, Blandine Émilien, and Jorge Carrillo

Introduction

This chapter seeks to understand how various actors (firms, trade unions, private and public intermediaries, etc.) at different levels experiment with their institutions to create good jobs. It examines how power dynamics shape the capacity of actors to co-construct inclusive regional governance institutions that support the aerospace industry in Mexico and are likely to foster better work.

The development of the aerospace industry in Mexico has been resting on contrasting trends. On the one hand, it is a high value-added industry well integrated into the global economy which requires a highly skilled workforce (Casalet 2013, 2016). On the other hand, the competitive advantage of the Mexican manufacturing industry continues to be based on a low-wage and low-skill model within which the existence of flexible workplaces acts as a basis for international comparative advantage (Caufield 2010; Carrillo et al. 2017; Bayón 2019). These contrasting trends reinforce the classic example of a low-skills equilibrium trap (Schneider and Soskice 2009): workers do not invest individually in acquiring skills because firms do not offer high-skill jobs, and firms, in turn, have few incentives to invest in production processes requiring high-skill jobs because skilled workers are scarce.

This problem is particularly salient in Mexico where there is an ongoing employment crisis (Bayón 2013, Mancini 2019). The formal labour market is unable to absorb the strong demographic growth that characterises Mexico's young workforce. As a result, a high proportion of young labour market entrants must find work in the informal economy, where roughly 50% of the population works (Bayón 2019). There is thus great pressure to attract new foreign direct investment (FDI) and create sustainable, highly skilled jobs.

Over the last few decades, the appeal of FDI has been based on two pillars. The first is the maquiladora model which, through tax exemptions,

DOI: 10.4324/9781003001089-10

relies on the manufacturing or assembly of imported components or raw materials that are then exported to the United States (Carrillo and Hualde 1996). The second is employer protection contracts that favour the expansion of 'ghost unions' and limit grassroots union organising (Bensusán and Middelbrook 2012).

In this chapter we focus on two regions engaged in the aerospace industry that have followed different paths for economic and social development. Baja California is the oldest aerospace cluster in Mexico and its expansion has been based on the maquiladora model and union exclusion. The industry is dominated by US multinational companies (MNCs) with weak ties to local businesses (Gomis and Carrillo 2016). Activities within the region are coordinated by the state and public agencies that focus mainly on attracting FDI. The development of the aerospace industry in Queretaro is relatively recent (early 2000) and includes firms of different productive complexity and sources of capital. These firms nurture strong links with local institutions (Casalet 2013). The presence of trade unions in the workplace is also significant (Salinas 2014) and these trade unions are able to develop some form of pattern bargaining. Activities within the region are coordinated by MNCs and are geared towards increasing firms' capabilities and resources within the cluster.

To understand the power dynamics and the role of various actors in the co-construction of regional governance institutions in each region, we draw on relevant documentation and interviews conducted with government officials, representatives of innovation and training centres, and with production and human resources managers from a number of MNC subsidiaries. In Queretaro, we also conducted interviews with industrial union representatives and union delegates, spread across eight MNC subsidiaries. These subsidiaries account for nearly 70% of employment in Queretaro's aerospace industry.

The chapter is divided into five sections. First, we briefly describe our theoretical approach and then outline the main institutional legacies in Mexico with a special focus on power dynamics. This is followed by an account of the Mexican aerospace industry and a description of the aerospace industry in Baja California and Queretaro. What follows is a comparison of the contrasting regional governance institutions within each region. The last section analyses how power dynamics shape regional governance institutions and the capacity of workers and trade unions to foster better work in terms of skills and wages.

Power Dynamics, Regional Governance Institutions, and the Quality of Work

This chapter draws on a multifaceted power approach to disentangle the capacity of various actors, particularly trade unions, to engage in the co-construction of regional governance institutions for better work. The analysis is rooted in the dynamic interplay between structural and dispositional power. Structural power is associated with an actor's position in the economic field (workplace and marketplace bargaining power) and political field (influence over politics through the set of dependencies between capital, the state, and civil society) (Wright 2000; Culpepper 2015). Hence, trade union positions within economic and political fields can shape their capacity to act by allowing them to access and benefit from strategic resources. Dispositional power refers to the collective forms of organisation of various interest groups such as trade unions and business associations. With regards to trade unions, several scholars draw a distinction between associational and organisational power (Silver 2003; Lévesque and Murray 2005; Hyman and Gumbrell-McCormick 2017). Associational power refers, for example, to legal rules and labour rights, while organisational power relates to trade union resources and capabilities. It is our contention that these various forms of power are interrelated in a complex way and can either undermine or reinforce a trade union's capacity to engage in the co-construction of regional governance institutions.

The co-construction of regional governance institutions involves processes of organisational experimentation where actors renew their practices, resources, and networks, and institutional experimentation, where actors recombine old and new rules, norms and cognitive frames to develop new ways of acting and thinking (Murray et al. 2020). Zukauskaite et al. (2017)[1] differentiate two stylised types of regional governance institutions: thick and thin institutions. Regions with thick institutions have a variety of industrial and mediating organisations supporting innovation and knowledge transfer. These organisations are well connected to each other and coordinate their actions among themselves. Power is dispersed instead of being concentrated, and actors share a common identity that focuses on the production of collective goods. In contrast, in regions with thin institutions, there are few mediating organisations such as research centres and vocational training infrastructure. Interactions between firms, and with mediating organisations, are limited and power tends to be concentrated in a few dominant organisations, generally large firms. There is no collective agenda binding the various actors to coordinate their actions to produce collective goods. Hence, the provision of private goods is paramount.

There is growing evidence suggesting that the more coordinated approach supported by thick institutions is more inclusive and opens more space for workers and trade unions to voice their concerns (e.g. Menéndez et al. 2018). One key question is whether trade unions can mobilise various sources of power to foster experimentation that leads to thick regional governance institutions. Another is whether these institutions can favour better work, particularly in terms of wages and skills. These are daunting questions especially in Mexico where the competitive advantage of the manufacturing industry continues to be based on a low-wage and low-skills model. Figure 7.1 maps out our approach to studying the process of experimentation for better work.

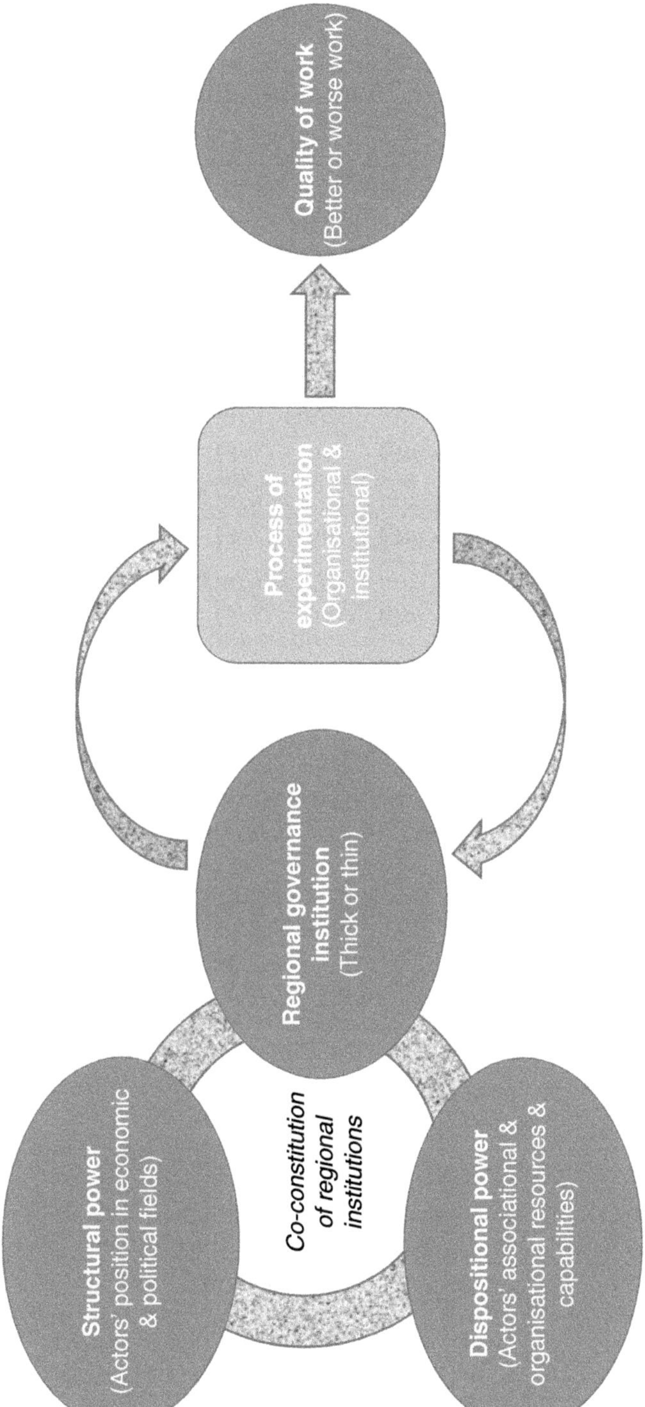

Figure 7.1 Processes of experimentation for better work[2].

Institutional Legacies and Power Dynamics in Mexico

Since the early 1920s, Mexico's official unions, notably the 'Confederations de Trabajadores Mexicanos' (CTM), have built close links with the state. This regime has been labelled 'authoritative corporatism' by several analysts (Bizberg 1999; Bensusán and Middelbrook 2012). The Institutional Revolutionary Party (PRI), which prior to the election of Vincente Fox in 2000 had held federal power since the early 1930s, has always maintained very close ties with the official unions, notably the CTM. This tight relationship between labour and the state has enabled the adoption of socially progressive labour legislation that has increased associational power for workers.

In this classic example of a corporatist political exchange, union representatives have had access to greater financial resources and played an important role within the state administration in return for their cooperation in industrial and political matters. This has particularly been the case with regard to labour courts, which have significant decision-making power in areas such as the determination of union representativeness, the registration of unions, and the legality of strikes. These same powers have contributed to the continued importance of official unions within the overall administration of the Mexican industrial relations regime, but they also highlight the vulnerability of workers' bargaining demands to overarching political considerations.

This regime of 'authoritative corporatism' evolved hand in hand with a model of economic growth relying on import-substitution of industrialisation (ISI). Policies and measures supporting this model of development have included restrictions on FDI, direct import controls, and credit and tax incentives for local entrepreneurs. State-owned enterprises (SOEs) have also played an important role in the economic development of the country. By 1982, the number of SOEs reached 1,155 (Villarreal and Ferguson 2014).

The 1982 Mexican debt crisis forced the government to rethink its state-led development strategy. By the end of the decade, import permits had been relaxed and practically eliminated while many SOEs were privatised: between 1983 and 1993, the number of SOEs decreased to 258 (Villarreal and Fergusson 2014). The dismantling of the ISI model was further accelerated with the North American Free Trade Agreement (NAFTA). This reinforced Mexico's integration into the global economy and established Mexico as a major player in North America. The development of the maquiladora model, which eases cross border trade through FDI, also expanded significantly from the mid-1960s and particularly through the 1990s. This model, based on the generation of currency (added value), employment (intensive, unskilled), and exports (raw materials and components imported for assembly or manufacture and later exported to the United States), allowed for sustained growth of FDI (Carrillo and Hualde 1996). By 2017, MNC subsidiaries adopting the maquiladora model employed 2.6 million people in Mexico (INEGI 2018). Despite its growth, this model was never able to develop solid ties with local businesses nor create high-skill and high-wage jobs.

Economic reform and political change since the early 2000s have not dismantled the complex arrangement of legal and administrative controls regulating labour relations. Official unions continue to play an important role within the state administration and, notably the CTM, in supporting the government's economic strategy, which relies on low wages and flexible workplaces as a basis for international comparative advantage (Bensusán and Middelbrook 2012). The CTM actively promotes this strategy and condemns any action from its affiliates that could undermine it. More precisely, the CTM and COPARMEX (Confederación Patronal de la República Mexicana), the Mexican employers' confederation, promote a work culture characterised by workplace flexibility and a community of interests between workers and employers.

The Mexican industrial relations model has evolved from authoritative corporatism, in which workplace behaviour was dictated from on high, towards micro-corporatism where the official unions, in return for the recognition of their presence in new factories, have accepted the competitive logic of their export-oriented employers (Lévesque and Murray 2005). State openness to FDI and the weakening of trade unions have given much leeway to MNCs. In such a permissive institutional context, MNCs can easily avoid institutional constraints or adapt them to their particular needs (Lévesque et al. 2015). Since NAFTA, despite continuous growth in productivity, workers have lost half of their purchasing power (Bayón 2019), reflecting the weakening power of labour. The 2008 financial crisis has exacerbated pressure on wages.

Despite the creation of the UNT (Union Nacional de Trabajadores) in 1997 (Bensusán and Middelbrook 2012) and the emergence of a more radical form of unionism exemplified by Los Mineros (Adanhounme and Lévesque 2013; Soul 2019), institutions in Mexico appear to be quite resilient and they lock actors into a logic of action that constrains workers' capacity to express their needs, defend their interests, and develop autonomous collective organisations. The election of Andres Manuel Lopez Obrador in 2019 seems, however, to have opened political opportunities for a restructuring of the Mexican labour movement (Marinaro and Ness 2019). First, the Mexican senate has ratified ILO Convention no. 98, which promotes the right to organise and bargain collectively. The ratification of this convention means that it is now possible to challenge employer protection contracts. Second, at the national level, the hegemony of the CTM has been diluted by the creation of two new confederations: the CIT (Conferacion Internacional de Trabajadores), led by the general secretary of Los Mineros (Senator Napoleon Gomez), and the CATEM (Confederacion Autonóma de Trabajadores y Empleados de Mexico), led by another senator (Pedro Miguel Haces Barba). Thirdly, in January 2019, more than

30,000 workers in Northern Mexico (in Matamoros, Tamaulipas), who had joined a CTM branch union (Sindicato de Jornaleros y Obreros Industriales y de La Industria Maquiladora, SJOIIM), went on strike demanding a 20% salary increase and a bonus of approximately $1,700 (US). This grassroot movement involved massive rallies and a strike involving 48 factories (Marinaro and Ness 2019). Instead of bargaining individually with each factory, SJOIIM union delegates decided to join forces and negotiated directly with the local government and the association of maquiladora employers. This movement has not yet reached Baja California and Queretaro.

The Aerospace Industry in Mexico

Over the last decade, Mexico has increased its role in the global aerospace industry. FDI has increased significantly, from $250 million (US) in 2004 to $1.1 billion (US) in 2014, while employment has surged from 13,000 in 2004 to 45,000 in 2014 (Ornelas 2015). The industry had a cumulative growth of 108% (from $482 US million to $1 US billion) between 2009 and 2016,[3] and its weight in manufacturing GDP doubled, going from 0.37% to 0.76% (Gobierno de la República de México 2016). Second, the total workforce increased from 11,061 to 41,151 between 2008 and 2018 (see Table 7.1). As a share of the manufacturing sector, employment in the larger aerospace industry went from 0.35% in 2009 to 0.68% in 2016, which amounts to a 94% increase (Gobierno de la República de México 2016). The number of aerospace companies also increased. By the end of 2018, there were 127 firms involved in Mexico's aerospace sector[4]. Table 7.1 describes the main features of the Mexican aerospace industry and of Baja California and Queretaro.

Four main aspects characterise the development of the aerospace industry in Mexico. First, the vast majority of the firms operating in Mexico's aerospace sector are subsidiaries of multinational companies and were set up using foreign capital (Gomis and Carrillo 2016). Some of these subsidiaries stem from leading aerospace firms. Airbus, Bombardier, Cessna, Beechcraft, Bell Helicopters, MD Helicopters, Embraer, Gulfstream, and Fokker (all of them 'Original Equipment Manufacturers' – OEMs) are among the companies that have subsidiaries in Mexico. Mexico is also home to subsidiaries of other top-tier companies of global industry, namely Honeywell, General Electric, Safran, Daher, Senior, and Sargent, among others.

Second the activities within the industry may be depicted as the manufacturing of 'aeroparts' rather than 'aerospace'. Economic activities focus on processes with varying degrees of integration. More generally, however, the sector is concerned with low value-added manufacturing processes. MNCs not only take advantage of the lower costs of labour (Bamber and Gereffi 2013), but also of the manufacturing capabilities developed over several decades of industrialisation, mainly in the electronic and auto parts

Table 7.1 Main Features of the Mexican Aerospace Industry

	2008			*2013*			*2018*		
	Mexico (Total National)	*Queretaro*	*Baja California*	*Mexico (Total National)*	*Queretaro*	*Baja California*	*Mexico (Total National)*	*Queretaro*	*Baja California*
Companies	43	3	9	94	14	18	127	18	33
		6.98%	20.93%		14.89%	19.15%		14.17%	25.98%
Employment	11,061	878	3,872	27,513	4,362	8,171	41,151	6,108	12,572
		7.94%	35.01%		15.85%	29.70%		14.84%	30.55%
Gross production (US$ millions)	590.15	135.9	97.4	1,262.40	166.9	275.5	1,830.70	459.7	389.0
		23.03%	16.51%		13.22%	21.82%		25.11%	21.25%
Gross value added (US$ millions)	352.04	73.9	67.9	555.85	77.2	159.2	932.64	257.4	230.4
		21.00%	19.28%		13.90%	28.64%		27.60%	24.70%
Total investment (US$ millions)	23.58	12.4	1.0	8.73	4.9	8.2	53.39	36.2	4.1
		52.63%	4.27%		55.80%	93.96%		67.79%	7.71%

Sources: *INEGI. Censos económicos 2008, 2013 and 2018* (https://www.inegi.org.mx/app/saic/). *Business sectors considered: 3364 aerospace manufacture NAICS code.*

maquiladoras (Contreras and Bracamonte 2013). Most of this industry's output is export oriented. Illustratively, in 2006, 95% of everything produced by the industry in Queretaro was meant for export (Universal 2016). Based on data from the Observatory of Economic Complexity (Simoes and Hidalgo 2018), for the period 1995–2014, Mexico had almost quadrupled its contribution in the global market for aircraft parts (from 0.4% to 1.9%), moving it from 29th to 9th place globally, and exports have diversified. The number of countries of destination rose from 16 in 1995 to 66 in 2014 and the United States became by far the most important country of destination, absorbing 83% of Mexico's exports between 1995 and 2016.

Third, there is no specific policy regulating the aerospace industry in Mexico, but various government agencies, such as Pro Mexico,[5] and private organisations such as FEMIA (*Federación Mexicana de la Industria Aeroespacial*) support the development of the industry. FEMIA is an employer-representation structure created in 2007 by leading firms across Mexico, and provides a framework through which employers are able to develop a common vision for the industry. It includes 106 members (82 associates and 24 affiliate members) representing more than 90% of all employment in the industry (FEMIA 2010).

Fourth, 77% of the firms in the sector are concentrated in five Mexican states with distinctive features and specialisations: Baja California, Queretaro, Sonora, Chihuahua, and Nuevo León. In the next two sections we describe in more detail the aerospace clusters of Baja California and Queretaro

Baja California Aerospace Cluster

While maquiladoras are spread across the country, the northern states of Mexico have been their main bastion, particularly Baja California where the largest number of maquiladoras are concentrated. They are spread across a variety of strategic industries including the electronics industry, automotive and auto parts, information technology, medical products and devices, and aerospace.

Rockwell Collins, Jonathan Engineered Solutions, and Skyworks Solutions were the first aerospace companies to set up in the region (Hualde and Carrillo 2007). Over the past decade, the industry has registered significant growth. Between 2008 and 2018, the number of companies and employment increased significantly, as highlighted in Table 7.1. There are currently 12,571 direct jobs distributed across 33 aerospace manufacturing companies located mainly in Tijuana and Mexicali. Roughly three-quarters of these companies are owned by American MNCs. Production activities are not concentrated in specific activities or parts of the aircraft but are instead quite diversified. However, the majority of firms in the industry are not involved in complex production processes and workers perform relatively simple subassemblies and final assembly tasks (Hualde and Carrillo 2007).

There is a significant presence of Economic Development Councils in Tijuana and Mexicali, and several private agencies operate at the municipality level to promote the development of the aerospace industry. The industry is mainly organised around two cluster associations: the Aerospace Cluster of Baja California in Tijuana and the Aerospace Alliance of Baja California in Mexicali, with little interaction and collaboration between the two (Robles Cortés 2013). These clusters include various private companies and associations, government entities (national and regional), universities and research centres (Conacyt 2016). They were created by the federal government, and promoted by the federal, and particularly the state governments to play multiple roles. These roles range from service providers, to regulators, to market advocates (Hernández and Carrillo 2018). However, the actors managing these associations mention that the resources offered by government agencies are limited, which reduces their ability to achieve these various roles (Robles Cortés 2013).

For the government of Baja California, these cluster associations should pursue two complementary goals: attract FDI and support the development of local suppliers. Government agencies as well as business associations have paid ongoing attention to the development of the local supply chain, not only because these groups are economically linked to the territory, but also because they can support knowledge spillover effects within the region. To develop local supply chains, cluster associations promote special events that aim to match the requirements of large aerospace companies with the capabilities of local small and medium-sized enterprises (SMEs). Even though all actors recognise that developing a local supply chain is a priority, the development of local suppliers has remained a secondary concern for large companies (Robles Cortés 2013). There are therefore some tensions between the priorities set by government agencies and the strategies of MNC subsidiaries.

These cluster associations also seek to increase both the value-added activities of the firms and the skills of the workforce. Out of 193 existing university education institutions in Baja California, seven are committed to supporting the aerospace sector. These are Autonomous University of Baja California (UABC) (with offices in Tijuana and Mexicali), Center for Technical and Higher Education (CETYS) (based in Tijuana and Mexicali), Technological University of Tijuana, Technological Institute of Tijuana, Technological Institute of Ensenada, Digital Technology Research and Development Center, and Technological Institute of Mexicali (Conacyt 2016). However, only two of these institutes offer specialised studies, namely the aerospace engineering course at UABC and the Master's degree in the same specialisation at CETYS (CETYS 2007). Furthermore, educational institutions tend to complain about a lack of depth in their relationships with the industry. Although companies will host students for professional and vocational training, they do not tend to commit further and their investment in research projects, technological development and even the management of new business with shared risk is limited. Despite the efforts of educational institutions, there is still a dearth of aerospace engineers in the state of Baja California.

Hence, the maquiladora model seems ill-equipped to deal with the dilemma of the low-skill equilibrium trap identified by Schneider and Soskice (2009). In this relatively centralised model, only a few incentives exist for MNC subsidiaries to develop horizontal links with other firms and to partner with educational and training institutions to upgrade skills. The complexity of the production process, which relies overall on simple subassembly tasks, does not favour skill upgrading either. Furthermore, these subsidiaries are highly dependent on their parent organisation for decision making and resource allocation (be they financial or technological resources). To add to this rather bleak picture, there is no space for workers to voice their collective concerns and interests. Trade unions are absent at the regional level while, at the workplace level, the diffusion of protection contracts and 'ghost unions' are widespread.

Therefore, in Baja California actors are engaged in a limited form of organisational experimentation. As a result, regional governance institutions remain relatively thin and do not foster a high level of coordination between actors and organisations. Despite their dynamism, the two cluster associations are mainly geared towards attracting FDI through comparative advantage based on geographical location, tax exemptions, low labour costs, and union exclusion. Upgrading skills is strictly addressed through the lens of the market and the provision of private goods. The alliance between foreign capital and the federal and state governments, combined with the compliance of trade unions at the state level, and the absence of grassroot trade unions in the workplace gives much leeway to MNCs and restricts workers' capacity to voice their concerns and to shape skill development and, more generally, the quality of work.

Queretaro Aerospace Cluster

While the industry revolved for many years around the activities of two foreign companies, from 2005 onwards, the Queretaro aerospace industry has experienced significant growth in investment with the arrival of major players such as Bombardier, Safran, and Airbus. To attract FDI, governments at both the state and federal levels have developed a range of incentives, from tax credits on imports for foreign companies to R&D funding and financial support for SMEs for industrial certification (Villavicencio et al. 2013; Casalet 2016). As of 2018, 18 firms with more than 6,000 employees work in aerospace-related production activities (see Table 7.1). The industry is specialised in propulsion systems, airframe structural assembly, engine components, landing systems as well as maintenance, repair and overhaul (MRO). Approximately 50% of the companies operating in the cluster are of European origin. The concentration of both North American and European companies is a defining feature of the Queretaro cluster.

In 2007, a number of actors affiliated with large firms, universities, and research centres set up an alliance (Alianza Estrategica y Red de Inovacion – AERI) to coordinate activities within the Queretaro aerospace cluster. The alliance aimed to build stronger ties among various stakeholders, stimulate R&D, facilitate human resources deployment, provide further access to funding sources, and accelerate certification processes for SMEs. All stakeholders in the industry (educational and training institutions, research centres, companies, etc.), with the exception of trade unions, are involved in the governance of the association. Since its creation, the association has been run by locally-based MNC managers that change after serving a three-year mandate. These managers play a crucial role in building networks and ties within and outside the region and in framing common issues for the Queretaro aerospace industry.

Through the new association, there have been attempts to develop the local supply chain, notably domestic SMEs. Several research centres dedicated to the industry were created, such as CENTA (Centro Nacional de Tecnología Aeronáutica), which became the new incubator for advanced research devoted exclusively to the aerospace sector. In 2014, a new laboratory (Laboratorio de Pruebas y Tecnologías Aeronáuticas (LABTA)) was set up to facilitate the certification of SMEs in accordance with aerospace requirements. While 20 Mexican SMEs obtained the required certification, they eventually faced barriers to integrating into the industry as MNC subsidiaries kept seeking suppliers from outside the local and regional supplier pool. MNC subsidiaries have therefore had difficulty reconciling their international integration with local and regional integration.

In 2007, public and private organisations worked jointly to create a new training institute that would henceforth be dedicated to aerospace, UNAQ (Universidad Aeronáutica en Querétaro). UNAQ has drawn on the experience of MNCs in their home country to transfer to Queretaro training models and practices developed in Montreal, Toulouse, and Wichita. Considered the cornerstone of this skills development model, UNAQ acts as an important provider of demand-driven training by offering courses that encompass several of the skill levels required for the industry and that adjust to the multiple needs of companies. Courses include basic technical training for top-level assembly, advanced technical training in the fuselage and more complex assembly, and finally university programs for engineers.

In 2006, a new trade union affiliated with the CTM (Sindicato Nacional de Trabajadores de la Industria Arnesera, Eléctrica, Automotriz y Aeronáutica de la Republica Mexicana) was created. It represents roughly 70% of the unionised workers in the aerospace industry in Queretaro. The presence of this union has led, through workplace collective bargaining, to the standardisation of several practices, including staffing, training, compensation, performance appraisal, and employer-employee relations. Illustratively, one of this union's initiatives has been to negotiate the convergence of staffing and training practices across the MNC subsidiaries whereby young, unionised workers are granted access to a three-month initial training program at UNAQ in an attempt to guarantee them employment upon completion of their training period. In collective agreements a lot of emphases is put on worker training and on linking wages to skill requirements. In some firms, this creates tension when there are insufficient opportunities for training.

The trade union is also pushing for new forms of work organisation that foster team working and flexibility. As such, the trade union agenda is very much aligned with management's narrative on new production imperatives. This model of trade unionism has much in common with Lucena's (2000) description of 'pactism' or Lévesque and Murray's (2005) account of micro-corporatism. It must be stressed, however, that this form of trade unionism does not share the same characteristics as the protection unions or white unions described by Salinas (2014). The local sections of this trade union in the aerospace industry can draw on a variety of organisational resources. In addition to basic mechanisms promoting worker participation in trade union activities (e.g. regular assembly, shop steward system, formal elections, paid release time for union delegates), they have developed mechanisms that nurture their external networks. The trade union has established regular relations with other trade unions in the community and participates in an information-sharing network on working conditions in the aerospace industry. As such, they have developed internal and external resources to increase their organisational power. In 2019, this trade union left the CTM and joined a new confederation, the CATEM (Confederation Autónoma de Trabajadores y Empleados de Mexico) which fosters partnerships between management and labour.

Actors in Queretaro have been engaging in a form of organisational experimentation that has resulted in the creation of thicker institutions. Various actors and organisations are involved in the coordination of collective action, creating new networks and providing collective resources such as a skilled workforce. MNC subsidiaries play a crucial role and are clearly capturing resources for the benefit of their own firm, but they are also at the centre of networks to upgrade collective and individual skills towards the needs of the industry. However, subsidiary engagement in this experimentation process does not go beyond the boundaries of large firms and is not having many spillover effects within SMEs and more generally within the local supply chain.

Trade unions are also engaged in this process of experimentation, but their actions are confined mainly to the organisational as opposed to the regional level. They are rule-takers rather than rule-makers and adapt to managerial strategies. Nevertheless, trade unions play an active role and mobilise their associational and organisational powers to reinforce their capacity to contribute to the development of workers' skills.

Understanding Skill Traps and Wage Gaps in the Aerospace Industry

Our results highlight contrasting processes of experimentation in the Baja California and Queretaro clusters with regards to how actors co-construct regional institutions for better work and to develop skills. In Baja California, actors have built thin regional governance institutions that grant MNCs significant leeway. Firms rely mainly on market mechanisms and an individualised approach that considers skills a private good. In Queretaro, the various actors develop a more collective and coordinated approach to experimentation that results in thicker regional governance institutions. They are more likely to define skills as a collective good that firms collectively produce and have access to. Table 7.2 depicts the main characteristics of each cluster.

Table 7.2 Characteristics of Regional Governance Institutions in Baja California and Queretaro

Dimensions	*Baja California*	*Queretaro*
Density of regional organisations (firms, business associations, trade unions, regional mediating organisations, etc.)	Two main associations representing government agencies, firms, and university and research centres	One association representing firms, research centres, and educational/training organisations
Dynamics and structure of power relations (decision-making process, distribution of resources, etc.)	Centralised through government and state agencies; concentration of power among MNCs	Decentralised through MNC managers; power distributed across various organisations
Identity and common agenda (actors' mutual awareness of their being involved in common endeavour)	Fragmented identity focusing on the provision of private goods and the attraction of FDI	Shared understanding of the need for coordination to produce collective goods to increase cluster capabilities
Levels of interaction (density and intensity of formal and informal interactions between actors and organisations)	Weak interactions between MNCs and with SMEs; no interaction with trade unions: research and education organisations weakly connected to the industry	Formal and informal interactions between MNCs and with trade unions; weak interaction between MNCs and SMEs; research and education organisations connected to the industry

In both clusters, several private and public actors are involved in the regional governance institutions and in both, MNC subsidiaries play a leading role. However, in Baja California the decision-making process is more centralised and the federal and state governments play a crucial role while in Queretaro, the decision-making process is more decentralised and managers of MNCs run the association. In Baja California, attracting FDI is paramount, whereas in Queretaro, governance institutions are geared towards increasing firms' capabilities and the provision of collective resources. In contrast to Baja California, which is larger, more diverse, and dispersed, actors within the Queretaro cluster display a stronger sense of cohesion and identity. Spatial proximity and the small number of MNC subsidiaries certainly help, but this cohesiveness is also linked to dense networks and activities developed within the cluster.

Both clusters have developed various research centres as well as training and educational organisations. However, in Queretaro, links with the industry are stronger. This does not imply that in Baja California firms do not invest in training and R&D. However, in each of these areas they adopt an individualised approach with a focus on their internal needs. This individualised approach also manifests in the types of relationships that exist between firms. Indeed, in Baja California, subsidiaries have strong relations with their parent organisation but very weak interactions with other MNCs. Interactions with SMEs and trade unions are non-existent. In Queretaro, while the relations between subsidiaries and their parent organisations are also overriding, they nevertheless develop strong relationships with other MNCs as well as with trade unions. However, ties with SMEs remain limited.

A striking difference between the two clusters lies in the role of trade unions. In Baja California, trade unions are absent in the workplace as well as at the regional level, while in Queretaro, despite the absence of union representation within the cluster association, trade unions can voice workers' concerns and interests through workplace bargaining and regular interactions with both general and HR managers of MNC subsidiaries. Through these formal and informal interactions, trade unions are able to introduce some form of coordination at the regional level. However, the commitment of trade unions to labour stability and industrial peace undermines their willingness to disrupt production to push forward workers' concerns and demands.

Queretaro, in contrast to Baja California, creates regional capabilities and resources that foster sustainable conditions to deal with the low skill trap equilibrium dilemma. The capacity of trade unions to voice workers' concerns and interests in terms of skill development is crucial. This capacity is linked to the ability of trade unions to mobilise associational power and develop their organisational power. The trade union narrative is framed around the presumption that upgrading skills will lead to wage increases and better jobs. However, an increase in workers' skills does not seem to affect workers' wages.

Data on annual salaries in the aerospace industry by state are not available, but the latest figures suggest that monthly salaries in 2018 in the aerospace industry in Mexico reached 675 US$ in comparison with 490 US$ in other manufacturing industries (INEGI 2021). Our own estimate, based on the content of collective agreements in the aerospace industry in Queretaro, suggests that monthly wages in 2019 for operators vary from 510 US$ to 660 US$ while for specialised workers they vary from 830 US$ to 990 US$. These salaries remain very low by international standards but, perhaps most importantly for our purpose, figures on compensation suggest that salaries are higher in Baja California than in Queretaro. The latest figure on workers' compensation in 2018 shows that monthly salaries in Queretaro represent 62% of the monthly salaries in Baja California (630 US$ in Queretaro versus 1,014 US$ in Baja California) (INEGI 2021).

These data must be interpreted with caution since many factors come into play in the settlement of wages (geographic location, labour market conditions, etc.). They nevertheless suggest two preliminary conclusions. First, in Baja California, workers lack both associational and organisational power, but they are not completely defenceless. Their geographic proximity to the US border gives them some marketplace bargaining power in their transactions with employers that they can mobilise to obtain material advantages. In Queretaro, trade unions' dispositional power, both associational and organisational, appears to favour the development of workers' skills, which helps resolve the low skill trap equilibrium dilemma, but it seems insufficient to deliver both high-skills and high-wage jobs. Hence, trade unions cannot convert upgrades in skills into wage increases. Accordingly, it appears that organisational and associational powers may be sufficient to deal with the low skill trap equilibrium dilemma, but it is insufficient to fill the wage gap. Structural power in economic and political fields limits the capacity of trade unions to provide high wages and high-skilled jobs, even though they have some form of associational and organisational power.

Concluding Remarks

Our analysis of these processes of experimentation with regional governance institutions for better work in the aerospace industry shows how structural and dispositional power are interrelated in complex ways. The alliance between the State, foreign capital, and labour at the societal level shapes other forms of power. The openness of the State to FDI gives much leeway to MNCs to avoid institutional constraints or to adapt them to their particular needs. In such a context, MNCs can develop a wide range of responses that can reinforce or challenge existing institutions, while trade unions and labour are subordinate, but not totally powerless.

The market-driven approach and thin regional institutions developed in Baja California fit well with these arrangements at the societal level.

MNC strategies focus on their individual needs while workers express their concerns through their marketplace bargaining power. In the absence of trade unions, workers cannot express their interests through associational or organisational power, and they engage in individualistic approaches. Hence, skill trap and wage gap issues are not addressed as a collective good issue, but as a private and individualised good.

The coordinated approach and thick regional institutions developed in Queretaro seem to open up more space for workers and trade unions to shape these issues collectively. The mobilisation of associational power and the development of organisational power provide trade unions with more opportunities to voice their concerns. However, these sources of power are not sufficient to overcome the pressures to conform to the export-oriented imperative of the State and foreign capital. This alliance between the State and foreign capital also limits the capacity of trade unions to mobilise their structural power to restrain production. In such a context, trade unions have developed a narrative which fosters industrial peace and collaborative union-management relations. This posture enables the trade union to be proactive in their participation in solving the low skill trap equilibrium dilemma through a discourse that defines skills as a public good. However, they are not able to transpose the upgrading of skills into wage increases.

Baja California and Queretaro follow different approaches and patterns of experimentation, but both focus on organisational over institutional experimentation. Indeed, in both cases, to varying degrees, these experiments foster the creation of new resources and networks but are not changing the rules of the game be it in terms of regulative, normative, or cognitive frames.

It remains to be seen whether both these approaches to regional economic and social development are sustainable. In Baja California, the State apparatus and firms, particularly MNCs, have been able to resist so far, the expansion in their region of the grassroots mobilisation of workers in Northern Mexico (in Matamoros, Tamaulipas) to increase wages and workers' voices through collective bargaining. The success of this movement may, however, trigger the enhancement of both associational and organisational trade union power. In Queretaro, the development of a militant form of trade unionism, exemplified by the action of the CIT (Conferacion Internacional de Trabajadores), may also compel trade unions to revisit both their repertoire of collective action and their narratives. Organisational power is as much about developing new repertoires of collective action as it is about framing a counter-narrative to the dominant managerial discourse. Trade unions in Queretaro have not yet developed such a narrative and this inability locks them into a path-dependent approach that limits their capacity to promote better work.

Notes

1 Zukauskaite et al. (2017: 337–338) have identified four dimensions to characterise regional governance institutions: the presence of a variety of organisations and actors (e.g. firms, unions, trade associations, training bodies), patterns of interaction between actors and organisations, the distribution and structure of power and the presence of a common agenda.
2 The graphic was conceived by Kai Hsin Hung from the CRIMT network.
3 Official data related to the GDP of the sector are presented in Mexican pesos. The conversion to dollars was done using data from Banxico. We used the month of May as the value of exchange rate for each year. (https://www.banxico.org.mx/SieInternet/consultarDirectorioInternetAction.do?sector=6&accion=consultarCuadro&idCuadro=CF86&locale=es).
4 The data on the aerospace industry varies from one study to another because these studies are based on more or less inclusive definitions of the industry (see Ornelas 2015; Casalet 2016). In order to compare the data across regions and time, we are using the data from INEGI even though they may underestimate the number of firms. The INEGI data includes aerospace companies whose activities correspond to the NAICS Code classification 3364 that are directly involved in 'Aerospace Product and Parts Manufacturing'.
5 ProMexico was abolished in 2018 by the new Mexican federal government since 2018 but their activities were transferred to Mexican Embassies and Consulates.

References

Adanhounme, A. & Lévesque, C. (2013) L'action syndicale à l'international vue du Sud: du global au local ou du local au global? *Relations industrielles/Industrial Relations*, 68(2), 239–260.

Bamber, P. & Gereffi, G. (2013) *Costa Rica in the Medical Devices Global Value Chain. Opportunities for Upgrading*. Durham: Duke University, Center on Globalization, Governance and Competitiveness.

Bayón, M. C. (2013) Hacia una sociología de la pobreza: la relevancia de las dimensiones culturales. *Estudios Sociológicos*, 31(91), 87–112.

Bayón, M. C. (2019) *Las grietas del neoliberalismo Dimensiones de la desigualdad contemporánea en México, (dir.).* Universidad Nacional Autónoma de México Instituto de Investigaciones Sociales México.

Bensusán, G. & Middelbrook, K. J. (2012) Organized Labour and Politics in Mexico. *The Oxford Handbook of Mexican Politics*. London: University of London: Institute of Latin American Studies.

Bizberg, I. (1999) Le syndicalisme mexicain face à la mondialisation et à la décomposition du régime politique. *La revue de l'IRES*, 29, 131–165.

Carrillo, J., Bensusán, G. & Thirion, J. M. (2017) *¿Es posible innovar y mejorar laboralmente? Estudio de trayectorias de empresas multinacionales en México*. Mexico: Universidad Autónoma Metropolitana.

Carrillo, J. & Hualde, A. (1996) Maquiladoras de tercera generación. El caso de Delphi-General Motors. *Espacios*, 17(3), 747–757.

Casalet, M. (2013) *(dir.) La industria aeroespacial: complejidad productiva e institucional*. Mexico: FLACSO.

Casalet, M. (2016) Meeting growth challenges of Mexico aerospace: the Querétaro cluster. *Space & Defense*, 9(1), 39–47.

Caufield, N. (2010) *NAFTA and Labor in North America*. Chicago: University of Illinois Press.

CETYS (2007) *Centro de Enseñanza Técnica y Superior*, https://www.cetys.mx/

CitiBanamex (2019) *Histórico Precio del Dólar Americano*, https://www.banamex.com/economia_finanzas/es/divisas_metales/dolar_interbancario.htm

Conacyt (2016) *Consejo Nacional de Ciencia y Tecnología*, https://www.conacyt.gob.mx/

Contreras, O. & Bracamonte, Á. (2013) Capacidades de manufactura global en regiones emergentes. La industria aeroespacial en Sonora. La industria aeroespacial: complejidad productiva e institucional, (dir.) M., Casalet et al. (coords.). Mexico: FLACSO, pp. 199–223.

Culpepper, P. D. (2015) Structural power and political science in the post-crisis era. *Business and Politics*, 17(3), 391–409.

FEMIA (2010) *Federación Mexicana de la Industria Aeroespacial, A.C.* https://www.femia.com.mx/

Gobierno de la República de México (2016) *Presidencia de la República*, https://www.gob.mx/presidencia/

Gomis, R. & Carrillo, J. (2016) The role of multinational enterprises in the aerospace industry clusters in Mexico: The case of Baja California. *Competition & Change*, 20(5) 337–352.

Gregor, M., Lévesque, C., Morgan, G. & Roby, N. (2020) Disruption and reregulation in work and employment: from organisational to institutional experimentation. *Transfer: European Review of Labour and Research*, 26(2), 135–156.

Hernández Chavarria, J. & Carrillo, J. (2018) Possibilities of Mexican SMEs insertion in the aerospace industry value chain, the Baja California case. *Estudios Fronterizos*, 19(38) 1–20.

Hualde, A. & Carrillo, J. (2007) La industria aeroespacial en Baja California. *Características productivas y competencias laborales y profesionales*. México: El Colegio de la Frontera Norte.

Hyman, R. and Gumbrell-McCormick, R. (2017) Resisting labour market insecurity: old and new actors, rivals or allies? *Journal of Industrial Relations*, 59(4), 538–561.

INEGI (2018) *México - Estadística del Programa de la Industria Manufacturera, Maquiladora y de Servicios de Exportación 2018, Datos al mes de diciembre*, 2017–2018, https://www.inegi.org.mx/default.html

INEGI (2021) Economic Census, 2018. Aguascalientes: Instituto Nacional de Estadística, Geografía e Informática, https://www.inegi.org.mx/app/saic/

Lévesque, C., Bensusán, G., Murray, G., Novick, M., Carrillo, J. & Gurrera, M. S. (2015) Labour relations policies in multinational companies: a three-country study of power dynamics. *Journal of Industrial Relations*, 57, 187–209.

Lévesque, C. & Murray, G. (2005) Union involvement in workplace change: a comparative study of local unions in Canada and Mexico. *British Journal of Industrial Relations*, 43(3), 489–514.

Lucena, H. (2000) 'El cambio en las relaciones industriales en América Latina' En: De la Garza, Enrique (coordinador) Tratado Latinoamericano de Sociología del Trabajo, FCE. México, 422–449.

Mancini, F. (2019) Movilidad social intrageneracional en México La herencia social del primer trabajo, (dir.) Bayón, M. C., in *Las grietas del neoliberalismo Dimensiones de la desigualdad contemporánea en México*, Universidad Nacional Autónoma de México Instituto de Investigaciones Sociales México, 67–107.

Marinaro, P. & DiMaggio, D. (2019) Strike Wave Wins Raises for Mexican Factory Workers. *Labor Notes*, 480, https://www.labornotes.org/2019/02/strike-wave-wins-raises-mexican-factory-workers.

Marinaro, P. & Ness, I. (2019) Introduction: Mexican labour movement in transformation. *Journal of Labor and Society*, 22(1), 5–7.

Menéndez, M. C. G., Almond, P. & Murray, G. (2018) Regional Business Systems and the Governance of Foreign Direct Investment in Canada, Spain and the UK. *Revista Española de Investigaciones Sociológicas (REIS)*, 3(163), 3–20.

Middelbrook, Kevin J. (1995) *The Paradox of Revolution: Labor, the State, and Authoritarianism in Mexico*, Baltimore: JHU Press.

Murray, G., Lévesque, C., Morgan, G., & Roby, N. (2020) Disruption and re-regulation in work and employment: from organisational to institutional experimentation. *Transfer: European Review of Labour and Research*, 26(2), 135–156, 10.1177/1024258920919346.

Ornelas, S. L. (2015) Inside Mexico's Processed Food Industry: Appetizing Potential & Challenging Value Chain Recipe, *MexicoNow*, November–December, https://www.mexico-now.com/index.php/article/20-magazine/editor-main-article/19-inside-mexico-s-processed-food-industry

Robles Cortés, R. (2013) *El Clúster Aeroespacial en Baja California: Diagnóstico y Propuesta metodológica para analizar su evolución y medir el desempeño*, Tesis, Maestría en Administración, Tijuana: Universidad Autónoma de Baja California.

Salinas, J. (2014) *Labor Relations and the Development of the Aerospace Industry in Mexico*. Los Angeles: UCLA Institute for Research on Labor and Employment, University of California.

Schneider, B. R. & Soskice, D. (2009) Inequality in developed countries and Latin America: coordinated, liberal and hierarchical systems. *Economy and society*, 38(1), 17–52.

Simoes, A. & Hidalgo, C. (2018) *OEC: The Observatory of Economic Complexity*, https://atlas.media.mit.edu/en/5

Silver, B. J. (2003) *Forces of Labor: Workers' Movement and Globalization since 1870*. Cambridge: Cambridge University Press.

Soul, J. (2019) Local unions in a transnational movement: the role of Mexican unions in the making of international networks. *Labor and Society*, 22, 25–43.

Toledo, S. E. (2019) El sindicalismo mexicano: ¿hacia un nuevo pacto social? *Economíaunam*, 16(46), 241–250.

Universal (2016, May 9). Una década en la aeronáutica. Retrieved February 26, 2018, from http://www.eluniversalqueretaro.mx/portada/09-05-2016/una-decada-en-la-aeronautica.

Villavicencio, D., Hernández, J. & Souza, L. (2013) Capacidades y oportunidades para el desarrollo de la industria aeronáutica en Querétaro. (dir.) Monica Casalet, Monica La Industria Aeroespacial. Complejidad Productiva E Institucional (The Aerospace Industry. Productive and Institutional Complexity). DF, Mexico: FLACSO and Conacyt, pp. 49–92.

Villarreal, M. A. & Ferguson, I. (2014) *NAFTA at 20: Overview and Trade Effects*. Washington, DC: Congressional Research Service.

Wright, E. O. (2000) Working-class power, capitalist-class interests, and class compromise. *The American Journal of Sociology*, 105(4), 957–1002.

Zukauskaite, E., Trippl, M. & Plechero, M. (2017) Institutional thickness revisited. *Economic Geography*, 93(6), 325–345.

Part IV

The Interconnections between Organisational and Institutional Experimentation

8 An Instance of Tripartite Successful Institutional Experimentation: Dual Vocational Education and Training in Spain

María C. González and Aroa Tejero

Introduction

The aim of this chapter is to analyse an instance of successful institutional experimentation and connected union action via social concertation in a European region (Asturias, Spain) in the context of a national reform that weakened labour power in the workplace and of crisis-induced restrictive funding of employment policies. Specifically, it examines the extent to which the innovative new institution created was a combination of institutional experimentation and inertia.

Sub-national regions in Spain are autonomous communities with substantive self-government in economic matters, particularly on regional development policy and active employment policies. Asturias is a distinctive case within the country in terms of its comparatively high membership of trade unions (predominantly class-based general unions, characteristic of Mediterranean countries) and employers' associations, and in that successive social-democratic regional governments have fostered a dynamic of collaboration and consensus on economic policy with employers and trade unions (González Menéndez et al. 2018). As a result, Asturias has established a coordinated model of socio-economic governance based on employment-focused tripartite social pacts every three or four years since 2000, governing a quarter of the region's budget, and with a high participation of trade unions and employers in tripartite governing boards of key regional institutions such as the Public Employment Services and the Institute for Economic Development.

While social concertation in the region is much wider, the chapter focuses on the development of a program to foster Dual Vocational Education and Training (VET) in 2014/2017. During the 2008–2014 economic crisis, the promotion and improvement of VET became a priority to improve the qualifications and employability of the young population in Spain, at that time facing record levels of unemployment (it peaked in 2013 at 55%). Activating employers to engage with VET and improving VET's perception among prospective students and their families

DOI: 10.4324/9781003001089-12

was at the core of the 2012 national reform that grafted Dual VET onto an education-based system.

In the case under study, a key sector in the regional development strategy in which employers had often voiced concerns about future skill shortages, the metalworking sector, was chosen by the regional unions, employers, and government to carry out an innovative Dual VET experiment. The innovative design of the scheme – targeting low-skilled youth, promoting their being at the workplace from week one, and being paid workers – was the result of negotiation among the parties. Also, all parties combined efforts in attracting prospective student-workers and trainers-employers and in supervising the scheme. Based on interviews with key decision-makers, the chapter will reflect on these and other aspects of design and implementation, on the assessment by the social actors of the scheme's impact on activating the regions' employers and youth to engage with Dual VET, and on the policy learning outcomes.

In a regional context with a high level of institutionalisation of dialogue among trade unions, employers, and government, marked by a generally cooperative attitude, such as can be found in Lombardy in Italy (Locke 1995; Ballarino 2006), trade unions shaped regional policy on VET. The chapter addresses why and how in the discussion section, using the concepts of institutional work (Lawrence et al. 2011; Hampel et al. 2017), trade unions' strategic capabilities (Lévesque and Murray 2010) and associational power (Wright 2000), and triggers and drivers of common knowledge creation (Culpepper 2008).

The Metalworking Sector in Asturias

With 1,155 companies in 2018, the metalworking sector accounted for nearly half of the total industrial employment and 7% of the total employment of the region, as well as for 11% of the GDP and 67.9% of the region´s exports. While most companies are small domestic firms (95%), medium and large firms employ 70% of the sector's workers (FEMETAL 2019a; 2019b). In 2016, 5.6% of total job offers in the region were in the metalworking sector, almost twice the national rate, and the highest in the industrial sector in the region (Adecco 2017). The metalworking sector of Asturias is specialised in the manufacture of metal products (63% of firms), the reparation, manufacture and installation of machinery and equipment (22% of firms) and in the manufacture of other metalworking, electric, and ICT products (FEMETAL 2019a). As to the structure of employment, most of the jobs are skilled, with 53.6% of the new contracts in 2015 requiring upper secondary academic (23%) or vocational (25.2%) education, or a university degree (5.4%) (SEPEPA 2015).

In a region with high trade union membership (31.4% or twice the national average (MESS 2011)) and high employers' associations membership (26.5% in Asturias vs 21.5% in Spain (INE 2018b)), the sector is characterised by a strong trade union membership (mostly the two large confederations, UGT and CCOO, also the most representative unions at national level) and employers' association (FEMETAL), and a long tradition of sectoral-regional collective bargaining. According to one of the main trade unions, CCOO, 38.2% of its membership in Asturias corresponds to the industrial sector, almost twice the national share (20%) (CCOO, Comisiones Obreras 2015). According to the main employers' association, 90% of the metalworking sector firms in Asturias were members of FEMETAL, directly or through another association in 2018 (FEMETAL 2019a). The employer membership rate in the industrial sector for Spain in 2018 was 28.3%, the second highest after Transport (INE 2018b).

The industrial sector overall has high collective bargaining activity. For example, 37.6% of all collective agreements signed in Spain in 2018 and 21.7% of all workers covered by collective agreements signed that year were in the industrial sector (MTMSS 2018). It is also one of the best paying sectors. In 2018, the industrial sector had a mean yearly wage of 30,307 €/year in Asturias, higher than the average for the region and for the country (23,915 €/year and 24,009 €/year, respectively) and higher than the average in the industrial sector at national level (28,097 €/year) (INE 2018a).

In 2017, 25.8% of VET students in the region were enrolled in industrial programs and 22.9% of all VET graduates obtained an industrial-related VET certification (CAFP 2017). The demand of upper secondary VET certified skills in the region expanded rapidly with economic recovery (5.1% in 2014 and 16.6% in 2018 of total job offers required VET certification), as in the country (7.1% in 2014; 17.8% in 2018) (Adecco 2015, 2019). The share of upper secondary students in VET in Asturias (35.6% in 2017/2018; 35.8% in 2019/2020) is above the national average (33.7% and 35.3% same academic years) (MEFP 2021); it is still much lower than the EU's average (48.4% in 2018) (European Commission 2020).

For many years, employers had voiced concerns about an ageing staff and the lack of a skilled industrial workforce to replace it. A report of the regional employment service estimated in 2010 that the average age in the metalworking sector would be 53 by 2015, and that problems to fill in jobs in several occupations, from boiler-makers, welders, machine operators, and mid-level technicians to university graduated engineers were expected (SEPEPA 2010). To adjust and reinforce the supply of training, the report recommended to unify criteria as to the goals and contents of Dual VET among the administration, training providers, and firms (SEPEPA 2010).

Five years later, with the new Dual VET programs underway and in a cycle of economic growth, the problems to fill in posts in the same and some other occupations were still reported by metalworking sector employers; now these were attributed more to the lack of experience of prospective workers, and to an inadequacy of VET programs (both by 47% of employers), than to a lack of trained personnel (43%); employers also voiced a need to recover the apprentice figure so the young could learn from more experienced workers (SEPEPA 2015), all of which could be interpreted as mounting support for Dual VET.

The Dual VET in Asturias

Currently there are three models of Dual VET in Asturias: (1) Labour-based, through the Training and Apprenticeship labour contract, a full-time contract for youth without a VET or university degree for a minimum period of a year and a maximum of three to obtain a professional certification connected to the work carried out and the connected training received in at least 25% of the time in the first year and 15% of the time in subsequent years; (2) Education-based, through a collaboration agreement between training centres and firms of a given industry, with a duration of two or three years and a minimum of 33% of the training hours in firm placements, which can be scholarship-based, conducive to a VET degree; and (3) a combination of both developed in the region (the 2014/2017 experimental program and a subsequent one). The first is nationally regulated. The second is regulated by the regional governments, it is considered experimental by definition and can vary from year to year and from region to region. The third is a variant developed in Asturias at the forefront of experimentation that combines the other two.

The third type, in its first program (2014/2017), focused on a specific business sector (metalworking) and a specific group of youths (aged under 25, neither in employment nor in education, with no degree above compulsory education obtained in the past five years). It enrolled 49 student-workers, 5 Integrated VET centres, and 15 companies in a three-year program of vocational education on Electric and Automatic Installations (11), Electromechanical Maintenance (10), Machining (11), or Welding and Boiler-making (17), with the students working with an employment contract at one of the participating firms from the first week, paid above the sector minimum wage, obtaining an Occupational Aptitude Certificate each year and, at the end, also obtaining a VET full-degree. The young applicants were selected by the participant companies and subscribed to a training and apprenticeship contract for one year with a firms' commitment of renewing yearly for up to three years. The student-workers acquired the training and qualification of one Occupational Aptitude Certificate per year working (three days a week), attending face-to-face classes at VET centres (two days a week), and passing exams. Via distance learning, the student-workers could take and pass some transversal competence units necessary, on top of the three Occupational Aptitude Certificates, to obtain an Intermediate Vocational Training degree.

The Labour- and Education-based Dual VET of Asturias

This section describes the processes of design, implementation, and appraisal of the first labour- and education-based Dual VET program focusing on the role of the social actors. It is the result of interviews carried out in February 2019 with representatives from the trade unions (one from each union), from the regional employer association (one), and representatives of the region's Council of VET (two) who were directly involved in all tripartite negotiations leading to the set-up of the program as well as on its supervision, i.e. from conception to appraisal. It starts by offering a chronology of the negotiations that led to the design and launch of the program, explaining the main issues that created tensions and the positions of all the actors. Then, it briefly covers some salient aspects of implementation, the collaborative tripartite follow-up of the scheme, and the social actors' appraisal of the scheme.

The Making of the Agreement within Social Concertation (2005–2014)

Social actors had been talking about the need for a Dual VET program in the region from 2005 and, according to the CCOO representative, a first proposal, inspired by the experiences of Basque Country, Madrid and the Valencian Community, was put forward by the trade unions in 2007. The first experiments were carried out in 2009/2010 with money from the European Social Fund for employment being devoted to some plans of specific firms (ALSA) and employers' associations (metalworking, ICT, automotive) but social actors thought these programs weak in terms of the professional certification obtained and of the oversight of progress and, in fact, they became very diluted. Yet, these initiatives spurred social actors to work, within the framework of regional social concertation, on draft proposals that would be the basis of the 2014–2017 program. For both unions and employers, social concertation is, in the words of the employers' representative interviewed, 'a crucial forum for dialogue with the government and for information on available funds, giving the social actors a global view of the region's budget'.

The metalworking sector was from then on the focus. The main reasons for this, besides its weight on the regions' employment, were, from the viewpoint of the employers' association, that problems in finding skilled personnel, and the diminishing number of students of VET in the relevant areas were clear by 2011, and that in 2012/2013 production in the sector started to recover from the crisis, which gave impulse to negotiations. The unions also stressed, as further factors, the availability, over several towns, of VET public sector schools providing degrees in occupations required by the metalworking sector, and that it was a sector with a strong collective agreement as an anchor and with interested firms that could offer posts.

Drafts were proposed by the social actors in 2011, in the framework of social concertation, that would be later taken to the newly created tripartite Dual VET Committee, composed of representatives of the trade unions and employers, of the regional labour administration and of the regional education administration. Negotiations would continue for some time afterwards. The negotiations involved technicians of both branches of regional administration and of the VET Council of Asturias, representatives of CCOO and UGT (two from each trade union) and representatives of the employers (two). For the trade unions, a scheme that allowed the students to obtain a degree while in a connected labour contract was a negotiating red line from the beginning. The employers did not specifically contemplate a labour contract, a scholarship with social security would have been an acceptable option.

Then, national regulation in 2012 regulated the two possible types of Dual VET: within the education system (with more hours at the workplace than previously) and within the employment system (via a training and apprenticeship contract requiring no VET or university degree obtained in the past five years). The idea of combining these newly regulated two branches of Dual VET to fit the trade unions' demand was then proposed by the employment administration. The new regulation also allowed firms to provide the education component of VET within their own schools, with little oversight from social partners. Faced with the marketisation of VET provision, trade unions gave even greater importance to strengthening the role of the public education system in the region's VET.

Subsequently, a commitment to a new Dual VET combining the education and labour branches of VET in experimental programs with the participation of government, trade unions, and employers was made explicit in the region's social pact Agreement for the Employment and Progress of Asturias 2013–2015 (GPA 2013), signed in February 2013. However, there was no explicit budget committed since quite tough negotiations were still ongoing and would go on until late in the summer of 2014. The agreement was finally signed by all parties on 8 October 2014 and the program started in November 2014.

The main successive tensions in the negotiation pertained to:

1 Tensions between the industry and education regional administrations as to paying for the education side of the scheme (which meant more hours of teachers, among other costs). This ended when the regional labour administration accepted to pay for the yearly professional certifications (12, eventually, in total) via active labour market employment policies; the education administration would only pay for the transversal modules needed, on top of the three yearly certificates, to obtain the degree (teachers, materials).
2 The labour administration offered to do this if the scheme was connected to the Youth Guarantee (YG), a national youth employment policy, in

turn, connected to a European Commission policy, which meant targeting those not in employment, education, or training. The connection to the YG also allowed the regional employment administration to fund 50% of the labour costs of the employers, specifically the training and apprenticeship contract with the students in the first two years. With the contract, the students would become, at the same time, workers, a non-renounceable demand of the trade unions that saw the scheme as a true opportunity to directly create employment at a time when the focus of employment policies was mostly on providing training for the unemployed.

In combination, the restrictions for participation in the YG (age under 25, without a job and not at training or education) and for entering the training contract (no VET or university degree obtained in the past five years) created a very specific population target: (1) age under 25 with compulsory education completed (2a) without a degree beyond compulsory education or (2b) with a degree obtained five years before, (3) not studying or in training, (3a) unemployed for at least a month, (3b) three months if the last contract had been open-ended, or (3c) six months if the last contract had been temporary. This meant that the most likely profile would be the hardest to reach youth, and both trade unions and employers had serious doubts about this arrangement. First trade unions and then employers eventually chose to see this as an opportunity for labour market inclusion of the most disaffected youth. Employers were particularly concerned as to being expected to keep a labour contract for three years irrespective of the performance of the student-worker. Once agreed with the trade unions that the contract would be as any other as to reasons for dismissal and that it would only be renewed if the student-worker also passed the year exams, the final number of placements rose from the initially foreseen 15 in one occupation, to 60 in four occupations, another trade union demand.

3. At this point of the negotiations, with the regional government elections looming (they were to take place on May 2015), the regional administration was keen on launching the pilot as soon as possible, i.e. for it to start in the academic year 2014/2015. With the employers very much on board, trade unions remained an obstacle. For the trade unions, the 2012 labour reform had radically deregulated and precarized employment and, in that context, they opposed the regional government funding the firms' training contracts. The unions, and particularly CCOO, strongly bargained for a wage for the student-workers above the national minimum wage (645.3€ in 2014) as a condition for signing. The economy was coming out of recession and employers and the regional administration conceded late in the summer of 2014. The student-workers were to be paid as 'specialists', a level 12, then the lowest but for one occupational category in the sector

collective agreement, which did not have at that time an apprentice category as such. All in all, with a wage of around 900 euro per month, the participants would be the best-paid student-workers in Dual VET in Spain, a victory for the regional branches of both trade unions. The agreement was finally signed in the first week of October 2014, after four years of negotiations that had been particularly intense in the latter two. The scheme was to start in November 2014, and it had no precedent in the public sector in Spain. According to a representative of the Council of VET of Asturias, only SEAT, the carmaker, had established something similar previously.

Implementation, Follow-up, and Main Results (2014–2017)

The process of implementation was marked by urgency at the start. All actors collaborated in intense activities of dissemination of the program to attract participants within a month. The employment administration via employment offices reached as many candidates for student-workers as they could at a time that the national YG registry was only starting. This meant there was no available list of prospective candidates and work at the regions' employment agencies was frantic, particularly since most of those contacted as unemployed under 25 did not fulfil other requirements of the YG.

The employers' association informed firms about the funding structure via its webpage and in specific sessions organised with technicians of the employment administration but regretted not having had more time to inform firms on-site. Participating firms also used their web pages to attract candidates. Some, like Thyssen, Daorje, or Daniel Alonso were companies that had always voiced the need for this sort of scheme and did not require convincing. The interviewed representative of UGT and directors of the participating VET schools used their relational networks in convincing some firms to participate. Both unions disseminated information among its members and 'answered many phone calls from parents that had read or heard about it' (CCOO's representative). A newspaper called *La Nueva España* was particularly active in reporting on the Dual VET pilot. All actors became, as a result, very aware of how difficult it was to reach the targeted youth via traditional publicity means, and interested parents often became the bridge to them.

Finally, 15 participant firms did the selection of prospective student-workers among the 150 persons that applied. The selection process fell entirely on the human resource managers of the participant firms with the acquiescence of trade unions, and trade union representatives found no fault with the selection process or its results: the initial number of 60 placements was decreased to 49 by the firms' selection process.

The follow-up committee, of which all negotiating parties were also members, had 14 formal meetings during the program and issued nine follow-up reports (CAFP 2017). It also took many decisions as problems or doubts arose, which involved a lot of informal contacts among the members of the committee, with tutors at the firms and at the training schools, and some informal one-to-one interviews with participating student-workers at risk of dropping out. The first year was fraught with difficulties: six student-workers were fired, four dropped out (some because of being offered another job, although not necessarily for a better one in the long-term in the view of the social partners), and nine were not offered a renewal of the labour contract. As a result, only 11 of the initial 15 firms and 30 of the initial student-workers continued in the program in the second year. In the second year, one student-worker dropped out. In the third and final year, three student-workers were fired, two because of the firm's closure and the other for objective reasons (not arriving on time to work and not attending class). Although at the end of the program 14% of the firms' respondents thought that the program could be improved, appraisal of the program by the participant firms was overall positive (81%), and the firms expected to continue to employ 19 of the 25 student-workers that had fully completed it (a student that started later was left out of this assessment) (CAFP 2017).

Appraisal by the Social Actors and Implications (2019)

All the interviewees expressed a general positive view on the program. There was, however, some disappointment with the direct results, given the economic resources devoted to the scheme and the personal effort put in by all that intervened in it. For the CCOO representative, the most critical, it had become more of a social program than an employment program: 'How many completed it? Around half? If you think of it as a social program, great. Some people with serious labour market inclusion problems did really well and now have a degree and job experience and some even a job. If you think of it as an effective training for employment program, which is what we had in mind, the results are not great. It depends on how you want to see it.' The UGT representative was much more positive: 'I'm in no doubt: it fostered employment in the region.' For the employers' representative, the appraisal of the program was firmly positive: 'Twenty-nine had a degree at the end, and twenty-six of them with an associated labour experience of three years. It also helped firms with recruitment: only six [of the student-workers] were not expected to [be offered to] renew [the labour contract] and for one of the six, the firm [where he had been working] said it may well happen down the line.'

For the unions, expansion of the program to other sectors was an aim in two key aspects: conducive to a degree (two years minimum) and with a wage (not a scholarship). However, immediate followers in the region (meat and automotive sectors) did not follow in the combination with formal education: 'they teach it in their own schools, not in the public system, making money out of it, and give certificates, not a degree'

(UGT representative). This is what the employers' representative termed the labour model: 'a year training contract plus one professional certification.' While the employers' representative supported this as a very valid alternative for some jobs, another interviewee pointed out the disadvantage of taking that route: 'The jobs they can aspire to only with professional certifications will be low in the occupational scheme, and even with three certifications, it will be hard for them to do the remaining units that would lead to a VET degree. They often don't even have the information about the possibility of getting a VET degree' (Council of VET of Asturias representative).

In more general terms, lessons were drawn out from the weaknesses of the first program that informed the approach of all actors to the following program approved for the period 2018–2021. The clearest weakness identified by all actors was the profile of the young participants as to their lack of training. In the words of the employers' representative: 'You need to have a minimum training base. When you get to the workplace you must be able to understand documents, to know something about the machine.' She identified another lesson learnt, that participants need to be already interested in the sector: 'Those that dropped out for another job … they went to sectors such as retail.' She added that the program had given them all a new perspective: 'There is a problem of orientation of the youth: they only get orientation on education options, not on labour options, and that affects their motivation to participate in programs like this one.'

Yet, in its main aspects, the program is to be replicated and can thus be considered a successful case of institutional experimentation. The new program will be carried out in the same sector, with the same occupational profile as to curricula plus two new ones, mechatronics and networked computing systems. Participant firms will repeat again, even if it is most likely that those that took most students will take fewer now: 'The first-year results were seriously demotivating for some firms. Although they value that now the workers will have to study first, they are offering fewer initial placements.' The structure is rather similar to the three-year composition of the scheme and the same as to the weekly distribution of hours between workplace and school. The most important difference here is that the first year will be school-only. Then, in the second year, students can choose to take the labour- and education-based type, which will mean two (instead of one) more years for completing the degree but that will give the students two years of labour experience with it. In the previous program, student-workers gained three years of labour experience while obtaining an intermediate-level VET degree, also gaining firm-specific training that helped them to stay employed in the same firm once they completed the program; in the new program, participants will be students for one year and student-workers for the following two. The follow-up process and supervising committee functions and structure remain similar.

Improvements have been made as to the mechanisms of communication between firms' and schools' tutors, now formalised; the role of tutors at the firm has been strengthened, and training for tutors at the firms will be provided. As to the wage of the student-workers and their occupational classification, trade unions tried to get the same occupational classification and wage level as in the previous program, but the employers association could not commit that firms would do it with a new sectoral collective agreement in place. The new collective agreement now includes a category of 'apprentice', with wage varying with age and increasing from level 15 (16-year-old), to level 14 (17-year-old), and level 13 (18–25-year-old) which participating firms will use. If the student is older than 25, she/he will receive a scholarship. Funding from the labour administration will remain the same as to 50% of the labour costs of firms for two years of the contract, also from YG funds, with the associated much less restrictive condition for student-workers' participation of having been unemployed for at least one day before entering the contract. In the new program, the education administration will pay for all the costs of certification. In fact, this program has been the result of a draft proposal led by the education administration and negotiations proceeded much faster: they started in April 2018 and were nearly finalised by November of the same year.

Discussion: Strategic Associational Capabilities, Institutional Work, and Triggers and Drivers of Common Knowledge Creation

There is little doubt about the influence of trade unions on shaping the program. Its defining characteristics – that the program would be conducive to a full degree (a VET cycle) and that its students would be, at the same time, waged workers – were trade union demands. The program used only public vocational education schools' resources, of particular importance for the trade unions' policy of defence of the public sector, but also for the social democrat regional government. The wage was also higher than in any other scheme in the country, the toughest bargaining issue and finally a concession of both employers and the government to a 'wounded' (by the labour reform) labour movement. Trade unions' capacity to dominantly frame issues in a very unfavourable political and economic national context is remarkable, even when connected to the existing dialogue capabilities of all actors and the social concertation tradition of the region. The sources of such union vigour in experimenting with innovations can be traced back to strategic capabilities (Murray 2017), and trade unions used here all four identified by Lévesque and Murray (2010): intermediating between contending interests to foster collaborative action and activate networks; framing; articulating actions over time and space; and learning.

The sources of trade union power are here both structural and associational (Wright 2000; Lévesque and Murray 2010; Fairbrother et al. 2013).

Structural, because of the high membership in the sector and more generally in the region, and associational, because the two unions presented a common front as to their demands, and because of the very close ties of one of the unions (UGT) to the party in government in the region. The relationship between UGT and the party in government is a two-way street, however, in that the government could also have requested that UGT stood down on the matter of the wage level. The result was likely a combination of several factors: that CCOO was not ready to concede on the wage level issue, the labour unrest that followed the national labour reform, the perception of economic recovery in the industry, and that elections were close.

The program may be seen as a case of multi-actor or collective institutional entrepreneurship (DiMaggio 1988) in that all actors collaborated in creating a new institution (the education- and labour-based VET) that, already with a new program in progress, may well survive the test of time. Yet, for Battilana et al. (2009: 68), social entrepreneurs must initiate *divergent* changes, that is, changes that break with the institutionalised template for organising within a given institutional context. The new institution, although innovative, does not break apart from the institutional logic or shared understanding of the goals to be pursued and how they are to be pursued in the region. In expanding the remit of social concertation to a new area, Dual VET, in the 2013 social pact, the creation of the new Dual VET is better analysed as collaborative *institutional work* of heterogeneous actors concerned with shaping large-scale institutions tied to major social challenges (Hampel et al. 2017) than as a case of institutional entrepreneurship.

Following Culpepper (2008) in that institutional experimentation and common knowledge creation on the basis of ideas that have analytical and distributive appeal to both unions and employers happens when existing institutions are in crisis, and that actors' negotiation preceded the 2012 national regulation introducing Dual VET as such, the main trigger for negotiations was the failure of the extant system of VET to reproduce a numerous enough skilled industrial workforce in the region, and employers' pressures in that regard, supported by ideas on German Dual VET that had been in the imaginary of the social actors since the 1980s (Martin Artiles et al. 2019), that fitted well the social dialogue practices in the metalworking sector. In terms of the drivers that made possible reaching an agreement in support for the new institution, trade unions' associational power was key: it is unlikely that employers on their own would have rallied the support of government to the program. This is an example of the basis for class compromises that Erik Olin Wright (2000) theorised: that high workers' associational power has a positive impact on capitalists' interests and helps them with collective action problems they face. Crisis-induced restrictive funding of active employment policies for youth was the enabling driver of the agreement in that it made it possible to partially fund the new institution via the YG. The high aggregate level of youth unemployment in Europe that gave impulse to the YG was thus more of a trigger (if indirect) for the creation of the new VET institution than the local rate of youth unemployment.

Once the program concluded, and with the relaxation of the conditions for youth participation in the YG, the payoffs associated with different institutional outcomes (labour market inclusion vs employment) also changed (Culpepper 2008). This can be linked to new political challenges social actors and social concertation faced at that time. The results of the 2015 election gave wings to the questioning of social concertation in the region from both the right and the new left parties in parliament, which resulted in the abolition of the advisory Economic and Social Council of Asturias in 2017 (González Menéndez et al. 2018). The changed political climate, along with a 2015 national reform that marketised training services, has eroded the role of social actors as regional and sectoral regulators of the labour market. Maintaining the social democratic practices associated with social dialogue in Europe (Fairbrother et al. 2013), and the power as policymakers the actors derive from them may have led the class-based general unions to accept a lower wage in the second program, and both unions and employers to focus on improving its employment outcomes in a key economic sector for the region and for trade union power.

The degree of experimentation involved in the design of the 2014–2017 Dual VET program by the government, trade unions, and employers was substantive. Connecting the education- and labour-based types of VET was totally new in the public sector in Spain, with only a similar known precedent of a large firm in the private sector, and has not yet been adopted elsewhere in Spain. Although, as in Spain overall (cf. Martin Artiles et al. 2019), replicating the German model was never an explicit objective in Asturias, the result was very similar to German Dual VET but for the absence here of a role for local chambers of commerce in skill certification (cf. Locke and Jacoby 1997).

The new program will not be an exact replica of the first, however. Some aspects have been changed with the goal of improving the proportion of student-workers that obtain the degree and labour experience, i.e. the program's employment outcomes. The actors' policy-learning process with the newly created institution and the changes introduced in a second program to reinforce the institution were also collective endeavours necessary to keep the legitimacy of social concertation and of the social actors' role as regional socio-economic policymakers. Despite the presence of institutionalised and informal channels allowing for cross-learning, explicit policy borrowing among Spanish regions is unusual for political reasons (González-Menéndez et al. 2015). It remains to be seen if the new government of Spain gives national impulse to the combined labour and educational approaches to VET as promoted by the trade unions in Asturias.

References

Adecco (2015) *Informe Infoempleo Adecco. Oferta y demanda de empleo en España 2014.* Madrid: Infoempleo. The Adecco Group. Available at: http://iestatic.net/infoempleo/informe-infoempleo/Informe_Infoempleo_Adecco_2014.pdf (accessed 24 September 2021).

Adecco (2017) *Informe Infoempleo Adecco. Oferta y demanda de empleo en España 2016.* Madrid: Infoempleo. The Adecco Group. Available at: https://iestatic.net/infoempleo/documentacion/Informe-Infoempleo-Adecco-2016.pdf (accessed 24 September 2021).

Adecco (2019) *Informe Infoempleo Adecco. Oferta y demanda de empleo en España 2018.* Madrid: Infoempleo. The Adecco Group. Available at: https://cdn.infoempleo.com/infoempleo/documentacion/Informe-infoempleo-adecco-2018.pdf (accessed 24 September 2021).

Ballarino, G. (2006) Between Institutionalized Concertation and Experimentation. The Regulation of New Forms of Labour in Lombardy. In Regalia, I. (ed.) *Regulating New Forms of Employment. Local experiments and social innovation in Europe.* NY: Routledge, pp. 110–140.

Battilana, J., Leca, B. and Boxembaum, E. (2009) How actors change institutions: towards a theory of institutional entrepreneurship. *The Academy of Management Annals,* 3(1), 65–107.

CAFP, Consejo de Asturias de la Formación Profesional (2017) *Memoria de la Formación Profesional en Asturias.* Oviedo: CAFP.

CCOO, Comisiones Obreras (2015) Afiliación y representación. Madrid: CCOO. Available at: https://www.ccoo.es/0106a77ec7bd5bedca76386125efd507000001.pdf (accessed 24 September 2021).

Culpepper, P. D. (2008) The politics of common knowledge: ideas and institutional change in wage bargaining. *International Organization,* 62(1), 1–33.

DiMaggio, P. J. (1988) Interest and agency in institutional theory. In Zucker, L. (ed.) *Institutional patterns and organizations.* Cambridge, MA: Ballinger, pp. 3–22.

European Commission (2020) *Education and Training Monitor 2020. Spain.* Luxembourg: Publications Office of the European Union. Available at: https://op.europa.eu/en/publication-detail/-/publication/c9527d62-2497-11eb-9d7e-01aa75ed71a1/language-en/format-PDF/source-171316235 (accessed 24 September 2021).

Fairbrother, P., Levesque, C. & Hennebert, M.-A. (2013) Understanding transnational trade unionism. In Fairbrother, P., Levesque, C. & Hennebert, M.-A. (eds.) *Transnational Trade Unionism: Building Union Power.* Routledge: New York, pp. 21–40.

FEMETAL (2019a) *Informe de Actividades 2017–2018.* Asturias: Federación de Empresarios del Metal y Afines del Principado de Asturias, Available at: https://www.femetal.es/ckeditor_assets/attachments/10733/memoriafemetal2019_imp0407web_2.pdf (accessed 24 September 2021).

FEMETAL (2019b) *Informe de Coyuntura Económica y Laboral del Sector Metal de Asturias.* Asturias: Federación de Empresarios del Metal y Afines del Principado de Asturias. Available at: https://www.femetal.es/ckeditor_assets/attachments/13054/informe_de_coyuntura_4t202190_4152.pdf (accessed 24 September 2021).

González-Menéndez, M. C., Guillén, A. M., Cueto, B., Gutiérrez, R., Mato J. & Tejero A. (2015) Barriers to and triggers of policy innovation and knowledge transfer in Spain. *STYLE Working Paper*, WP4.1/ES. CROME. Brighton: University of Brighton. Available at: https://www.style-research.eu/publications/working-papers/ (accessed 24 September 2021).

González Menéndez, M. C., Luque Balbona, D., Pruneda, G. & Almond, P. (2018) Embedding multinational firms in regional business systems: neoliberal and social-democratic models in Spain. *Industrial Relations Journal*, 49(1), 50–68.

GPA, Gobierno del Principado de Asturias (2013) *Acuerdo por el Empleo y el Progreso de Asturias 2013-2015*. Asturias: GPA. Available at: https://www.idepa.es/detalle-publicacion/-/asset_publisher/t2oaIuup7miq/content/acuerdo-por-el-empleo-y-el-progreso-de-asturias-2013-2015 (accessed 24 September 2021).

Hampel, C. E., Lawrence, T. B. & Tracey P. (2017) Institutional Work: Taking Stock and Making it Matter. In Greenwood, R., Oliver, C., Lawrence, T. B. & Meyer, R. E. (eds.) *The SAGE Handbook of Organizational Institutionalism* (2nd Edition). Thousand Oaks, CA: SAGE Publications, pp. 558–590.

INE, Instituto Nacional de Estadística (2018a) *Encuesta Anual de Estructura Salarial*. Madrid: INE.

INE, Instituto Nacional de Estadística (2018b) *Encuesta Anual Laboral*. Madrid: INE.

Lawrence, P. R., Suddaby, R. & Leca, B. (2011) Institutional work: refocusing institutional studies of organization. *Journal of Management Inquiry*, 20(1), 52–58

Lévesque, C. & Murray, G. (2010) Understanding union power: resources and capabilities for renewing union capacity. *Transfer: European Review of Labour and Research*, 16(3), 333–350.

Locke, R. M. (1995) *Remaking the Italian Economy*. Ithaca: Cornell University Press.

Locke, R. M. & Jacoby, W. (1997) The dilemmas of diffusion: Institutional transfer and the remaking of vocational training practices in Eastern Germany, In Turner, L. (ed.) *Negotiating the New Germany: Can Social Partnership Survive?* Ithaca: ILR Press, pp. 33–68.

Martin Artiles, A., Barrientos, D., Moles Kalt, B. & Lope Peña, A. (2019) Política de formación dual: discursos con Alemania en el imaginario. *Política y Sociedad*, 56(1), 145–167.

MEFP, Ministerio de Educación y Formación Profesional (2021) Alumnado matriculado en Enseñanzas de Régimen General. *Estadísticas de Enseñanzas no Universitarias*. Madrid: MEFP.

MESS, Ministerio de Empleo y Seguridad Social (2011) *Encuesta de Calidad de Vida en el Trabajo. Año 2010*. Madrid: MESS. Available at: https://www.mites.gob.es/estadisticas/ecvt/ecvt2010/index.htm (accessed 24 September 2021).

MTMSS, Ministerio de Trabajo, Migraciones y Seguridad Social (2018) *Estadística de convenios colectivos de Trabajo 2018*. Madrid: MTMSS. Available at: https://www.mites.gob.es/estadisticas/cct/welcome.htm (accessed 24 September 2021).

Murray, G. (2017) Union renewal: what can we learn from three decades of research? *Transfer: European Review of Labour and Research*, 23(1), 9–29.

SEPEPA, Servicio Público de Empleo del Principado de Asturias (2010) *Estudio ocupacional del sector del metal en el Principado de Asturias. Informe de resultados del sector metal 2010*. Asturias: Consejería de Industria y Empleo del Principado de Asturias. Available at: https://www.asturias.es/RecursosWeb/trabajastur/Actualizaci%C3%83%C2%B3n%20Metal%202010.pdf (accessed 24 September 2021).

SEPEPA, Servicio Público de Empleo del Principado de Asturias (2015) *Estudio ocupacional del sector del metal en el Principado de Asturias. Informe de resultados del sector metal 2015.* Asturias: Consejería de Industria y Empleo del Principado de Asturias. Available at: https://trabajastur.asturias.es/documents/36440/57148/Metal_Actualizacion_2015.pdf/0d77c3a7-4946-d6b5-f098-b7c7a840cf0c?t=1589198749071 (accessed 24 September 2021).

Wright, E. O. (2000) Working-class power, capitalist-class interests, and class compromise. *American Journal of Sociology*, 105(4), 957–1002.

9 From Organisational to Institutional Experimentation in the Montreal Aerospace Industry: Understanding the Role of Trade Union Strategic Capabilities

Christian Lévesque, Cassandra Bowkett, Marc-Antonin Hennebert, and Lucie Morissette

Introduction

This chapter seeks to understand how actors are involved in organisational and institutional experimentation for the development of inclusive and democratic governance at the regional level. It puts a special focus on a regional trade union body in the aerospace industry in Montreal, District 11, affiliated with the IAMAW (International Association of Machinists and Aerospace Workers). Several chapters in the book examine how power dynamics are shaping the processes of experimentation at the regional level. This chapter aims to contribute to this endeavour by analysing how trade union involvement in these processes of organisational and institutional experimentation intersects with the deployment of trade union strategic capabilities.

Over a 40-year period, actors in the Montreal aerospace industry, with trade unions in the foreground, have been engaged in the co-construction of regional governance mechanisms to deal with uncertainties and problems confronting the industry. They have developed various intermediating organisations, provided collective resources, and fostered the development of strong networks between various actors. This process of organisational experimentation has led gradually to a process of institutional experimentation where actors develop new rules, norms, and frames that diffuse new collective habits of thinking and acting.

The chapter draws on a database of 100 interviews conducted with a variety of actors in the Montreal aerospace industry, including workplace and industrial trade union representatives, managers, government officers and representatives from public and private organisations. Interviews were conducted between 2005 and 2019 with peaks in 2008–2009 and 2015–2019 to capture the main features and challenges of the industry, the initiatives and organisations implemented to deal with these challenges, the

DOI: 10.4324/9781003001089-13

trade union responses and involvement in the experimentation processes, and the strategic capabilities they have deployed.

Our aim is to contribute to the debates on the process of experimentation for the development of inclusive and democratic governance at the regional level by linking two strands of literature. First, we build on institutional theories (Kristensen and Morgan 2012; Murray et al. 2020) to gain more insight into the differences between organisational and institutional experimentation. We propose that organisational experimentation refers to a process where social actors seek to modify or renew their resources, networks, and alliances. In comparison, institutional experimentation involves a collective process where new rules, norms, and frames are scaled up, and spread new habits of thinking and acting amongst actors. Second, we seek to contribute to the literature on the role of trade unions at the regional level (Barton 2018; Bosch and Schmitz-Kießler 2020; Barton and Fairbrother 2014) by showing how the engagement of trade unions in processes of experimentation with regional governance requires the mobilisation of specific capabilities, in particular their capacity to create a shared meaning and vision (framing capabilities), to link and connect actors and institutions across various levels (articulating capabilities), to arbitrate and reconcile conflicting interests (mediating capabilities), and to learn from their own experience and that of others so that they can position themselves in the present and anticipate the future (learning capabilities) (Lévesque and Murray 2010).

The chapter is divided into four sections. First, we set out the main lines of our analysis and discuss the concepts which have guided our research. Second, we describe the composition of the Montreal aerospace industry. This is followed by an analysis of the processes of experimentation over four decades. We then explore the implications of our results for a more complex understanding of the transition from organisational to institutional experimentation through the mobilisation of strategic capabilities. The conclusion outlines the main findings and avenues for future research.

The Role of Trade Unions in Processes of Experimentation at the Regional Level

There is a growing body of research that highlights the importance of regional institutions as a source of social and economic development (Coe et al. 2008; Zukauskaite et al. 2017; Rutherford et al. 2018). The capacity to attract investment and preserve 'good jobs' resides increasingly in institutional arrangements at the regional level. These institutions provide various resources such as R&D infrastructure, networks of suppliers, and local labour pools (Torre and Rallet 2005; Coe et al. 2008). They also provide actors with an aggregate of norms and practices that may help them to cope with uncertainties (Crouch et al. 2009). These norms and practices stimulate and stabilise communication and cooperation between firms, trade unions, schools, universities, research and development facilities, and political and administrative actors (Heidenreich 2005).

Union engagement with forms of regional governance presupposes the capacity to act. Crouch's (2005) work puts much emphasis on the varieties of norms and practices within a given national context and notes how this degree of variety allows actors to undertake a 'bricolage' of new institutions by recombining existing ones. This approach injects agency into institutional analysis and considers that institutions establish a set of constraints on, as well as opportunities and resources for, actors as they seek to modify existing institutions. These institutions can limit prospects for change by constraining actors, locking them into particular path-dependent repertoires of action and constraining the range of their future options. However, these same institutions can also facilitate agency and be mobilised to reshape patterns of relationships and actor behaviour. Kristensen and Morgan (2012) propose a theory of co-constitution of institutions and actors where actors are continuously developing and adapting institutions to cope with uncertainties. More specifically, they develop the notion of experimental institutions to depict such forms of change processes. Herrigel (2012, 2018) also places much emphasis on the capacity of actors to creatively and reflexively experiment with institutions to cope with uncertainties.

In relation to experimentation, it is necessary to distinguish between two types: organisational and institutional (Murray et al. 2020). Organisational experimentation refers to a process where social actors seek to modify or renew their resources, networks, and alliances, while institutional experimentation refers to a process where new understanding, norms, and rules are scaled up and institutionalised over time. Drawing on the work of Dewey (1991), Garneau (2021) suggests that a constitutive dimension of institutional experimentation is the development of new habits of thinking and acting. This mirrors the work of Bourdieu on habitus, which he defines as to set of arrangements, schemes of action and perceptions acquired through social experience (Bourdieu, 1994). Through their socialisation and social trajectories, individuals incorporate an enduring way of thinking, feeling, and acting. Dewey (1991) believed in the power of collective social intelligence to transform ideas and patterns of behaviour and relationships. Institutional experimentation, in contrast to organisational experimentation, thus involves a collective process where new rules, norms, and frames scale up and spread new habits of thinking and acting amongst actors.

The uncertainties caused by economic restructuring, the reconfiguration of global production networks, and the adoption of disruptive technologies have compelled trade unions to experiment with new repertoires of action and narratives at the regional level. This process, however, is contested and uneven. In his study of Western Australia Pilbara iron mining, Ellem (2003) shows how industry restructuring has prompted the trade union to create a new internal organisational structure and to redefine its role in relation to the safeguarding of the community. Barton's (2018) work on the mining sector in Tasmania concretely shows how the trade union was able to renew its narrative and mobilise community support. She highlights that the union had the capacity to frame a new narrative around work, place, and landscape by engaging with community unionism. Barton and Fairbrother (2014) in their study of trade union strategies in response to plant closure and redundancies by two multinational corporations in Northwest Tasmania show, however, that trade unions can also be locked into past patterns. They argue that both trade unions were unable to renew their repertoires of action and their power resources and strategic capabilities, leading them to reproduce the same repertories and narratives.

The partners involved in such experimentation are varied. Bosch and Schmitz-Kießler (2020) examine how IG Metall, the German metalworkers' union, has leveraged existing rules of codetermination and works councils, to shape the adoption of Industry 4.0 (I4.0). The union partnered with both traditional (works councils) and non-traditional actors (management consultants) to set up an experimental pilot project involving workers in the design and implementation process and is working to develop an industry union response to I4.0. Rutherford and Frangi (2020) in their study of the process of implementation of I4.0 in the Canadian auto industry in Southern Ontario also show how some local union representatives from UNIFOR have developed more experimental approaches. They have not only negotiated with plant managers via traditional procedures such as technological change language in workplace agreements, but also by using plant-level mechanisms such as health and safety committees, to shape or modify work organisation practices.

The state can be an important actor in the process of regional governance. Rutherford et al. (2018) in their study of two sub-regions in Canada show that local experimentation has produced dense private and public networks working with provincial and federal governments to attract and retain multinational corporations (MNCs). They argue that the role of trade unions in these processes in terms of skill development is far more important in Quebec than in Ontario. Haddow (2015) argues that the two provinces have followed different patterns of development, leading to distinct social and economic policy choices. For instance, whereas Ontario has developed a firm-centric approach, Quebec relies more heavily on a concerted form of interest intermediation between various stakeholders.

These studies provide insight into how trade unions are experimenting with new repertoires of action and narratives and on their engagement in the co-construction of regional governance. In this chapter we seek to analyse the interconnection between trade union engagement in these processes of experimentation with regional governance and the deployment of trade union strategic capabilities. It is our contention that trade union engagement in this process of experimentation is intertwined with four strategic capabilities: framing, intermediating, articulating, and learning

(Lévesque and Murray 2010). *Framing capabilities* refers to the ability to craft frames of reference that define and legitimate repertoires of action. These frames can be more or less inclusive and may be part of a broader social project. Framing involves the connection of events and experiences and the process through which these are highlighted or excluded. *Mediating capabilities* entail reconciling contending interests, fostering collaborative action and accessing, creating and activating salient social networks by managing the interface between individuals or groups (or organisations). A context where substantial rescaling is occurring requires *articulating capabilities:* the ability to make links between different levels of action across time and space. *Learning capabilities* concern the ability within the union to learn and to diffuse that learning. Learning involves an ability to foster, reflect on, and build on past and current experiences. Through this analysis, we seek to show that the transition from organisational to institutional experimentation requires that actors, in our case trade unions, activate and mobilise these four strategic capabilities.

The Montreal Aerospace Industry

Prior to the COVID-19 pandemic, which had a devastating impact on the airline and aerospace industries, Montreal, together with Toulouse and Seattle, was one of the world's three aerospace capitals. In 2019, approximately 185 aerospace companies were operating in Quebec, and they have generated $17.8 billion in annual sales (Ministère de l'Économie et de l'Innovation Québec [MEIQ], 2020). The aerospace industry is important, not only because it is a large contributor of GDP, but also because the industry makes large investments in innovation activities. As an industry, Canadian aerospace's R&D intensity has remained significantly high – at least 15% more than the manufacturing average of 3% since 2014 (Lévesque et al. 2021: 16–17).

The Montreal cluster specialises in aeronautics, with production concentrated in the construction of business and regional planes, civilian helicopters, small turbine engines, and simulators (CAMAQ 2020). The cluster's structure has the pyramid shape typical of the industry. It is organised around three OEMs (Airbus, Bombardier, Bell Helicopter), more than a dozen Tier 1 system integrators (e.g. CAE and Pratt & Whitney) and a larger number (around 170) of small and medium-sized enterprises (SMEs) integrated into local and global supply chains (MEIQ 2020).

With over 40,000 jobs, aerospace is one of the most important manufacturing industries in Quebec. As of 2019, roughly 28% of these employees are scientific staff, 16% are technicians, 13% are administrative employees, and 42% are production workers (CAMAQ 2020). It is a highly skilled industry, with nine out of ten production workers having a qualified trade (CAMAQ 2020: 7). A third of these employees, mainly production workers, are unionised. About two-thirds of these workers are part of the

IAMAW and 30% of UNIFOR. Roughly 80% of the workers are men. Women comprise 21% of the workforce, but these employees are mainly (80%) concentrated in administration. Women represent only 12% of the workforce in trades and roughly 20% of both scientific and technical staff (Comité sectoriel de main-d'œuvre en aérospatiale au Québec CAMAQ 2016). There are several studies documenting that, even in fields with skill scarcity, women and immigrants face barriers to entry (Braham and Tobin 2020; Ng and Gagnon 2020).

The industry is also characterised by an ageing workforce, with an average age of around 45 years (Comité sectoriel de main-d'œuvre en aérospatiale au Québec CAMAQ 2016). This is partially correlated to the difficulty of attracting a younger generation of workers into Canadian aerospace. Prior to the COVID-19 pandemic, demand for labour outstripped supply in the industry, resulting in labour shortages in many occupations. According to the two dominant trade unions, IAMAW and UNIFOR, this trend is exacerbated by the fact that firms are often recruiting experienced workers, as opposed to young people via apprenticeships. Both trade unions argue that the recruitment of younger workers is problematic and requires the provision of good, stable jobs with meaningful work. To address this issue, they have been pressuring the federal government to develop a national strategy addressing the future of Canadian aerospace (IAMAW 2019; UNIFOR 2016). However, the aerospace industry does have several qualities that make it attractive to workers, as it is a high-tech industry that offers competitive salaries. In 2016, average hourly earnings were roughly 40% higher than the Canadian average (UNIFOR 2016).

The Process of Experimentation in the Montreal Aerospace Industry

One of the distinctive features of the Montreal aerospace cluster is its thick institutional architecture. Montreal has as many as ten international bodies involved in the aerospace industry, such as the International Civil Aviation Organization and the International Business Association Council. The cluster is also structured around several regional intermediary organisations that provide stakeholders with various resources. These regional intermediating organisations benefit from government financial support even though firms and other organisations, such as trade unions, contribute either financially or in kind.

This section describes the evolution of processes of experimentation in the Montreal aerospace industry over more than four decades, with a special focus on trade union engagement in these processes. We distinguish three phases of experimentation (1980–1994, 1995–2010, 2011–2019) and highlight the repertoires of action and strategic capabilities developed by the IAMAW during each phase of experimentation. Table 9.1 describes for

Table 9.1 Evolution of the Processes of Experimentation

	Experimenting with joint governance organisations (1970–1994)	*Building thick governance organisations (1995–2010)*	*Experimenting with new institutions (2011–2019)*
Main feature of the industry	State-owned enterprises, with a few large American companies Unions well implemented in large firms Employment in Canada drops from 48,000 employees in 1967 to 20,000 in 1990	Development of a network of large private companies and parts suppliers with Bombardier playing an anchor role played by Bombardier September 2001 and 2008 financial crisis Development of the C-series Growth of employment: 40,000 in 2010	Reduction in the number of suppliers Deployment of the global value chain. Acquisition of the C-Series by Airbus Stabilisation of employment. Labour shortage
Uncertainties and challenges	Shortage of skilled labour and a sharp decline in employment	Coordination within and between organisations and collective actors	Supply chain and SME capabilities
Regional governance intermediaries	Creation of union-management committees to develop a skilled workforce (CAMAQ)	Creation of various intermediaries' organisations (e.g. AQA, CRIAQ, District 11, Aéro Montréal)	Consolidation of various networks and development of new activities, programs, and rules (e.g. plant visits, MACH, MACH-FAB)
Machinist Union responses and involvement	Collective bargaining Lobbying to safeguard employment and to increase workforce skills Co-construction of joint governance intermediary organisation	Building regional union organisation Co-construction of regional skill infrastructure	Engagement in new areas (organisation of the value chain, technical innovation). Building transnational alliances Political mobilisation
Strategic capabilities • Framing • Articulating • Mediating • Learning	Capacity to advance a common frame about skill development Capacity to articulate skill issues at the workplace and regional scales Mediating labour-management conflicts at the workplace level Investing in a new domain (skill) at a new scale (region)	Capacity to develop a common vision of the industry Capacity to articulate the interest of various stakeholders Mediating the tensions between flexibility and security Integrating a plurality of interests	Capacity to frame an industrial policy for the industry Capacity to articulate employment and industrial policy issues Mediating workers short- and long-term interests Navigating across multiple scales

each period the main features of the industry, the main challenges and uncertainties, the regional governance organisations and initiatives implemented,[1] the trade union responses and involvement in these experimentation processes, and the strategic capabilities they have deployed.

Phase 1: Experimenting with Joint Regional Governance Organisation (1980–1994)

In the early 1970s, the aerospace industry was dominated by a few large integrated foreign MNCs such as General Dynamics and United Aircraft. As in many countries at the end of the 1960s and the beginning of the 1970s, Quebec experienced major social and industrial conflicts in both public and private sectors (Rouillard 2004). In the aerospace industry, the long and bitter United Aircraft strike involving the United Auto Workers (UAW) lasting almost 22 months came to symbolise workers' struggle for union recognition rights at the factory level (Gindin 1995).

During this decade, the entire aerospace industry was in sharp decline. In Canada, employment dropped from 48,000 employees in 1967 to 25,000 in 1976 (Zhegu 2007). At Canadair, from 1970 to 1972, about 4,000 hourly employees were laid off so that by 1972, fewer than 1,000 workers were employed in the bargaining unit and the number remained below this level until 1976 (Peach 1982). Following pressure from various trade unions, including the IAMAW, the federal government intensified its direct investment and bought Canadair in 1976, which was then acquired by Bombardier in 1986. In terms of employment, the industry was confronted by two contradictory trends: on the one hand, a sharp decline in employment, on the other, a shortage of a qualified workforce at various levels (machinists, technicians, and engineers) which forced companies to recruit qualified employees from abroad.

The IAMAW and other unions pressured the federal government to create a joint union-management committee, which became CAMAQ in 1982 (Comité sectoriel de main-d'oeuvre en aérospatiale). Throughout the 1980s, this joint union-management committee was the primary locus of coordination within the industry. The joint committee comprised the main trade unions in the industry (IAMAW and UAW) and HR directors of major firms. The work done through CAMAQ has enlarged the trade union network within the aerospace industry and with actors in the education and training system. As highlighted by one union representative, trade union involvement in CAMAQ gave them the opportunity to address aerospace issues from a different perspective:

> We had good discussions at CAMAQ. Me, I liked it because I took off my label of trade union representative. I was more looking at the whole context of the aerospace industry in Quebec. How we can gain more work in Quebec and shape the debates within firms.
>
> (Union representative, Quebec Machinist Union)

In the mid-1990s, the survival of CAMAQ was put into question when the federal government withdrew its financial support to this form of joint committee. The Quebec provincial government stepped in and decided to consolidate the joint union-management committee in the aerospace industry and to expand them across a larger number of industries. In 1989, several universities collaborated with industry to launch a master's degree in aerospace. This program, coordinated by CAMAQ, currently includes six universities. In 1994, under the leadership of CAMAQ, a specialised school for the aerospace industry was founded (École des métiers de l'aérospatiale de Montréal – EMAM) with the objective of creating a pool of qualified tradesmen for industry based on the school to factory principle. With these actions, CAMAQ consolidated the portfolio of specialised training from high school, to college, through to university. It has also developed various tools (for example, annual surveys) and services to track and anticipate the evolution of the labour market in the industry.

Even though IAMAW participated in the co-construction of a governance structure for the industry and in the development of training programs, it nevertheless remained strongly anchored at the local level. During this period, the focus was on its role as a bargaining agent and ensuring the application of the collective agreement. In large firms, it practised a form of job control unionism with detailed collective agreements to limit the rights of management and the discretion of managers on the shop floor. Occasionally, the trade union experimented with new forms of bargaining. This was the case at Canadair where the union and management negotiated an improvement productivity plan as early as 1968. The trade union had the capacity to mediate tensions at the workplace level and, at the turn of this period, had begun to frame employment issues at the industry level around skill upgrading. By enlarging this frame and connecting it to skill upgrading, the trade union was able to position itself as a key interlocutor.

During this phase, the IAMAW remained largely centralised at the Canadian level but more fragmented at the local level. The absence of a trade union intermediary structure in Quebec gave much leeway to business agents and union representatives at the factory level, particularly in large firms. There was little coordination between the various bargaining units, which remained relatively autonomous, and they conducted their work independently from one another.

Phase 2: Building Thick Governance Organisations (1995–2010)

This period was characterised by the consolidation of the Montreal aerospace industry. Employment grew steadily from roughly 23,000 jobs in 1997 to 40,000 in 2010 even though the industry went into crisis after 11 September 2001. According to Zhegu (2007), this steady growth was not only linked to investment from existing firms, but also to new entrants such as Bell

Helicopter and subsidiaries of foreign MNCs specialised in various segments. By the mid-2000s, the industry was structured around two major players (Bombardier and Bell Helicopter), a dozen integrators and 160 suppliers.

This period is also characterised by the increased density of intermediary organisations within the industry. In 1997, an employer association, AQA, was established to give a voice to SMEs and strengthen their position within the industry and vis-à-vis large firms. A consortium (CRIAQ) was founded in 2002 to foster more collaboration between MNCs, SMEs, and universities. This collaborative, open model of innovation was supported financially by industry, universities, and government, and sought to enhance the competitive position of the aerospace industry in Quebec.

In the mid-1990s under pressure from the International and Canadian union leaders of the IAMAW, District 11 was founded, which will be referred to as the Quebec Machinist Union. The creation of this intermediary structure regrouping the majority of local unions in the aerospace industry in greater Montreal was not an easy task. There was significant scepticism and resistance, particularly from the larger locals, which were self-sufficient. This intermediary structure reinforced the actions of the Machinist Union at the regional and industry levels. First, it fostered the conditions for more fairly distributing the financial resources across the various locals particularly towards smaller units. These smaller locals could thus rely not only on financial resources but also on technical expertise that was often lacking. Second, it favoured the creation of a deliberative space where representatives from large and small units could exchange information and share best practices. This deliberative space was also instrumental in the development of a common vision and policy for the industry. Machinist Union leaders were learning how to integrate a plurality of interests.

In 2006, Aéro Montréal was founded at the instigation of large companies with government support to represent the entire industrial cluster. Until then, CAMAQ was considered a major actor in the industry and trade unions through this joint committee were also considered as an essential interlocutor. Aéro Montréal includes all the industry's stakeholders (companies, training institutions, trade unions, government agencies, representatives from CAMAQ and CRIAQ) with a view to promoting dialogue, representing the cluster, and ensuring a common vision. The implementation of Aéro Montréal has led to a redefining of relations between the actors and organisations within the industry, as this interlocutor from Aéro Montréal points out:

> At first it was difficult because, well, Aéro Montréal arrived … CRIAQ existed, CAMAQ existed … then we tell them: 'Well there, come with us on the ice rink.' You know, at first, people didn't like it. Especially since we have the decision makers … [and] they do not have these people on their boards.
>
> (Representative, Aéro Montréal)

Out of the 35 members of the Board of Directors at Aéro Montréal, one is dedicated to a trade union representative from the Machinist Union and another to a representative of the Fonds de solidarité FTQ, a trade union pension vehicle protecting and promoting employment through risk-capital financing. Obviously, in comparison with the board of CAMAQ, which operates on a parity basis between employer and union representatives, it is more difficult for the trade union to influence decision-making processes. And yet, the participation of the Machinist Union in the Board of Directors of Aéro Montréal has opened up space for the trade union to not only voice their concerns, but also to participate in discussions related to strategic decisions concerning public policies in the industry, support for technological change and the upgrading of the value chain. At the turn of this period, the Quebec Machinist Union was fully engaged in regional governance (CAMAQ and Aéro Montréal), creating its own structure to act more efficiently at this scale, and developing a more encompassing vision of the industry.

Machinist Union leaders were engaged in intense bargaining with Bombardier's management to obtain the assembly of a new aircraft, the C-Series. There was intense international competition between the various sites of Bombardier to obtain the mandate to assemble these new aircraft. There was also intense negotiation with members of the union because it involved the reopening of the collective agreement in order to introduce flexible work rules. The leaders had to arbitrate between employment and flexibility on both short- and long-term horizons. The Machinist Union leaders were able to frame a proposition that articulated the promotion of local employment with Bombardier's requirements to attain cost savings through the outsourcing of segments of production to lower-cost locations. These union leaders were able to situate their proposition over a long-time horizon and to mediate between contending interests. Montreal finally secured the mandate to assemble the C-Series.

Over this period, various actors within the Montreal cluster have built a thick organisational infrastructure at the regional level. Each industry-intermediating organisation (Aéro Montréal, CAMAQ, CRIAQ) is relatively autonomous, but they do operate in a complementary and coordinated way. Each of these organisations develops their own projects independently, while also engaging in joint projects, depending on the issue at stake. This institutional diversity has created space for the involvement of a variety of actors: from large firms to SMEs, to trade union representatives, and research and education organisations. Power is not distributed evenly among the various actors, yet actors such as trade unions and SME representatives have a voice and can influence the course of events.

Phase 3: Experimenting with New Institutions (2011–2019)

During this period, employment in the aerospace industry stabilised at around 40,000 employees even though the number of firms declined. This was in part related to large firms' strategies to outsource activities previously carried out internally and to reduce the number of suppliers. SMEs were under pressure to integrate more complex processes and functions, and to strengthen their position within global value chains. SME suppliers had to set up more sophisticated management systems, adopt new production techniques such as 'lean production', and engage in partnerships with contractors and manufacturers. However, very few SMEs were able to rise to that challenge. Most of them were not very well structured. Their activities were concentrated around an entrepreneur who had the necessary technical capacity but had not always developed managerial skills.

There was a common understanding amongst the various stakeholders in the industry, including trade unions, that SMEs alone could not meet these challenges. By themselves, SMEs lacked the resources, skills, capabilities, and often the mindset necessary to upgrade their capabilities and collaborate with large firms on various projects. Several actors and organisations, in particular Aéro Montréal and CAMAQ, developed new resources, programs, and activities that gradually changed the rules of the game and led to the development of new ways of thinking and acting in the industry. CAMAQ was involved in improving human resource management practices among firms through an initiative encouraging sharing and disseminating best practices. This initiative was designed to promote the sharing of concrete experiences and the transfer of innovative practices between firms, while also facilitating networking among SMEs. One manager from an SME acknowledged how the sharing of concrete experiences was beneficial:

> But there's not an idea that can exist without being fuelled by what other companies are doing. As I mentioned, the visit to [redacted name of SME] really gave us ideas on how to do that, because they even suggested some kind of partnership.
>
> (SME, Manager)

Aéro Montréal has created programs targeting SMEs, such as the MACH/ MACH Fab 4.0 programs, to increase their management capabilities and to promote the adoption of new technology. These programs have included an auditing process and control mechanisms to ensure that SMEs participating in the programs comply with the new standards, which include new work organisation, human resource, and management practices. Roughly 70 SMEs have been involved in these programs and, as highlighted by this manager, they were a game-changer in the industry.

> For the last ten years, as I explained to you, it has been easier to share some things, because [before] we wanted to keep everything to ourselves, and we didn't want to share. But we realize that the competition is not between us. It's really global, and we can help each other. I think MACH had a lot to do with it.
>
> (SME, Manager)

During this period, Machinist Union leaders also gradually changed their ways of thinking and acting. They had to deal with offshoring issues that had important impacts on employment in the region. Bombardier opened a facility in Mexico to manufacture electrical harnesses and structural components. Initially, the facility employed 800 workers but by 2017 it had 3,000 workers. The transfer of jobs to Queretaro created significant frustration and complaints on the shop floor but the leader of the trade union argued that it was the only way to save jobs in the long run. This was, however, a hard sell:

> Bombardier is going to send manual, low-cost business there [Mexico], that's going to save more money, but there is some business (expertise) they can only do here. If I say, no, no, I'm against change, I want to build 100% of the plane, I'll do 100% of nothing or 50% of the 2,500 copies they'll sell in China or Russia. You have to have a vision that is unfortunately not shared by the people working every day on the factory floor. You have to look and explain where we're headed with all this.

The decision to invest in Mexico was not only criticised on the shop floor because it had a clear impact on the level of employment but by the trade union leaders who questioned the firm's strategy. According to union leaders, Bombardier was transferring training and education programs and know-how to Mexico. In their own words, Bombardier was exporting 'our institutional competitive advantage' built over a 30-year period.

In early 2015 when Bombardier encountered serious financial problems, the union leaders stepped up to support the company and put pressure on both levels of government, provincial, and federal, for financial support to save the firm. Once again, union leaders were walking a thin line since the rank and file and more generally the public opinion was very critical towards Bombardier's management and further government support.

Machinist Union leaders have also extended their repertoire of action at the international level. Drawing on the experience of several global works councils (e.g. Rolls Royce), the Quebec Machinist Union has been instrumental in creating forums that seek to bring together all local and industrial unions of Bombardier. The leaders have developed strong ties with a variety of unions in Europe and in North America and these ties are collaborative, despite the obvious competition between sites to obtain new product mandates. The acquisition of the C-series by Airbus in 2017 compelled the district to further invest in international alliances with various trade unions representing Airbus workers in Europe. In spring 2018, Machinist Union leaders organised a tour of various facilities in Europe to exchange and open channels of communication with European trade unionists. This initiative was widely diffused both within and outside the Machinist Union and was considered to be an essential part of their strategy:

> Despite the fact that our unions operate in different environments, we have found that we have many issues in common and that collaboration between our unions has become essential to the pursuit of our demands. This alliance currently includes unions from the two largest aerospace clusters in the world with Montreal and Toulouse, which is unheard of in this sector.
>
> (Machinist Union leader)

This first encounter was followed later that year by a three-day meeting in Montreal between the Machinist Union and representatives from 'Force ouvrière', which represents roughly 60% of the unionised workers at Airbus plants in France. Following these meetings, both trade unions formalised their alliance and Airbus accepted the enlargement of its European work council to include representatives from the Quebec Machinist Union. Since then, the union leaders have increased communication and exchanges with European trade unions. These meetings and site tours in Europe gave the Machinist Union representatives the opportunity to learn more about labour relations systems and trade union practices in Europe, and to better understand the challenges and strategies of several aerospace MNCs. These meetings and visits also allowed the union representatives to see that aerospace companies in Montreal were lagging behind their counterparts in the implementation of new technologies, particularly in relation to I4.0.

Even though the Machinist Union has strengthened its international links, it is still committed to increasing the quality of jobs through strong collective agreements and labour standards and seeking to frame narratives in new areas such as technological innovation and the coordination of the value chain. It has started to build on the idea that value chain weakness, lack of technological investments and firm inefficiencies are as much a challenge for workers and trade unions as they are for management. In 2019, the Quebec Machinist Union contributed to the IAMAW aerospace national strategy report for the development of the Canadian industry. This report outlines the trade union vision for the industry and puts forward a series of recommendations on R&D, labour, training and education, financing, and cluster policy development (IAMAW 2019). According to a representative from CAMAQ:

> In the last ten to fifteen years, I've seen the role of the unions change, and now they really want to be partners in their own way, you know, with the issues of the workers they represent, but with the desire to keep an industry that is strong. To find solutions.
>
> (Representative, CAMAQ)

Over the last decade, the Machinist Union has learned to navigate across multiple scales, to mediate between contending interests, to bring together workplace trade unionists from different sites and to connect their needs, and to frame a clear vision about the development of the industry.

Understanding the Role of Trade Union Strategic Capabilities in the Transition from Organisational to Institutional Experimentation

The description of each period shows that actors in the Montreal aerospace industry have been engaged in the co-construction of regional governance architecture to deal with the changing uncertainties and problems confronting the industry. They have developed various intermediary organisations, provided collective resources through a number of programs, and fostered the development of strong networks between a number of actors. This process of organisational experimentation has led to a process of institutional experimentation where actors develop new collective habits of thinking and acting. Firms, trade unions, and representatives from intermediary organisations have gradually changed their way of thinking about the industry and have put more emphasis on the creation of collective goods. Even though there are still many tensions and conflicts between the various stakeholders, there is also greater space for collaboration between actors in various fields. Actors are incorporating an enduring way of thinking and acting through a process of collective intelligence (Dewey 1991) where actors they collectively solve the problems they are confronted with.

The Quebec Machinist Union has played an important role in these processes of organisational and institutional experimentation for the development of inclusive and democratic governance at the regional level. Through its involvement in intermediary organisations, particularly CAMAQ and Aéro Montréal, the union was able to participate in the development of policies and programs aimed at the whole industry. This includes union participation in initiatives to foster skill upgrading for various categories of employees but also in new areas, such as R&D and supply chain development. The Machinist Union also developed its own intermediary structure in Quebec to expand exchanges and links between workplace unions and was actively involved in the creation of company works councils and international alliances, giving the trade union a global reach.

The involvement of the Machinist Union in these processes of experimentation intertwines closely with the deployment of strategic capabilities (mediating, articulating, framing, and learning). These strategic capabilities reinforced each other and enabled the transition from organisational to institutional experimentation through a collective process where new rules, norms, and frames scale up and spread new habits of thinking and acting amongst actors.

The Machinist Union developed a common frame about skill development and gradually enlarged this frame to develop a common vision of the sector and industrial policy. The shift from a firm-specific narrative to a national industrial policy meant the union had to develop and connect their position on issues such as employment and economic development. In their eyes, production and industrial policy issues were too important to leave solely in the hands of government. Union leaders were also able to articulate various issues (e.g. skills, technological development) at different scales and to connect the interests of a variety of stakeholders. Union leaders found themselves increasingly called upon to mediate between conflicting interests and articulate them across time and space. They had to mediate conflicts beyond the and traditional labour relations issues such as firms' strategic investments. Through these gradual changes, the trade union leaders were engaged in a learning process, reflecting on their own practices and identifying and acting upon opportunities to change.

The Machinist Union was thus engaged in a reflexive process, moving them outside of their comfort zone. By doing so, they were able to experience new ways of thinking and acting. Through these processes of experimentation, the Machinist Union has gradually transformed itself.

Conclusion

This chapter has sought to contribute to the literature on actors' engagement in processes of organisational and institutional experimentation for the development of inclusive and democratic governance institutions at the regional level. Over a 40-year period, actors have built thick regional governance institutions (Zukauskaite et al. 2017) encompassing various intermediary organisations and tight networks involving multiple actors that share a common agenda (Lévesque et al. 2021; Pérez-Lauzon 2021).

The prospects for unions to engage at a regional governance level is marked. The chapter characterises and locates the role of trade unions in these processes and assesses how they can give voice to workers' concerns and increase their influence at multiple scales. These processes are complex, involving multiple actors. Moreover, in these processes unions must have the capability to act and implement practices at multiple levels, in collaboration with the state and other actors.

The task facing unions is to be able to engage in organisational and institutional experimentation. Our study highlights how the achievement of active engagement in regional governance may involve unions developing their own strategic capabilities in relation to framing, articulating, mediating, and learning. By building coalitions with other actors at both regional and international scales, the Machinist Union has expanded their traditional repertoire of action. This has required them to develop their capabilities in framing and articulating in new arenas, including skill development, new technology, employment, and industrial policy. They have also had to mediate and develop common interests among their members within and across various workplaces and trade unions. Building new coalitions is in itself a challenging feat, as conflicting or competing interests emerge.

The shift from organisational to institutional experimentation for the Machinist Union has emerged from their developing of learning capabilities, as they have been able to build on previous organisational experiments, and to apply what they have learnt from these to the other fields that they operate within. Trade unions are embedded in multiple fields across several scales. As such, their actions within one field can create ripple effects if they can transpose their new ways of thinking and acting into the other fields.

Hence, our study makes an important contribution, as our findings suggest that the transition from organisational to institutional experimentation involves a reflexive process where actors collectively reassess their ways of thinking and acting. This analysis undoubtedly raises more questions than answers. Nonetheless, this study opens avenues for future research to better understand how organisational experiments that foster inclusive and more democratic regional governance can be scaled up and institutionalised. This examination is an initial step in demonstrating how the voice of workers can be amplified by unions at a regional governance level.

Note

1 For a more detailed description of the initiatives and the regional governance organisations developed, see Lévesque et al. (2021).

References

Association Internationale des Machinistes et des Travailleurs et Travailleuses de l'Aérospatiale (AIMTA) (2019) *Propulser le Québec vers de nouveaux sommets: pour un engagement renouvelé en aérospatial.* Montréal: AIMTA.

Barton, R. (2018) 'Our Tarkine, our future': the Australian workers union use of narratives around place and community in West and North-West Tasmania, Australia. *Antipode*, 50(1), 41–60.

Barton, R. & Fairbrother, P. (2014) What can unions do? Addressing Multinational relocation in North West Tasmania. *Journal of Industrial Relations*, 56(5), 691–708.

Bosch, G. & Schmitz-Kießler, J. (2020) Shaping Industry 4.0 – an experimental approach developed by German trade unions. *Transfer: European Review of Labour and Research*, 26(2), 189–206.

Braham, E. & Tobin, S. (2020) *Solving the Skills Puzzle: The Missing Piece Is Good Information.* Future Skills Centre (FSC), Ryerson University. https://fsc-ccf.ca/wp-content/uploads/2020/01/SolvingTheSkillsPuzzle-PPF-JAN2020-EN.pd

Bourdieu, P. (1994). *Raisons pratiques : sur la théorie de l'action.* Paris: Éditions du Seuil.

Comité sectoriel de main-d'œuvre en aérospatiale au Québec (CAMAQ) (2016) Recensement des emplois au 1er Janvier 2015 et prévisions du nombre d'emplois au 1er Janvier 2016 et au 1er Janvier 2017. Industrie aérospatiale au Québec. CAMAQ. https://camaq.org/wp-content/uploads/2019/12/Rapport-Recensement-Fabrication-2015–2017.pdfCAMAQ 2016

Comité sectoriel de main-d'œuvre en aérospatiale au Québec (CAMAQ). (2020) Recensement des emplois, au 1er Janvier 2019, et prévisions des emplois aux 1er Janvier 2020 et 2021. Industrie de la Fabrication Aéronautique et Spatiale au Québec. CAMAQ. https://camaq.org/wp-content/uploads/2020/02/Rapport-Recensement-Fabrication-2019–2021.pdf CAMAQ 2020

Coe, N. M., Dicken, P. & Hess, M. (2008) Global production networks: realizing the potential. *Journal of Economic Geography*, 8, 271–295.

Crouch, C. (2005) *Capitalist Diversity and Change: Recombinant Governance and Institutional Entrepreneurs.* Oxford: Oxford University Press.

Crouch, C., Schröder, M. & Voelzkow, H. (2009) Regional and sectoral varieties of capitalism. *Economy and Society*, 38(4), 654–678.

Dewey, J. (1991) *Liberalism and Social Action.* Delhi: Prometheus Books (first published 1935).

Ellem, B. (2003) New unionism in the old economy: community and collectivism in the Pilbara's mining towns. *Journal of Industrial Relations*, 45(4), 423–441.

Fairbrother, P. (2017) When politics meets economic complexity: doing things differently in the Gippsland Region, Australia. *The Australasian Journal of Regional Studies*, 23(3), 400–420.

Garneau, J. (2021) *Relations d'emploi à l'ère de l'industrie 4.0: Un cas d'expérimentation institutionnelle dans le secteur manufacturier de l'aérospatiale au Danemark*, Thèse de doctorat, Québec: Université Laval

Gindin, Sam (1995) *The Canadian Auto Workers: The Birth and Transformation of a Union*, Toronto: James Lorimer & Company.

Haddow, R. (2015) *Comparing Québec and Ontario: Political economy and public Policy at the turn of the millennium.* Toronto: University of Toronto Press.

Heidenreich, M. (2005) The renewal of regional capabilities. Experimental regionalism in Germany. *Research Policy*, 34(5), 739–757.

Herrigel, G. (2012) *Manufacturing Possibilities. Creative Action and Industrial Recomposition in the United States, Germany, and Japan.* Oxford: Oxford University Press.

Herrigel, G. (2018) Experimentalist systems in manufacturing multinationals. German automobile and machinery examples. *Critical Perspectives on International Business*, 14(4), 362–382.

International Association of Machinists and Aerospace Workers (IAMAW) (2019). Grounded potential: An IAMAW report on a national aerospace strategy. IAMAW. http://www.iamaw.ca/wp-content/uploads/2019/02/6Feb2019_IAM_Aerospace_Strategy_2018.pd

Kristensen, P. H. & Morgan, G. (2012) From institutional change to experimentalist institutions. *Industrial Relations: A Journal of Economy and Society*, 51(1), 413–437.

Lévesque, C., Bowkett, C., Perez-Lauzon, S. & Émilien, B. (2021) *Industry 4.0, the Future of Work and Skills: Building Collective Resources for the Canadian Aerospace Industry*. Toronto: The Future Skills Centre.

Lévesque, C. & Murray, G. (2010) Understanding union power: resources and capabilities for renewing union capacity. *Transfer: European Review of Labour and Research*, 16(3), 333–350.

Ministère de l'Économie et de l'Innovation Québec (MEIQ) (2020) Présentation de l'industrie de l'aérospatiale. Government of Québec. https://www.economie.gouv.qc.ca/bibliotheques/secteurs/aerospatiale/presentation-delindustrie-de-laerospatiale/ Ministère de l'économie de l'innovation (MÉIQ) (2016) *Stratégie québécoise de l'aérospatial*, Québec: Gouvernement du Québec. Tiré de https://www.economie.gouv.qc.ca/objectifs/informer/par-secteur-dactivite/aerospatiale/

Murray, G., Lévesque, C., Morgan, G. & Nicolas, R. (2020) Disruption and re-regulation in work and employment: from organizational to institutional experimentation. *Transfer: European Review of Labour Research*, 6(2), 135–156.

Ng, E. S. & Gagnon, S. (2020) *Employment gaps and underemployment for racialized groups and immigrants in Canada: Current findings and future directions. Public Policy Forum.* https://ppforum.ca/wp-content/uploads/2020/01/EmploymentGaps-Immigrants-PPF-JAN2020-EN-Feb7.pdf

Peach, D. A. (1982) The Canadair-I.A.M. Productivity Improvement Plan. *Relations Industrielles/Industrial Relations*, 37(1), 177–197.

Pérez-Lauzon, S. (2021) *L'adaptation des PME de l'aéronautique à la lumière d'une perspective de champ: l'initiative MACH à Montréal et en Wallonie*, Doctoral thesis, Montréal: HEC Montréal.

Rouillard, J. (2004) *Le syndicalisme québécois. Deux siècles d'histoire*. Montréal: Éditions du Boréal.

Rutherford, T. D. & Frangi, L. (2020) Is Industry 4.0 a good fit for high performance work systems? Trade unions and workplace change in the Southern Ontario Automotive Assembly Sector. *Relations industrielles/Industrial relations*, 75(4), 751–773.

Rutherford, T. D., Murray, G., Almond, P. & Pélard, M. (2018) State accumulation projects and inward investment regimes strategies. *Regional Studies*, 52(4), 572–584.

Torre, A. & Rallet, A. (2005) Proximity and localization. *Regional Studies*, 39(1), 47–59.

UNIFOR. https://www.unifor.org/sites/default/files/documents/document/aerospace_sector_strategy_20180410_eng.pdf

UNIFOR (2016) Aerospace sector profile. UNIFOR. https://www.unifor.org/sites/default/files/documents/document/unifor-aerospace-en.pdf

Zhegu, M. (2007) *La coévolution des industries et des systèmes d'innovation: l'industrie aéronautique*. Montréal: UQAM.

Zukauskaite, E., Trippl, M. & Plechero, M. (2017) Institutional thickness revisited. *Economic Geography*, 93(4), 325–345.

10 Unions Interrogating Regions and Regionalism in Australia: The Challenges of Experimentation

Peter Fairbrother and Ruth Barton

Unions have a long history of engaging with industrial (sectoral) governance and less so with sub-national forms of regional governance. Nonetheless, unions have interests and concerns that are grounded in sub-national regional fortunes and futures. To illustrate, unions frequently will be concerned with regional skills or employment issues, often in the context of major worker displacement. Moreover, it is in regions where workers live, work, and relax. But surprisingly, there is little evidence of sustained engagement in promoting and formulating social and economic policies; rather it is *ad hoc*, often responsive and not systematic. In this chapter, we explore these themes.

The challenge facing unions is how to represent and advance members' interests within and of a region; it may be that sectional occupational and industrial interests are at the forefront of union concerns. In effect, unions may be faced with choices which make demands on their capacities as well as refining their purpose. This conundrum will be addressed via a comparative study between two sub-national regions in Australia, Gippsland in the State of Victoria and North West Tasmania in the State of Tasmania. These two regions have long histories as areas with a strong resource base, an industrial base and, in each case, complemented by an expanding service sector. Both regions have undergone major restructuring in recent decades thereby occasioning challenges for unions as regional actors.

This chapter addresses the difficulties that unions face in embedding experiments in relation to regional governance. As noted above, in chapter one, an institutional analysis requires a consideration of agency, exploring constraints and opportunities (see Crouch 2005). By developing new habits of thinking and acting, in the context of organisational experimentation, modifying or renewing their resources, networks, and alliances, unions may be in a position to move towards inclusive and democratic governance at the regional level (see Chapter 1). The argument here is that for such steps to be successful, unions must address the question of embeddedness, that is, the implanted or firmly established strategic economic and political practices of unions in relation to regional governance (see Culpepper 2008). The chapter

DOI: 10.4324/9781003001089-14

addresses this dimension in the two cases, one (Gippsland), where the experiment was compromised because the union leadership failed to achieve a common and agreed understanding and narrative of a policy and practice of change allowing a power struggle over the direction and scope of engagement; the second, where unions lacked the resource to achieve an inclusive and democratic form of regional governance, so that unions in effect remained marginal to regional policy initiatives and practice.

Conceptual Questions

Unions in liberal democracies have long histories as key actors in regulating work and employment. Often this takes the form of addressing terms and conditions of employment, including wage levels and related employment requirements. The focus tends to be on industrial concerns, as workers with specific jobs and skills are recognised over time via negotiations and related activities. Often, there is a place-based dimension to these actions, reflected in the places where members work, ranging from fixed workplaces (factory sites) to mobile workplaces (transport) to more disaggregated forms of working places (home-based care work). Over time, unions have built their capacities and developed the resources to represent their members in these varied settings, not always equitably and effectively, but nevertheless in ways that ground unions as collective organisations.

One dimension that is often overlooked is the way that sub-national regions matter in terms of the focus and processes of economic development and transition. Increasingly, regions have become a focus of economic policy, dealing with the consequences of industrial decline as well as the sites for innovation and the reconstitution of these areas as sites of employment. On the one hand, decision-makers may seek to attract inward investment and, on the other, reposition themselves following the decline of sectors such as manufacturing. Of note, there is a long-standing debate about constituent features and parameters of the sub-national region. These debates have been distilled into questions relating to the multidimensionality of a region (Jessop et al. 2008). Recent contributions, moreover, identify questions relating to territoriality, scalarity, and network-connectedness (e.g. MacLeod and Jones 2007; Mackinnon 2011).

Two related themes focus the analysis. First, regional levels of governance matter for unions. Such arrangements often involve a constellation of institutional forms, comprising local government, provincial ('State' in Australia) government, regionally-based economic elites, and other participants such as educational institutions and the like. Regional governance may involve shifting institutional arrangements that fall both within and outside formal government structures, as well as involving cross-national flows and relationships (Amin 2004). The decisive feature is that governance involves 'binding decision-making in the public sphere', distinguished as general-purpose jurisdictions or task-specific ones (Hooghe and Marks 2003: 236, f/n[1] and f/n[5]). These arrangements can provide diverse actors with the capacities to focus and shape regional economic and social matters or they may limit the capacities of some actors, such as locally-based community groups, and hence act as a barrier to involvement and engagement in regional socio-economic development. The different forms of engagement draw attention to the spatial boundaries of regions, the patterns of relations within regions, the way regions cut across and are connected to local, national, and international space, and the place of various actors in the regional governance process.

Second, regional progress and development require 'purposive agency' (Sotarauta and Beer 2017). The challenge is that place-based governance often involves limited sets of actors, usually reflecting the interests of regional economic and political elites (Pape et al. 2016). Hence, when employers leave an area or reduce their operations, it has largely been left to those in the region to somehow determine future economic directions (see Barton and Fairbrother 2014). In these situations, it then becomes the question of who governs and how power is exercised in determining the direction and beneficiaries of regional development (Jacobs 2007; Pike et al. 2007). In this respect, interventions by place-based actors are important and draw attention to purposeful collaborative leadership (e.g. Eversole 2016). Such steps may require network arrangements to stimulate and locate place-based action (theorised by Jessop et al. 2008; Eversole and McCall 2014).

Unions face challenges in addressing and engaging at the regional policy level. The proposition that guides this analysis is that unions as collective actors are often in the process of developing, adapting, and even forming new institutions to address this level of governance (analytically elaborated by Kristensen and Morgan 2012). As regions pursue policy initiatives to address the socio-economic structures and arrangements that define a region, unions representing members in a region face choices about what to do, if anything. In this respect, the forms of experimentation that unions pursue may be organisational (using existing institutions in novel or adapted ways) and institutional (changing or creating understandings, norms, and rules) to address these developments (see Murray et al. 2020). As noted, these forms are not necessarily clear cut, and blur into each other (see discussion in Chapter 1).

While the above considerations lay out the scale and scope of regional practice, the task facing unions is how to realise the opportunities to play an active and progressive part at a regional governance level. The argument here is that there are at least two conditions to ensure success. First, it is critical that unions develop a shared narrative about the direction and the way that they want to organise and operate to realise their purpose (Fairbrother 2015). This step of institutional experimentation involves what Culpepper refers to as 'common knowledge' (2008). While Culpepper characterises such 'knowledge' as born out of crisis, events, and sets of activities that stimulate the development and articulation of 'persuasive ideas' (7), this understanding of the relations underpinning institutional experimentation can be applied beyond Culpepper's focus on industrial negotiations. Second, organisational experimentation requires resources that will allow the experiments to be embedded, resources such as time, finance, personnel, appropriate infrastructure, and ways of effectively representing members so that the experiment can be secured both on a day-to-day basis as well as in the long term. As noted by Murray and colleagues (above), unions may be able to experiment in ways that are 'typically deliberate but it may also be emergent as actors come to realise in process that they are engaged in such experimentation' (Murray et al. 2020: 8). Hence, experimentation may provide a foundation for and an approach towards the long-term realisation of union purpose in varying contexts and in relation to changing goals and aspirations (Fairbrother 2015).

For us, the overarching question is whether and how can unions play an active and engaged role in promoting policy development and achieving regional transition and improvement? The answer will provide insights into the ways in which regionally active unions, and their confederations can address the relation between immediate sectoral (wage and employment) concerns and the more long-term and transformational or defensive concerns associated with debates about regional futures.

Approach and Method

These themes are examined via an analysis of two challenged regions in Australia, Gippsland and North West Tasmania. These regions have distinctive histories, both born out of the settler and colonial past that defines Australia. Each has a long history of trade unionism, and these unions and their members face challenging futures.[1]

Gippsland

The Gippsland region is spatially defined by the sea to the south, the mountains to the north and the east, and the metropolitan area of Melbourne in the west, the major conduit in and out of Gippsland. In 2021, the region comprised six local councils with a population in 2016 of 266,020 (Australian Bureau of Statistics ABS 2016). The economy has long been based on four major resources: coal; oil and gas; forestry; and agriculture (Fairbrother et al. 2012b). Much public attention has been given to the place of coal in this regional economy with far less attention to either the expanding employment areas (health and social care) or the industries responsible for half the regional gross domestic product, namely food, and fibre (Fairbrother et al. 2012a and Coles et al. 2017).

For much of the 20th century, the major employer in the Latrobe Valley sub-region was the State Electricity Commission of Victoria (SECV). As the single major employer in the region, the SECV was the focus of union organisation and activity. Following the restructuring of the industry in the early 1990s, and the subsequent privatisation of the generating companies, the form and pattern of industrial relations in the area was transformed. The unions in the area faced not only the break-up of the industry but also falling membership and a demoralised and increasingly impoverished community (Fairbrother and Testi 2002). Recently, attention has begun to focus on the transition of energy and mining away from a high carbon economy as well as recognition of the importance of growth sectors for the region such as health and social care and food and fibre (Coles et al. 2017).

The analysis is based on a decade of research work undertaken about Gippsland. More than 120 policy and related reports have defined the social and economic profile of Gippsland, and the sectors that comprise the local economy (Tyler et al. 2012). Complementing the analysis of these and other relevant public documents, 60 semi-structured interviews have been conducted with union leaders between 2008 and 2017. Of note, all members of the Gippsland Trades and Labour Council (GTLC) were interviewed between 2012 and 2014, focusing on the rebuilding of the confederation after privatisation. In addition, 20 semi-structured interviews have been conducted with personnel from State and local government, businesses, and community groups. These interviews were recorded and transcribed. The analysis is also informed by a stakeholder event titled 'Transition and Transformation Working Conference', providing the occasion for over 50 key leaders, activists, and commentators to reflect and engage in debate and discussion about the prospects for the Gippsland region (Coles et al. 2017). In addition, since 2009, Fairbrother has been an active participant in the area of promoting union experimentation and reflection on socio-economic transition in the context of the climate crisis. It is also important to note and remember that Fairbrother was an active player with the GTLC until 2017, when the confederation changed direction, as outlined below.

Tasmania

Tasmania is an island State south-east of the Australian mainland. North West Tasmania comprises nine local government areas (LGAs), with a combined population of 113,834 (Australian Bureau of Statistics ABS 2016). LGA populations range from 1,500 to 25,500 people. The population and industrial centres are concentrated along the north coast, mainly between the port cities of Devonport (population around 25,500) and Burnie (population around 20,000).

The region has undergone industrialisation, deindustrialisation, and a process of uneven regeneration. In the early 20th century, the Tasmanian government embarked on a strategy of hydro-industrialisation to attract heavy industry with the promise of cheap electricity with growth in resource-based (timber, agriculture, and minerals) and manufacturing industries.

This boom was replaced by a period of overall industrial decline beginning in the 1980s. It saw unionised large-scale manufacturing and processing businesses downscaled and/or closed, as have some mining operations. This decline was accompanied by out-migration, profound social and economic disadvantage and community and political divisions over the economic direction and future of the region and the State more generally (RDA 2017). Meanwhile, the core economy shifted to niche and value-added produce (dairy, agriculture, aquaculture), advanced manufacturing, and service provision (health care and social assistance, retail, education, tourism) (Walker and Fairbrother 2015).

The research is based on documentary analysis of public sources (newspapers; official reports) and 92 semi-structured interviews and three focus groups with union leaders conducted in 2014–2016 in North West Tasmania. Prior to 2014, preliminary research was carried out involving 25 interviews with key respondents. Interviewees for the current analysis included representatives from State and local government, businesses, unions, and community groups. In addition, Barton has a long history of engagement with unions and the region, an experience that informs the analysis.

Summary

The evidential base for both areas was analysed using a thematic framework based on regional governance and union capacities. For both areas, transcripts (related documents, including fieldnotes) were analysed through repeated reading by two members of the research team. A coding framework was developed, identifying key themes. This coding framework and illustrative quotes were checked by other research team members for coherence and reliability. The transcripts were coded using NVivo software. The practice for quotation selection is that quotations generally are indicative of a cluster of respondents, at least four in any single category, such as union leadership, unless otherwise noted.

Unions, Regional Governance, and Challenges

The unions in each area tended to articulate their regional concerns either as a coordinated union body, along with individual union representation, as was the case in Gippsland, or in *ad hoc* ways, event by event, union by union, as was the case in Tasmania. In each case, forms of institutional and organisational experimentation were initiated by the unions.

Gippsland

The unions in Gippsland have a long and active history. Nonetheless, unions such as the Australian Manufacturing Workers' Union (AMWU) and the National Union of Workers (NUW) represented workers across Gippsland in the food processing and horticultural industry respectively. Other unionised clusters of workers were employed in the off-shore oil facilities, as well as in educational and health facilities across the region. These unions and others sought to defend their members and improve working conditions, often via the long-standing and changing juridical processes that mark Australian industrial and labour relations, and hence trade union representation and activity (Weller 2007 and Creighton and Stewart 2010).

Many of the unions in Gippsland have long been centred on the Latrobe Valley sub-region. Beginning in the early 20th century, open-cut coal mining and power generation defined the area as the industrial hub of the whole region. In 1918, the Victorian government established the State Electricity Commission of Victoria (SECV) as the government-owned electricity supplier for the State and developed the industry into a major employer in the region. In the 1990s, the SECV was corporatised and privatised, precipitating economic and industrial decline (Birrell 2001). The then directly employed 9,000 strong workforces in the SECV (mid-1970s) was reduced to around 1,800 by 2002, with further reductions over the next 20 years (Duffy and Whyte 2017; Wiseman et al. 2020).

Prior to 1983, the SECV-based unions were organised via the Central Gippsland Trades and Labour Council, a confederation viewed as mainly representing SECV workers, and in the late 1970s and early 1980s, it extended the co-ordination of inter-union industrial action within the SECV to include the broader region (see Benson 1991). Renamed the Gippsland Trades and Labour Council (GTLC) in 1983, and with the privatisation of the SECV in the 1990s, it went into a near-fatal decline. Nonetheless, in the early 2000s, a small group of union activists (leaders in several former SECV based unions and others) re-established the confederation. From the early 2000s, the GTLC pursued a policy of institutional experimentation, presenting the confederation as a regionally-focused union organisation. The leadership of the GTLC articulated a persuasive narrative as the voice of workers and their households across the region. This experiment placed the GTLC as a key player in regional governance across the region.

Alongside their industrial focus, unions in the region were active in a range of activities related to climate change and community-based concerns, such as transitional policy development in relation to coal and energy. These unions, via the GTLC, took steps to educate their members about global warming, and develop progressive policy positions (Snell and Fairbrother 2010). In effect, the GTLC leadership developed a form of 'common knowledge', pursuing a 'high road' development strategy to enable the establishment of secure forms of 'decent' work and environmentally responsible investment across the region. The confederation held a series of Climate Change Forums from 2007 untill 2012, involving national and State union leaders as well as a range of other social actors, including local and State government representatives (Snell 2018). Under the rubric of the confederation, union leaders and activists attending the workshops articulated a just transition knowledge framework. Their support for 'green transition' initiatives, especially in relation to coal and energy production, attracted the attention of environmental organisations such as Environmental Victoria. Hence, the GTLC looked to the possibility of a future beyond coal involving a just transition for the coal and energy sector in the region as well as more broadly across the region.

Thus, the unions, via the GTLC, embarked on an institutional and organisational experimentation. On the one hand, as indicated, the GTLC became a voice of worker interests in the region; on the other hand, the unions, together via the GTLC, embarked upon forms of institutional and organisational experimentation. In relation to the latter, the member unions of the GTLC embraced a division of capacity, with individual unions pursuing the immediate and industrially-based concerns in the region associated with work and employment, while the confederation, the GTLC, became a regional advocate for regional transition, if not transformation.

An important aspect of this was the GTLC campaigning and lobbying activities between 2011 and 2016 to establish a Workers Transition Centre. A formal proposal was presented first in a report in 2012 about the possible impact of the then projected closure of at least one coal-fired generator in the Latrobe Valley coalfield (Fairbrother et al. 2012b). While closure did not occur at this time, over the next three years, as the GTLC anticipated the possibility of closure of at least one coal-fired generator, it reached out into the region to forge links with other major social actors, arguing a case of a just transition. This engagement is demonstrated by membership of the Latrobe Valley Transition Committee (Latrobe City 2009) and co-sponsorship of a range of transition awareness workshops with Latrobe City Council (see also Snell 2018). Moreover, the GTLC also opened up discussions with other regional actors, such as food and fibre businesses, represented by Agribusiness Gippsland, a major advocacy body. The GTLC, for example, spoke on behalf of this sector, alongside the East Gippsland Food Network, advocating on behalf of the precarious and seasonal horticultural workforces in the east of the region. It also was a partner to the 'Transition and Transformation' Working Conference in November 2016 (Coles et al. 2017). The qualified realisation of the lobbying for a Centre, and an embedded partnership promoting a just transition ultimately saw the GTLC partner in the establishment of a Worker Transition Service, with the State government and others. The GTLC thus became a notable contributor to the narrative on social and economic transition and active partner of the Gippsland regional governance fora.

But this experiment remains unfinished and was circumvented by power dynamics within the confederation in 2016–2017. With the announcement of closure of one of the four power stations in November 2016, the GTLC turned away from this recent trajectory. When the French multi-national Engie foreshadowed the closure of Hazelwood, the Department of Premier and Cabinet announced the establishment of the Latrobe Valley Authority, and tasked it with a program of reconstruction and transition. Chaired by the Premier, the Authority administered a $22 million support package and established a Worker Transition Service in a partnership with the GTLC, unions, employers, employment agencies, adult education providers, and training agencies (Wiseman et al. 2020). The Service provides and enables education, counselling, and financial advice, as well as subsidised training for displaced workers, provided business support to expand job opportunities and develop transition plans and expanded the established 'Back to Work' employer support scheme to employ retrenched workers, from the mining and energy industry and extended to timber and food (Wiseman et al. 2020).

In the midst of this, the GTLC turned away from its broader regional accomplishments and embraced a more narrowly focused and immediate set of policy initiatives (Fairbrother 2017). With the announcement of the closure, one of the two major impacted unions affected a 'take-over' of the GTLC and accelerated the departure of the then President. At least three of the eight-member executive were from the same union (permitted by the rules), including the Secretary; there were no members from the care economy, the largest employment area across the region, and the education representative was employed outside the region, at a university. Notably, some executive members withdrew (two women departed in 2017, leaving one woman as a member of the executive, still the case in 2021), while other executive members were 'no longer listened to' on executive matters (informal comment, 2017; records 2021). The new Secretary and his supporters rebuilt the executive as a power-based industry body (mining and energy). They secured agreement from the Latrobe Valley Authority to locate one outlet of the Worker Transition Service in the GTLC offices as a one-stop support and advice service. Initially a voluntary service on the part of the GTLC, it evolved into a significantly state-funded activity (Snell 2018). While this endeavour was focused on the closure, it could also be interpreted as a 'just transition' strategy (see Snell 2018), it was nonetheless a limited and narrow approach. The focus was on mining and energy employees and their households; it tended to overlook other employment areas such as forestry, health and education provision, and tourism. Moreover, the broader regional industrial base – the care economy and agriculture – no longer figured in GTLC deliberations. This reversion to older forms of engagement and focus was at the cost of the more broadly based engagement across the region and the further refinement of a long-term progressive approach to mine closures and other aspects of transition away from a carbon economy. As a confederation, it divorced itself from allies and coalitions that had been built up over a 10-to-15-year period and no longer played a proactive role in the broader region.

The Gippsland Experiments

With closure of the first major generator, and the partnership with the LVA, the GTLC changed direction, although still under the narrative of a union initiated just transition. In effect, with the change of leadership in 2016, the focus shifted to the short-term, in relation to job protection within the energy and mining sector and job transfer to like jobs outside the industry (*cf.*, Snell 2018). Nonetheless, it must be acknowledged that the partnership solution to the closure involved considerable support and sustenance to workers from the closed generator (direct and indirect workers) and importantly their households. A peer support model of assistance and support was developed, financial support for retraining was provided and a relatively comprehensive worker transfer scheme between the remaining generators was developed by the three major unions in the industry (Snell 2018). Despite the tensions within the union movement, the GTLC remains an important, albeit it limited, regional actor. The point to note is that the power struggle within the GTLC meant that the 'common knowledge' that had been moulded and focused over more than a decade was reframed after the 2016 closure.

More broadly, the federation failed to articulate and implement a sustainable narrative focused on the implications of the changes underway, in the mining and energy industry and across the region. The institutional experiment, which had the potential to change the face of unions in regional politics, involved a narrative for sustainable alternative jobs following projected closure of the coal-based energy sector and the diversification of the regional economy through new types of investment and sustainable regional development policies (Parker 2009/2010; see also Weller et al. 2011 and Weller 2012). In effect, the GTLC put content into the previously formal relations between regional governance actors, such as the local councils and regional advocacy bodies, to build networks and provide the union movement within the region with a voice amongst regional decision-makers. This development involved the articulation of a comprehensive inclusive narrative about a social and economic just transition. It also took the form of expressing a union perspective on the more specific concerns of the localities that made up the communities in this region. This narrative was well-developed and presented publicly in ways that other actors in the region responded positively to the invitations to engage, including advocacy bodies, local councils, and other networks in the region. The then GTLC secretary, supported by other union leaders, publicly explained the desirability of addressing the tough questions facing the region and the importance of working with others across the region (e.g. Parker 2009/2010).

It appeared that the GTLC had been able to transform itself from an economistic, industrial-focused union body to a community and transition-focused council. This elaboration of a 'community unionism' narrative involved a scaling up of the analyses by union leaders as the voice of members, not only in the workplace but also as members of communities. However, this way of developing a focus was effective, although not necessarily stable and long-term. It was focused and organised around particular leaders, and specifically the confederation Secretary, a leader of a non-mining and energy-based union group. When the Secretary retired because of ill-health in 2014, his successors and supporters, particularly the President, faced a fracturing of the common knowledge that underwrote the engaged narrative. Indeed, as time passed and the tensions in the community sharpened around power station closure and related events (e.g. campaigning over forestry and saw-milling matters as well as tourist-focused community proposals), the inclusiveness of the previous decade was abandoned. Instead, the GTLC turned to a more exclusive and economistic response to the public announcements on closure and its implementation. The confederation developed an agreed narrative that underwrote the immediate and focused on mining and energy. In this respect, the turn was enabled by the role of the Latrobe Valley Authority in developing a transition approach for the displaced energy workers in the locality.

The lesson from this example is that the saliency of experimentation rests in part on the union agreement about the narratives adopted and the common knowledge that was forged and elaborated. It remains the case that the immediate and the long term could have been embraced and developed further, rather than the limited Worker Transition Service. The fragility of this experimentation, with its focus on norms and values and the ways of looking at an inclusive future, was not sustained with a change in leadership and a sharpening of the tensions about employment and work in the region. The paradox is that the community-focused and positive approach to transition was cast as an unnecessary indulgence when closure of the first major generator was announced in 2016; in the event the confederation returned to its earlier role as an energy industry-based federation rather than one that engages with a wide range of industrial sectors and the communities associated with them in the region.

North West Tasmania

Unions have a long history in North West Tasmania. In 2019, there were 25 recognised unions in the State, representing 50,000 members affiliated with the Hobart-based State union confederation, Unions Tasmania (Unions Tasmania 2019). Of these five unions had offices on the North West coast in Devonport: Australian Education Union (AEU); AMWU; Health and Community Services Union (HACSU); Maritime Union of Australia (MUA); and NUW. Except for HACSU, all the unions had one staff member with three unions sharing a single office. Apart from the

NUW and the MUA, the remainder are sub-branches and report to State offices either interstate or in Hobart.

There also is a notable history of regional union confederations in North West Tasmania. Two confederations were established in the 1940s in Burnie and Devonport. They played an influential role in local political and community affairs as well as coordinating regional industrial campaigns. Nonetheless, a series of factional disputes between the 1950s and 1970s and an on-going process of deindustrialisation (Davis nd; Barton 2015) sapped the vitality of these regional councils. By the late 1990s, both councils had disappeared, leaving the Hobart-based Unions Tasmania the sole peak union body in Tasmania (Unions Tasmania 2011). In the mid-2010s, Unions Tasmania began to take a more active and visible role in the region, but had limited resources to achieve the programs of activity evident in Gippsland.

Of note, unions were impacted by the deindustrialisation of the North West coastal area. A number of unions such as the Textile, Clothing and Footwear Union and the Pulp and Paper Division of the Construction Forestry, Mining and Energy Union withdrew from the North West coast when factories closed. The manufacturing-based union, the (AMWU) in Tasmania, lost 57% of their membership between 2003 and 2018 (Registered Organisations Commission 2019) due to industry closures and technological change. In the context of these developments, some unions sought to have a say on regional economic development, but it was sporadic, reactive, and uncoordinated. To illustrate, Unions Tasmania was consulted by the State government for its Economic Development Plan and the AMWU was involved in representing manufacturing; some unions had been invited to participate with State and Federal politicians on a joint State/Federal body put in place to assess skills and regeneration on the North West coast.

Yet there were organisational opportunities for these unions to address socio-economic development policy and practice in North West Tasmania. This region had established a relatively robust form of regional governance. In the late 1990s, in the context of deindustrialisation, steps were taken to establish a regional development authority to overcome problems of parochialism and scale. The aim was to develop an inclusive body to 'build upon common regional interests in order to set common regional goals and objectives' (Broatch 1999: 7). In 2000, the nine North West Tasmanian councils established the Cradle Coast Authority (CCA) to coordinate economic development across the North-West. These councils sought to promote a 'stronger voice in the region … we need an economic driver' (Burnie Council official, October 2011; Cradle Coast Authority 2012a).

The Authority was successful in securing development funding and promoting industrial redevelopment in the region. It was governed through a two-tier structure comprising representatives from each Council as well as from industry, tourism, and education and training (Cradle Coast Authority 2012b). Funding was provided by the Tasmanian Government's Partnerships Agreement Program and the Commonwealth Government's Sustainable Regions Program (McDonald et al. 2013). For nearly a decade, the CCA was able to promote partnership governance. Nonetheless, as noted by McDonald et al. (2013), the Authority faced structural constraints, specifically in relation to State and Commonwealth government requirements, as well as relative invisibility within the region and no 'direct democratic accountability' (McDonald et al. 2013: 354). In the late 2010s, and following some internal council criticism, the Authority refocused 'to help connect communities, business and government to work together for the good of the region' (Cradle Coast Authority 2019) and it began a process of revising its strategic plan to address regional economic development more specifically. However, the Authority failed to address the question of inclusiveness, at least for the unions active in the region.

The CCA comprised a specific 'interplay between institutional forms and political forces' (Macleod & Goodwin, 1999: 523). It was structured with the objective of fostering an economic development perspective that complemented the economic approaches of each council. Moreover, it was and remains a limited form of regional governance, especially when compared with the Regional Development Agencies that were a feature of economic development initiatives in the United Kingdom (Bailey et al. 2010). Overall, this was a fluid and contested form of limited regional governance. While the aspiration was to be inclusive, there was no evidence of seeking to consult unions as economically-based actors, or indeed, other non-governmental organisations from civil society. Rather, unions were seen as part of 'old' large industrialised, militant workplaces that had paid a large role in Burnie's past but would play little part in its future, except perhaps to help workers in industries that were closing down transition to new jobs. In part, this seemed to derive from a sentiment that unions, for example, are concerned with 'industrial relations' and thus would only have a limited role to play. Thus, unions might have a subject-specific role in such discussions and planning, but little more.

Nonetheless, some unions realised that in a declining region they needed to change their approach and engage with the community in broader and more sustained ways and move outside the workplace. On occasion, unions were successfully able to mobilise the local community, and local politicians. This approach was evident in two cases, one, where the Australian Workers Union's campaigned to continue mining in the Tarkine (Barton 2018) and the other, the campaign to continue Australian crewed coastal shipping (MUA 2015; see also Fairbrother and Gekara 2016). In practice, such engagements were initiated by the unions and limited to the Australian Labor Party (ALP); these approaches were not reciprocated, with little evidence that politicians actively sought to engage with the unions. Thus, engagement was initiated by the unions, usually in short-term and issue-based ways rather than longer term and sustained involvements around broader regional policy formulation.

In some cases, unions were hampered by their member's aspirations and commitments. As with the shift in Gippsland in 2016, some members wanted their union to continue its traditional and sole focus of servicing the workplace. Others sought to articulate a broader focus but struggled to know how to engage with these groups (Unions workshop, 2 June 2015; Unions Workshop, 25 February 2015). As well, there was the complication that the unions representing relatively highly paid workers in a depressed region characterised by disadvantage and unemployment found it difficult to frame their arguments about jobs and employment effectively and equitably. At times in their bargaining campaigns, the unions had been disparaged by politicians and people in the community for being 'greedy' and jeopardising jobs in the region (*The Advocate*, 12 October 2014). Moreover, unions were often caught up in the tension between their desire for 'good jobs' (Unions Workshop, 25 February 2015) and the community's desire for any jobs.

Thus, in relation to socio-economic change and development, this regional form of governance was both institutionally fragmented, horizontally (between councils), complemented by the regional organisation of the state agencies (Regional Development Tasmania, Regional Development Australia, Tasmania and Departments, State and federal) and vertically (councils and the CCA). Within this 'space', regional actors articulated functionally socio-spatial interests, as well as expressing these interests via the integrating forum of the CCA. Nonetheless, this form of institutional experimentation was limited and under-developed by the unions.

The North West Tasmanian Experiment

The unions in the northwest of the State organised and operated as distinct unions, each with a designated area of activity and an associated membership. There has been no coordinating or organising arrangement across unions since the mid-1990s, when the then locally-based federation closed down. These unions often worked together, involving leaderships who were familiar with each other and who cooperated and exchanged information in line with the political allegiances of these leaderships. This pattern of rivalry had a long history, going back to the 1950s and into the 1970s (Quinlan and Lindley 2006). Remnants of these divisions occasionally showed up in the different sectors such as manufacturing, and as members of the different blocs that made up Unions Tasmania, based 200 km to the south in Hobart, Tasmania's capital city.

Institutional experimentation took the form of forging common understandings, norms and rules, scaling up and institutionalizing such arrangements. It concerned non-state and state actors and was triggered through bottom-up or top-down processes, often involving collective action and joint deliberative processes (Barton 2018). The experimentation took the form of extending union purposes, organising and campaigning around public concerns such as the logging of old forests or the defence of favourable employment legislation (Barton 2018). There was an informal organisational dimension to this type of activity, for example, involving the accommodation and related arrangements that brought union leaderships, organisers, and activists into shared activities and exchanges of information as well as planning, on occasion. Such occurrences were often targeted and focused, rather than sustained and long-term. As noted by Barton (2018), such forms of experimentation involved the articulation of narratives that were community-based and focused on specific local issues. Indeed, these happenings demonstrated the ways that unions could move beyond a narrow and exclusive focus on work and employment protections.

It was notable that, in the main, these events and occurrences did not entail organisational experimentation through an extension of union capacities via organisational initiatives and experiments. First, they were unable to develop a narrative that could sustain an engagement with the varied forms of regional governance in play such as the CCA. This meant they largely remained reactive and focused only on specific sectoral or industrial issues. Second, they lacked the institutional form of a regional confederation that would facilitate a coherent and long-term broader focus and narrative on regional and community issues. While successful in an episodic way, the unions were unable to extend and scale up their achievements from one set of activities to another. Thus, the unions in the region successfully came together around specific campaigns developing narratives of engagement, in episodic ways, but they were unable to extend and scale up these achievements via organisational experiments, for example, by establishing a confederal form of union participation and engagement to maintain a collective union presence in the region.

An Assessment

The challenge for unions is that, in situations where sub-national regional governance is fragmented and selective, there often appears to be a limited possibility for engaged and participative practice involving unions (Fairbrother et al. 2017). Given the thrust towards more devolved and seemingly consultative practices in relation to sub-national regional governance, this structuring often affirms the on-going relations between political and economic elites at this level. Nonetheless, if unions can develop 'common knowledge' affirmed by sustained and agreed commitments, then they may be able to take proactive steps to develop their capacities in ways that enable the development of a broad and layered sense of purpose. Such capacity-building, however, is tenuous in the sense that it rests on agreements that can become fractured in the context of a power struggle and different visions of strategy and tactics over immediate transition steps, as was the case in Gippsland, or underdeveloped because the fora for resolving and developing understandings between sovereign union groups does not exist, as in the case of Tasmania.

Unions require capabilities and the resources (or 'slack resources') to become effective sub-national regional actors capable of pursuing regional vision-setting. Unions face questions in relation to the exercise of their capacities (capabilities and resources), reconciling aspirations in relation to sectoral concerns and regional aspirations. The question is, do such leaders have time 'to devote to questions of regional strategic significance' (Beer and Clower 2014: 11)? When considering the collective aspect of trade union leadership, it is necessary to disentangle the meaning of slack resources in relation to the makeup of trade unions. It can be argued that, in the case of unions, slack resources refer to the ways that collective capabilities and resources provide for possible futures; the question is, do unions have the capacities to realise these futures (Fairbrother 2015), as indicated above, shaped in relation to general-purpose jurisdictions (Gippsland) or task-specific ones (North West Tasmania)? Of course, in the absence of 'systems of governance that are … fully representative, deliberative and willing to share influence' (Sotarauta and Beer 2017: 220), such prospects are challenging, no matter how capable the union and its leadership (see Hooghe and Marks 2003, f/n[1] and f/n[5]; Fairbrother 2015).

Taken together, these cases demonstrate the fragility of experimentation by unions, and their federations to address the challenges they face within sub-national regions. The analysis reveals three themes that require further study and exploration.

First, in situations where regional governance is fragmented and selective, there is a limited possibility for engaged and participative practice. Indeed, the structure of this form of regional governance is likely to be exclusive, involving limited sets of actors. Given the thrust towards more devolved and seemingly consultative practices in relation to regional governance, this structuring affirms the on-going relations between political and economic elites at a regional level. The question is, how and on what terms can unions become involved in such arrangements? This step will require careful and cautious reflection of the way forward and the experimentations that may be possible and fruitful.

Second, what is notable is that labour has been viewed as an object of regional development strategies, focusing on skilling, deployment, and utilisation. This conceptualisation of labour leads to partial outcomes and disengaged workers (and households), with possible challenging ethical, material, and political outcomes (for example, Ford and Goodwin 2014). For labour, the means to give voice to their interests may be by unions and related organisations, such as sectoral interest groups (for example, health advocacy bodies) and via alliances among unions in the form of confederations or other collective bodies. In this respect, the examples provided above offer insights into the challenges and opportunities that are in play.

Third, whatever the structure of regional governance, unions face considerable difficulty in exercising their capacities in relation to regional governance and thereby helping to shape the future of regions. The organisational challenge is to maintain the sectoral base of trade unionism while affirming the solidaristic concerns that unions embody. The problem is that our understandings of the conditions for reciprocal relations between different scalar levels of union organisation are usually cast in hierarchical rather than cooperative terms (Fairbrother and Gekara 2016). Hence, there is a tendency to accept current relations as given, rather than explore the organisational and capacity challenges created by the major changes that are taking place, such as the imminent closure of carbon-based mining and energy production in specific regions. Such explorations occur not only in relation to global value chains and networks, but also in the ways these changes play out in spatially based ways, in regions and other places. Hence, it is necessary to examine the role unions may play in reshaping regional governance, in particular, their capacity to frame issues, bridge, and span boundaries, and mediate between contending interests

There is an opaque, illusory dimension to these relationships. As noted elsewhere, when unions face their futures, they are often caught in tensions between the immediate and the long-term. On the one hand, union strategies are shaped by the processes of economic and social change, institutional arrangements, and their relationship to employers. On the other hand, unions can exercise agency and can open up new agendas, framing issues in distinctive ways that constitute a challenge to prevailing relations, as some of the recent actions by unions and their confederations have done in relation to 'green' jobs (Snell and Fairbrother 2010). The ways these operational logics are resolved in practice can be decisive for the prospects of more inclusive thus effective forms of regional governance.

Conclusion

The premise of the chapter is that unions face tests when they seek to address the trajectories of change in a sub-national region. These challenges encourage unions to address the tension between the immediate, or short-term, such as protecting jobs, and the long-term, namely the reconstitution of labour markets and the economies in which they are embedded. In general, the choices made by unions are cast in terms of reactive and pro-active measures. Unions may move from an implicit acknowledgement, often captured in national policy stances, for example, the recognition of global warming and its anthropomorphic nature and addressing the circumstances of upheaval precipitated by closure and transition to low-carbon economies. At this moment, industry-focused unions are taking understandably defensive stances or seeking to ensure a transition that leaves workers in a comparable (or improved) position to that before the change. Moreover, as demonstrated, there can also be a shift in focus, for example, from regional leaders seeking to address the challenges in inclusive and comprehensive ways towards more narrow and immediate gains for members. Such shifts can also be a part of an underlying power struggle within a union or confederation, or another form of union organisation. Such shifts can also be sanctioned by provincial (State) and national decision-makers who, in turn, may also be driven by short-term electoral expediency, rather than a commitment to long-term inclusive change. Thus, as always, there must be a recognition of who has power over what and when.

Unions are caught betwixt and between. To address this on-going dilemma, a clearer understanding of the relevance of governance arrangements on the way actors and institutions cope with a variety of issues such as restructuring, de- and re-location, and environmental policies. For unions, it means renewal as transition, and not as short-term accommodation. It means unions seeking to shape regional governance, exploring ways in which regional institutions can be recast, by whom, and for whom, with inclusive outcomes, both economic and social. The challenges for unions and their memberships are clear.

Note

1 The authors would like to acknowledge the support, assistance, and guidance of the following members of the research teams who worked with us, researching unions in both regions: Larissa Bamberry, George Cairns, Madelaine Pape, Richard Phillips, Darryn Snell, Dora Carias Vega, Matthew Walker.

References

Advocate (2014) Simplot Condemns Union as Industrial Action Escalates, *The Advocate*, 12 October 2014 https://www.theadvocate.com.au/story/2618781/simplot-condemns-union-as-industrial-action-escalates/

Amin, A. (2004) Regions unbound: Towards a new politics of place. *Geografiska Annaler*, 86 B(1), 33–44.

Australian Bureau of Statistics (ABS) (2016) Regional Population Growth, Australia (Cat no. 3218). Canberra, Australia: ABS.

Bailey, D., Bellandi, M., Caloffi, A. & De Propris, L. (2010) Place-renewing leadership: trajectories of change for mature manufacturing regions in Europe. *Policy Studies*, 31(4), 457–474.

Barton, R. (2015) 'Good riddance to the stinkin' place': deindustrialisation and memory at associated pulp and paper mills in Burnie, Tasmania. *Labour History*, 109, 149–167.

Barton R. (2018) 'Our Tarkine, our future': the Australian workers unions use of narratives around place and community in West and North West Tasmania, Australia. *Antipode*, 50(1), 41–60.

Barton, R. & Fairbrother, P. (2014) What can unions do? Addressing multinational relocation in North West Tasmania. *The Journal of Industrial Relations*, 56(5), 691–708.

Beer, A. & Clower, T. (2014) Mobilizing leadership in cities and regions. *Regional Studies, Regional Science*, 1(1), 5–20.

Benson, J. (1991) *Unions at the Workplace: Shop Steward Leadership and Ideology*. Oxford: Oxford University Press.

Birrell, B. (2001) *The Latrobe Valley: Victims of Industrial Restructuring*. Centre for Population and Urban Research. Victoria, Australia: Monash University.

Broatch, A. (1999) *North West Tasmania Building the Region*. Braddon Business Centre, http://www.aphref.aph.gov.au_house_committee_primind_rdinq_sub298-e.pdf, accessed 9 August 2019.

Coles, A., Fairbrother, P. Jovanovski, N., Macdonald, F., Prokopiv, V., Safari, D., et al. (2017) *Doing Things Differently: A Strategy for the Gippsland Region*. Centre for People, Organisation and Work, RMIT University. Accessed 14 September 2021. https://cpow.org.au/gippsland-transition-and-transformation/

Cradle Coast Authority (2012a) *Welcome to the Cradle Coast Authority*. Retrieved from http://www.cradlecoast.com/

Cradle Coast Authority (2012b) *The Board*. Retrieved from http://www.cradlecoast.com/board_members.html

Cradle Coast Authority (2019) Regional Economic Development. *Cradle Coast Authority*, Accessed 4 September 2019. https://www.cradlecoast.com/cca/regional-economic-development/

Creighton, B. & Stewart, A. (2010) *Labour Law*, Fifth Edition. Annandale, NSW: The Federation Press.

Crouch, C. (2005) *Capitalist Diversity and Change: Recombinant Governance and Institutional Entrepreneurs*. Oxford: Oxford University Press.

Culpepper, P. (2008) The politics of common knowledge: ideas and institutional change in wage bargaining. *International Organization*, 62(1), 1–33.

Davis, R. (nd) *A Hundred and Eleven Years Labor: The ALP in Tasmania, 1903–2014*, http://www.richardpdavis.com/tasmanian-labor-history.html. Accessed 5 December 2017.

Duffy, M. & Whyte, S. (2017) The Latrobe Valley: the politics of loss and hope in a region in transition. *Australian Journal of Regional Studies*, 23(3), 421–446.

Eversole, R. (2016) *Regional Development in Australia: Being Regional*. Abingdon: Routledge.

Eversole, R. & McCall, T. (2014) Constructing advantage in the Cradle Coast region, Tasmania: knowledge partnering as a regional development platform approach. *Regional Science Policy and Practice*, 6(3), 251–264.

Fairbrother, P. (2015) Rethinking trade unionism: union renewal as transition. *The Economic and Labour Relations Review*, 26(4), 561–576.

Fairbrother, P. (2017) When politics meets economic complexity: doing things differently in the Gippsland Region. *Australasian Journal of Regional Studies*, 23(3), 400–420.

Fairbrother, P. & Gekara, V. (2016) Multi-scalar trade unionism: lessons from maritime unions. *Relations Industrielles/Industrial Relations*, 71(4), 589–610.

Fairbrother, P. & Testi, J. (2002) The Advent of Multi-national Ownership of the Victorian Electricity Generating Plants: Questions for Labour. In Fairbrother, P., Paddon, M. & Teicher, J. (eds) *Privatisation, Globalisation and Labour*. Sydney: Federation Press, pp. 102–130.

Fairbrother, P., Snell, D., Cairns, G., Bamberry, L., Tyler, M., Pape, M., et al. (2012a) *Identification of Opportunities to Support Structural Adjustment in the Latrobe Valley: Final Report for Commonwealth Department of Regional Australia, Regional Development and Local Government*. Melbourne: Centre for Sustainable Organisations and Work.

Accessed 12 September 2021. https://cpow.org.au/identification-of-opportunities-to-support-structural-adjustment-in-the-latrobe-valley-region/

Fairbrother, P., Condon, L., Snell, D., McKenry, S., Bamberry, L., Winfree, T., Stroud, D. & Blake, J. (2012b) Jobs and Skills Transition for the Latrobe Valley: Phase 1: Benchmark Occupations and Skill Sets. Submitted to the Commonwealth Department of Education, Employment and Workplace Relations (DEEWR) and undertaken under the auspices of the National Centre for Sustainability (NCS) at Swinburne University of Technology, Centre for Sustainable Organisations and Work (CSOW) at RMIT University and the Centre for Global Labour Research (CGLR) at Cardiff University. Accessed 12 September 2021. https://cpow.org.au/jobs-and-skills-transition-for-the-latrobe-valley-phase-1-benchmark-occupations-and-skill-sets/

Fairbrother, P., Walker, M. & Phillips, R. (2017) Unions and regional governance: the case of North West Tasmania, Australia. *Regional Studies Journal*, 52(11), 1502–1511.

Ford, R. & Goodwin, M. (2014) *Revolt on the Right: Explaining Support for the Radical Right in Britain*. London and New York: Routledge.

Hooghe, L. & Marks, G. (2003) Unraveling the central state, but how? Types of multi-level governance. *American Political Science Review*, 97(2), 233–243.

Jacobs, K. (2007) Territorial modes of governance and the discourses of community reaction in the State of Tasmania. *Space and Polity*, 11(3), 263–277.

Jessop, B., Brenner, N. & Jones, M. (2008) Theorizing sociospatial relations. *Environment and Planning D: Society and Space*, 26(3), 389–401.

Kristensen, P. & Morgan, G. (2012) From institutional change to experimentalist institutions. *Industrial Relations: A Journal of Economy and Society*, 51(1), 413–437.

Latrobe City (2009) *Latrobe City Council CPRS Policy Position Consultation Draft Report*. Morwell: Latrobe City Council.

Mackinnon D. (2011) Reconstructing scale: towards a new scalar politics. *Progress in Human Geography*, 35, 21–36.

Macleod, G., & Goodwin, M. (1999) Space, scale and state strategy: rethinking urban and regional governance. *Progress in Human Geography*, 23(4), 503–527. doi: 10.1191/030913299669861026

MacLeod, G. & Jones, M. (2007) Territorial, scalar, networked, connected: in what sense a regional world? *Regional Studies*, I41(9), 1177–1191.

McDonald, C., Kirk-Brown, A., Frost, L., Van Dijk, P. & Rainnie, A. (2013) Partnerships and integrated responses to rural decline: the role of collective efficacy and political capital in Northwest Tasmania, Australia. *Journal of Rural Studies*, 32, 346–356.

MUA (2015) Shadow Minister Brendan O'Connor's Doorstop Transcript. *Maritime Union of Australia*, 19 July, Accessed 6 September 2021 https://muanational.nationbuilder.com/_shadow_employment_minister_brendan_o_connor_s_doorstop_transcript

Murray, G., Lévesque, C., Morgan, G. & Roby, N. (2020) Disruption and re-regulation in work and employment: from organisational to institutional experimentation. *Transfer: European Review of Labour and Research*, 26(2), 135–156.

Pape, M., Fairbrother, P. & Snell, D. (2016) Beyond the state: shaping governance and development policy in an Australian region. *Regional Studies*, 50(5), 909–921.

Parker, J. (2009/2010). No Time to Waste. *The Gippsland Bush Telegraph*. Morwell, Victoria, Australia: Gippsland Trades and Labour Council.

Pike, A., Rodriguez-Pose, A. & Tomaney, J. (2007) What kind of regional development and from whom? *Regional Studies*, 41(9), 1253–1269.

Quinlan, M. & Lindley, M. (2006) Trade Unions. In Alexander, A. (ed.) *The Companion to Tasmanian History*. Centre for Tasmanian Historical Studies, University of Tasmania. http://www.utas.edu.au/library/companion_to_tasmanian_history/T/Trade%20unions.htm

Registered Organisations Commission (2019) Automotive, Food, Metals, Engineering, Printing and Kindred Industries Union known as The Australian Manufacturing Workers Union (AMWU). *Registered Organisations Commission*, https://www.roc.gov.au/find-a-registered-organisation/amwu/amwu Accessed 6 September 2019.

RDA (2017) RDA Tasmania Regional Plan July 2017–June 2019. *Regional Development Australia*, https://www.rdatasmania.org.au/client-assets/documents/documents-and-reports/RDA%20Tasmania%20Regional%20Plan_2017%20-%202019%20(FINAL).pdf. Accessed 4 September 2019.

Snell, D. (2018) 'Just transition'? Conceptual challenges meet stark reality in a 'transitioning' coal region in Australia. *Globalizations*, 15(4), 550–564.

Snell, D. & Fairbrother, P. (2010) Unions as environmental actor. *Transfer*, 6(3), 411–424.

Sotarauta, M. & Beer, A. (2017) Governance, agency and place leadership: lessons from a cross-national analysis. *Journal of Regional Studies*, 51(2), 210–223.

Tyler, M., Fairbrother, P., Snell, D., Bamberry, L., Carroll-Bell, S. & Suraci, S. (2012) *Identification of Opportunities to Support Structural Adjustment in the Latrobe Valley, Briefing Report One – Assessing Current Knowledge*. Centre for Sustainable Organisation and Work. Accessed 12 September 2021. https://www.rmit.edu.au/research/research-institutes-centres-and-groups/research-centres/centre-for-people-organisation-and-work/projectsmams.rmit.edu.au/32vrogook3mjz.pdf

Unions Tasmania (2011) *Unions Tasmania Directory 2011*. Hobart: Unions Tasmania.

Unions Tasmania (2019) *Affiliated Unions*, https://www.unionstas.com.au/unions-tasmania-executive-affiliated-unions/ Accessed 12 September 2021.

Walker, M. & Fairbrother, P. (2015) *Labour Market Profile: North West Tasmania. People and the Economy Report No. 2*. Melbourne: RMIT University.

Weller, S. (2007) Power and scale: the shifting geography of industrial relations law in Australia. *Antipode*, 39, 896–919.

Weller, S. (2012) The regional dimensions of the 'transition to a low-carbon economy': the case of Australia's Latrobe Valley. *Regional Studies*, 46(9), 1261–1272.

Weller, S., Sheehan, P. & Tomaney, J. (2011) *The Regional Effects of Pricing Carbon Emissions: An Adjustment Strategy for The Latrobe Valley. Report to Regional Development Victoria*. Melbourne, Australia: Centre for Strategic Economic Studies, Victoria University. November.

Wiseman, J., Workman, A., Fastenrath S. & Jotzo, F. (2020) After the Hazelwood Coal Fired Power Station Closure: Latrobe Valley Regional Transition Policies and Outcomes 2017–2020. CCEP Working Paper 2010. Canberra, Australia: Crawford School of Public Policy, Australian National University.

Index

For Product Safety Concerns and Information please contact our EU representative GPSR@taylorandfrancis.com
Taylor & Francis Verlag GmbH, Kaufingerstraße 24, 80331 München, Germany

www.ingramcontent.com/pod-product-compliance
Ingram Content Group UK Ltd.
Pitfield, Milton Keynes, MK11 3LW, UK
UKHW022353190926
475702UK00015B/2260
9781032320090